Interaction:
Foreign Policy
and Public Policy

Interaction: Foreign Policy and Public Policy

Frank B. Feigert
Norman A. Graebner
Demetrios G. Papademetriou
Gerard J. Mangone
Harry Howe Ransom
Larman C. Wilson
James H. Wolfe

Edited by Don C. Piper and
Ronald J. Terchek

American Enterprise Institute for Public Policy Research
Washington and London

Library of Congress Cataloging in Publication Data
Main entry under title:

Interaction, foreign policy and public policy.

(AEI studies ; 381)
Includes bibliographical references.
1. United States—Foreign relations—1945–
—Addresses, essays, lectures.   2. United States—
Foreign relations—1945–   —Decision making—
Addresses, essays, lectures.   3. Policy sciences—
Addresses, essays, lectures.   I. Piper, Don C.
(Don Courtney)   II. Terchek, Ronald, 1936–
III. Series.
JX1417.I58 1983   353.0089   83–8810
ISBN 0–8447–3524–8
ISBN 0–8447–3523–X (pbk.)

1 3 5 7 9 10 8 6 4 2

AEI Studies 381

Printed in the United States of America

In Appreciation
Elmer Plischke

The authors of this volume are very pleased to dedicate it to Professor Elmer Plischke, who served for more than thirty years in the Department of Government and Politics at the University of Maryland. During that time he was a productive scholar and dedicated teacher in the field of American diplomacy and foreign policy. For some of us he is a congenial professional colleague and a valued friend. Others of us are also privileged to recognize him as a mentor and adviser for our own academic careers. In dedicating this book and our contributions to him we acknowledge his contributions to the study of American foreign policy and we express to him individually our thanks and appreciation.

Frank Feigert
Norman Graebner
Gerard Mangone
Demetrios Papademetriou
Don Piper
Harry Howe Ransom
Ronald Terchek
Larman Wilson
James Wolfe

Contents

Interaction: Foreign Policy and Public Policy

Introduction:
Foreign Policy as Public Policy

Ronald J. Terchek and Don C. Piper

Public policy can conveniently be divided into a domestic component and a foreign component. Accordingly, each component should be expected to possess characteristics common to public policy and each to possess its own distinctive properties as well. Domestic policies are those that are implemented primarily within the territorial and jurisdictional boundaries of the state. In contrast, foreign policy is implemented primarily outside the country and is directed toward the governing authorities or nationals of other states and international organizations. The basic constituencies of foreign and domestic policy have also traditionally been different, although for some issues, domestic groups may be quite active on behalf of foreign policy issues that affect the domestic well-being of their members or foreign groups with which they have a strong affiliation. In the same manner and for the same reasons foreign constituencies may be quite active in domestic issues. The policy processes also show some marked differences between the making of domestic policy and the making of foreign policy. Domestic policy has generally been more involved in public debate, political controversy, and group conflict than foreign policy, which frequently has been the province of a specialized elite operating against a background of public indifference or deference.

It is, however, inappropriate to conclude from these differences that foreign policy is distinct from or not a part of public policy in the United States. Foreign policy is public policy in the same way that domestic policy is public policy. Both constitute public policy because they involve the authoritative allocation of resources and the promotion or protection of values through governmental institutions and processes.

Foreign and domestic policy frequently present different aspects of the same issue, whether political, economic, or social. Although

1

there may be some issues of public policy, such as public housing, that have only a domestic dimension, it is difficult to conceive of any that have only a foreign dimension—although some, such as national intelligence gathering, clearly impinge on domestic politics in only a peripheral way at best. In many issues of public policy there are trade-offs between competing foreign and domestic goals; of some issues, the foreign policy dimension will be dominant and of others the domestic dimension will be dominant. The weight achieved by each dimension can never be regarded as absolute or unchangeable. Fluid situations, both foreign and domestic, and the adoption of new policy priorities will require adjustments in the public policy balance. Not surprisingly, there is likely to be a continuing tension among the various policy makers, constituency groups, and interested parties as they compete to establish a balance between the two dimensions.

Public policy today means more than authoritative allocations of values. It also refers to a way of studying both policies and their alternatives. Analysts of public policy attempt to generate standards for evaluating policies and their alternatives, study alternative ways of solving a problem, and assess the feasibility and costs of various policies and their alternatives.[1] In addition, those engaged in policy analysis have attempted to anticipate some of the unintended consequences of policy and determine whether those unintended consequences are beneficial or harmful to desired goals.[2]

In an important way, policy analysis is not a new component of the study of foreign policy. Government officials and scholars have long considered foreign policy to be a rational enterprise, one that was free from the pulls and pressures of domestic policy. National goals could be identified, strategies for implementation constructed, and resources collected to further foreign policy in ways that were not characteristic of the making of domestic policy, which had to deal with local constituencies, local pressures, and local trade-offs. To undertake a sound study of foreign policy meant that policy makers should be free of the constraints of narrow dogma, unreflective impulse, or group influence.[3]

The characteristics of the foreign policy process are generally identified as the effort to define national goals, to enumerate foreign and domestic obstacles to attainment of those goals, and to attempt to diminish the obstacles and increase the likelihood of policy success. The wild card in the foreign policy process is the potential volatility of the international arena in which isolated events may frequently change the opportunities or constraints facing policy makers. Even though they can generally count on some predictable patterns in the international environment, something akin to Machiavelli's *fortuna* threatens the best-laid plans of policy makers.

Domestic policy making is traditionally more apt to be characterized by a group-conflict model wherein predictions are more difficult, goals more diversified, unintended consequences more likely to arise, and the environment, if not more complex, is usually more crowded with competing interests.

The growth of public policy analysis has focused new attention on various aspects of decision making and option analysis that were previously left as separate concerns. Sometimes, however, we are excessively impressed with the novel and forget continuities in structures, processes, and goals of foreign policy in the United States. Policy analysis has served to emphasize the importance of reliable information in making sound decisions, in recognizing domestic political and cost constraints in evaluating alternative proposals, in searching for alternative policies to strengthen or replace existing policies, and in seeing the increasing connection between foreign and domestic trade-offs. In each of the essays presented in this volume, one or another of these public policy concerns is considered.

The role of the executive in the formulation of public policy that has a dominant foreign policy dimension will remain more substantial than that of Congress. This is in part because the president enjoys the functions of representation and communication, has access to critical information, and serves as commander in chief. These functions combine to give the executive the larger role in the initiation of the foreign-policy-making process and the implementation of established policy. Although the Congress has a lesser part in initiation of policy, its control of the appropriations process, the exercise of the legislative and oversight functions, and the responsibility of the Senate in the approval of treaties and appointments all combine to enable the Congress to contribute significantly to the public and governmental debate over appropriate foreign policy and the allocation of resources to foreign policy activities.

As the domestic dimension of public policy increases in relation to the foreign dimension, the role of the Congress correspondingly increases, and the policy-making process assumes more of the characteristics usually associated with the formulation of domestic policy. It is consequently instructive to observe those issues, such as foreign direct investment in the United States, wherein the domestic dimension appears to be assuming greater importance and the policy-making process to be evolving into more of a domestic policy process.

The contributors to this volume examine one or another aspect of foreign policy as public policy. The essays in part 1 are focused on the processes of the foreign policy decision-making system and identify opportunities and restraints that await foreign policy decision makers. In the essays in part 2 some important substantive issues in public policy that contain both foreign and domestic policy components are considered. In some of the issues, such as disarmament and human rights, the foreign policy dimension is clearly dominant. In others, such as illegal immigration, the domestic policy dimension is dominant. And in a third group of issues the delicate balance between foreign and domestic policy goals is in a state of flux, and the public policy is consequently in a process of evolution—the law of the sea and foreign direct investment in the United States, for example.

Norman Graebner finds that the president has had virtually a free hand in constructing major foreign policies. The great issues of war and peace and strategic commitments have emerged out of a consensus formed by a small elite in the executive branch, and the public has largely been deferential to the president's foreign policy. Because of the dominant executive role, foreign policy decision makers are able to generate their own views and cling to them without direct reference to the public much more successfully than can the makers of domestic policy.

In addition, there does not appear to be any systematic process for inserting public ideas into the foreign policy process. Consequently those in public office are on the whole free to accept or ignore the public discussion, depending upon whether it is in support of their own views.

The constitutional function of the Senate in the treaty-making process still remains important, as the delay of the SALT II treaty and the heated controversy over the Panama Canal treaties indicate. The powers of the purse, amendment, and hearings, moreover, give both houses of Congress the ability to influence administration policy proposals, and each of these legislative initiatives has been extensively studied. One area of legislative-executive conflict over control of foreign policy has not received attention, however, and that is the presidential veto and the congressional override of the veto. The veto becomes important when Congress initiates and passes legislation opposed by the administration—that is, when the negotiating processes between the two branches break down and the legislative branch votes its will contrary to the president's preference. Frank Feigert analyzes the historical and contemporary importance of the veto and examines the way the veto and the veto-override process actually influence policy outcomes in defense and foreign policy.

Taken together, Graebner's and Feigert's contributions indicate continuation of presidential predominance in foreign policy. While not disputing this argument, Ronald Terchek finds that the foreign policy process has become more complex, that new participants are active, and that more and more foreign policy issues are linked to issues of domestic policy. The flexibility and independence that once characterized the foreign policy process now seem more appropriate at the level of global and strategic decision making but much less characteristic of a wide range of other foreign policy issues. Terchek argues that foreign policy elites must accommodate a growing diversity of interests—from economic to environmental to ethnic to energy. The increasingly intimate relations and frequent trade-offs between foreign and domestic policies, moreover, have produced less indifference toward certain foreign policy issues and less deference to foreign policy elites in certain sectors than there were in the past. With the nature of the issues changing, the number of participants increasing, and the linkages between domestic and foreign policy intensifying, some foreign policy issues appear to be facing some political constraints of the same kind that accompany much domestic policy. More and more foreign policy issues are resembling the bargaining and compromising that characterize the domestic political arena, and policy proposals in the international arena that might once have seemed politically feasible no longer seem destined for automatic acceptance.

Concerns about political feasibility are obviously central to the public policy process, but equally critical is the quality of information available to decision makers. Timely, reliable information does not produce good decisions by itself, but decisions based on faulty information rest on a weak foundation. Incomplete or misleading information has always been a problem in policy making but takes on special importance in strategic foreign and military policy, where many of the sources and much of the content of strategic intelligence occur outside public scrutiny. Harry Howe Ransom's discussion of information gathering highlights the pitfalls and the importance of strategic intelligence and the special dangers that come from a reluctance to examine mistakes made in the past. Like Graebner, Ransom finds that one of the principal weaknesses of a closed, nearly insular foreign policy elite is its unwillingness to sponsor criticism that would improve its own performance and the quality of its future decisions.

The chapters on substantive foreign policies all indicate the influence of past policies on present alternatives, policy trade-offs, and the problem of complexity and unpredictability in foreign policy. They also identify the importance of both foreign and domestic constituencies and the balance between foreign and domestic policy

5

that exists or is required for a responsive public policy.

These themes come together in an issue as old as immigration, as complex as foreign direct investment in the United States, and as apparently prosaic as the seabeds. Demetrios Papademetriou focuses on the domestic consequences of American immigration policy and the group forces that seek to influence that policy. Economic, social, demographic, and political considerations not only compete with one another but must be weighed in the policy equation when the consequences for other countries of alternative policies are faced. Papademetriou's chapter also reflects a theme developed earlier in Terchek's essay: certain important foreign policies, such as immigration, are not merely foreign policy issues, because their solution depends on the way various domestic, economic, social, and political issues are solved.

The problem of trade-offs assumes a somewhat different dimension in Don Piper's discussion of foreign direct investment in the United States. Public policy discussion in the past has been limited and dominated by the policy of promoting and protecting American foreign direct investment abroad. As a consequence of this successful policy there now exist constraints on the range of acceptable domestic policy options available for the federal and state governments that will neither place the American government in the position of presenting a dual standard in foreign and domestic policy nor jeopardize American investment abroad. Nevertheless, recent concern about possible undesirable consequences of foreign investment in the United States suggests that the dominant policy concern of protecting foreign policy interests abroad is being challenged and that the new policy debate will be focused on the appropriate balance that should be maintained in order to achieve both foreign and domestic policy goals.

According to the old formula of bipartisanship, politics should stop at the water's edge, and the nation should present a united front as it moves beyond the oceans. But what is happening in the waters and on the floor of the oceans is hardly an uncontentious affair. Gerard J. Mangone carefully details the conflicts between military imperatives and economic interests as well as the disputes among economic interests. The interests of the fisheries industry are not compatible with those of the mining industry, and neither is especially concerned about some important questions of scientific research and exploration or environmental safeguards. Mangone also highlights the importance of bureaucratic bargaining and compromise in the foreign policy process and shows that on this issue there is no clear elite consensus about the seabeds beyond the attempt to accommodate as many domestic interests as possible.

The problem of trade-offs is particularly important in Larman Wilson's article about human rights. Concern for human rights is the most recent expression of idealism in American foreign policy and, like other elements of idealism in foreign policy, creates both opportunities and dangers. We would all like to think that the United States is more than the sum of its economic interests, however they are defined, and that U.S. foreign policy seeks not only to protect and defend American democracy but also to enhance the respect for and observance of human rights abroad. Idealism makes support for U.S. policy more palatable, both at home and abroad. It can, moreover, give coherence to a policy that might otherwise be seen as reflecting domestic power configurations. Idealism may conflict with other goals, however, and be applied only selectively. And like other efforts at idealism in foreign policy, the human rights thrust has often been compromised and selectively applied. Violations of rights are more apt to be seen through the lenses of strategic requirements, and the Soviet Union is more likely to be found wanting than are some American allies. Wilson identifies the strengths and weaknesses of the approach of the Carter administration to the promotion of human rights and considers whether promotion of human rights has become institutionalized as a dimension of American public policy.

The drag of past policies on future options and the inability of the elite to review their past successes and failures critically can be seen in the examination of arms control and disarmament policies. Although some earlier attempts at arms control have had the result of capping some forms of armaments or delivery systems, they also opened the door simultaneously to intensive and expensive stockpiling of new, and usually more lethal, weapons. Indeed, the SALT II treaty is no exception to this generalization. As part of the price he was willing to pay to assure the votes he needed in the Senate, President Carter pledged new weapons systems to compensate for other systems that would be restricted in the proposed treaty. Given our inability to reach general disarmament and our tendency to redirect the arms race when agreements are reached, it may well be important to consider alternatives, some new, some not so new. The goal of widespread limitation of arms may be laudable, but experience indicates that it is not really feasible. James Wolfe's proposed regional, selective approach to arms control introduces an important element into the alternatives to global disarmament and takes into account trade-offs and the criterion of feasibility.

American foreign policy continues to face important challenges abroad, but along with the stock of traditional opportunities and constraints that have helped to shape policy, new challenges are rising, making policy analysis more difficult. New complexity has built on past complexity, on both the successes and the failures of previous policy initiatives. The successful pattern of earlier American foreign investment abroad has introduced constraints for considering current alternatives to regulation of foreign investment in the United States. At the same time, the failure of earlier comprehensive arms-control initiatives invites the serious consideration of alternative policies to regulate the spread and use of dangerous weapons. Along with a need to respond to foreign actors and international events, American foreign policy also faces increasing complexity at the policy-making level. More and more domestic issues are merging with international issues, and more and more foreign policies are having domestic consequences.

Notes

1. Duncan MacRae, Jr., "Concepts and Methods of Policy Analysis," *Society* (September-October 1979), p. 17.
2. Thomas R. Dye, *Understanding Public Policy* (Englewood Cliffs, N.J.: Prentice-Hall, 1975), p. 3.
3. Walter Lippmann, *The Public Philosophy* (Boston: Little, Brown and Company, 1955).

PART ONE
The Policy-Making Process

1

Public Opinion and Foreign Policy: A Pragmatic View

NORMAN A. GRAEBNER

The Historic Dominance of the Executive in External Affairs

The idea of democracy rests on the assumption that the public is the ultimate source of political power. Democracy claims superiority as a political system because policies democratically formed will be supported by the combined intelligence and virtue of the masses. Democracy proclaims majority rule, not because the majority possesses the greater power in society, but because with free expressions of opinion it is more apt to be right. Throughout modern times, however, the public's understandable deficiencies in essential knowledge and the difficulties it has faced in judging the costs and benefits of alternative policies have tended to eliminate questions of foreign policy from normal democratic processes. How was a people to know the possible effect of a revolution, a change in government, an act of aggression, or a variety of mundane events in distant lands on its own interests or those of other countries? Of what use, moreover, were public preferences that exceeded the possibilities of successful action abroad? Such opinion, if effective, could drive a nation to disaster. Thus, even in democratic states, external affairs evolved outside the boundaries of legitimate public discourse. Foreign offices determined the world's foreign policies; the masses could judge them but could not control them.

What challenged this elitist control of foreign policy was the tragedy of the Great War of 1914–1918. The failure of Europe's leaders to prevent the outbreak of that war and, thereafter, to curtail its destructiveness discredited the old diplomacy. "After the war," observed one member of the British House of Commons in 1918, "the old diplomacy of Court and upper classes will be in the eyes of most people, obsolete and inadequate."[1] The national and human sacrifices which that war levied on the populace made it clear that future decisions would require public support or fail. As Lord Strang, later undersecretary in the British Foreign Office, observed, "In a world where war is everybody's tragedy and everybody's nightmare, diplomacy is everybody's business." People who would man the barricades and make the sacrifices that would follow any breakdown of the peace had the right to approve or disapprove every policy proposal that involved a national obligation.[2]

After Versailles Western writers and statesmen anticipated the emergence of an *educated* public, prepared to exert its influence in behalf of a more peaceful future. Democratically controlled policies would be responsible; they would limit government actions to what the public regarded as decent and proper. Elihu Root, elder statesman of the Republican party, promulgated this encouraging view of the public in the first issue of *Foreign Affairs* in 1922:

> When foreign offices were ruled by autocracies or oligarchies the danger of war was in sinister purpose. When foreign affairs are ruled by democracies the danger of war will be in mistaken beliefs. The world will be the gainer by the change, for, while there is no human way to prevent a king from having a bad heart, there is a human way to prevent a people from having an erroneous opinion. That way is to furnish the whole people, as a part of their ordinary education, with correct information about their relations to other peoples, about the limitations upon their own rights, about their duties to respect the rights of others, about what has happened and is happening in international affairs, and about the effects upon national life of the things that are done or refused as between nations; so that the people themselves will have the means to test misinformation and appeals to prejudice and passion based upon error.[3]

This vision of an informed people, possessing cultural maturity, exerting its will through democratic procedures, was an appealing one. "There is no guarantee of peace," declared Idaho's William E. Borah, "like the guarantee which springs from the common sense of the people in those matters which contribute to peace or war."[4]

During the two long generations that followed Versailles countless writers and statesmen assumed that the government of the United States absorbed public opinion and embodied it in its foreign policies. Public opinion expert Martin Kriesberg once observed that the American people "ultimately make or break our foreign policy."[5] Historically any evaluation of the role of public opinion in the formulation of foreign policy raises two related questions: What was the extent of the public's influence? Was that influence beneficial, as Borah suggested, or destructive? Dean Rusk, addressing the American Political Science Association in September 1965, answered both questions in a classic definition of the public's role:

> The simple fact is that the long-range foreign policy of the United States is determined by the American people. . . . Throughout my long years in government, I have found that the American people expect their government to travel a broad highway of policy which responds to their simple and decent purposes and that when government wanders over toward the soft shoulders on either side of the road the people have a dozen ways to nudge the public vehicle back toward the hard surface.[6]

Some students of American opinion have recognized a more direct and restrictive public role in the country's external relations. The notion that public opinion actually determined the character of American policy after the Great War permitted such observers to assign to the public a large share of the responsibility for the breakdown of the Versailles order in the 1930s and for everything that went wrong thereafter. Alexis de Tocqueville, in his *Democracy in America*, had warned the American people a century earlier:

> Foreign policies demand scarcely any of those qualities which a democracy possesses; and they require, on the contrary, the perfect use of almost all those faculties in which it is deficient. . . . [A] democracy is unable to regulate the details of an important undertaking, to persevere in a design, and to work out its execution in the presence of serious obstacles.

Specifically, wrote Tocqueville, a democracy could not maintain the secrecy and patience necessary for the conduct of successful foreign relations; rather, it would sacrifice prudence and mature design to gratify a momentary caprice.[7] Walter Lippmann attributed the post-Versailles decline of the great democracies to the wartime derangement of power that permitted the public to impose a "massive negative" on the foreign policies of the Western powers. "The unhappy truth," he wrote, "is that the prevailing public opinion has been destructively wrong at the critical junctures. The people have imposed a veto upon the judgment of informed and responsible officials. They have compelled the governments, which usually knew what would have been wiser . . . to be too late with too little . . . too pacifist in peace and too bellicose in war, too neutralist or appeasing in negotiation or too intransigent."[8] Policy failed, believed Lippmann, because the public persistently challenged the soundness of official proposals and rejected them.

Such observations explain neither the nature nor the quality of the public's role. The anticipation that policies based on the will of the public would attain unprecedented levels of wisdom and responsibility ignored the inescapable limitations that even a democracy imposed on public opinion. These limitations were inherent in government itself. People in the mass could not make or influence foreign policy in any specific sense. Whatever the possibilities of public education, the masses continued to know little about questions that did not touch them directly. Only a tiny educated minority could command the facts required to pass firm judgment on most external decisions. That small public might criticize; it could not substitute policies of its own. It had no voice or institution through which it could act. Neither had the Congress. Only the executive, supported by specialists in foreign affairs, could assume responsibility for the foreign policies of the country. If the president failed to perform his function as the creator and defender of policy, no one else could do so, except perhaps those officials who shared the task of policy formulation. "It is not enough," admitted Secretary of State Dean Acheson, "to give the President wise, though tough, advice and expect him to create acceptance in Congress and the country for the resulting action. We also had a duty to explain and persuade."[9] Arguing for executive leadership in foreign affairs, Senator Hugh Scott of Pennsylvania once declared, "Wars cannot be fought and peace achieved by committee—certainly not a committee of 535." President Richard Nixon claimed a mandate "to articulate the nation's values, define its goals and marshal its will." To the extent that the public might resist an essential foreign policy decision, American leadership has failed.[10]

In its educative role the United States government never had the field to itself. After Versailles outsiders continued to compete for the public's attention. Public sentiment on any external issue can have existence only as foreign policy elites, inside and outside government, give it vitality, strength, and direction. Except for those engaged directly in the study of international affairs, Americans could be no wiser than those who instructed them. The public would become destructive of the national interest when its ignorance or prejudice was not attacked, but exploited. What rendered the task of exploitation easy was the public's primary concern for acceptable ends, not for the definition of means. Thus the troublesome element in public opinion was never its role as a factor in the creation of policy; it was rather the body of public expectation formed by those who influenced opinion and the extent to which widely held expectations would sustain external policies that were relevant to the country's limited interests as well as its limited power. What troubled Elihu Root in 1922 was the prospect that political demagogues would seek popularity and that newspaper editors would seek additional circulation by attacking the behavior of other countries and involving the public politically and emotionally in external matters that transcended the country's historic interests and thereby defied the creation of genuine policy. Equally troublesome were those editors, members of Congress, and spokesmen of the party out of power—none of whom carried any responsibility for national policy—who effectively aroused segments of the public by seizing upon the most demanding or most promising from among suggested alternatives and insisting that the government, to protect the nation's security or prestige, achieve no less, whatever the possibilities of success.

Still there is little evidence that public opinion, whatever its potentially troublesome qualities, has greatly influenced policy.[11] The public can scarcely reach, much less overwhelm, those concerned with the defense of national decisions. In Washington opinion exists only as officials choose to recognize it. Some outsiders, because of special knowledge or competence gained by virtue of education, connections, or occupational position that permits access to government, may have a measurable part in the formulation of policy. The New York Council on Foreign Relations, comprising largely business executives, bankers, and lawyers, has traditionally had close relations with official Washington. Not only has the council usually given the State Department its overwhelming support, but also many of its members have held high positions in government. Officials may seek the views of foreign correspondents of broad experience and proven knowledge. At the same time the State Department cannot ignore those whose views it does not seek. Positive opinion reinforces policy. To that extent officials may recognize and encourage the support of columnists, newspaper editors, scholars, and foreign policy groups such as the Foreign Policy Association. Adverse opinion may influence policy makers before they reach a decision; thereafter those responsible for policy will ignore contrary opinions and arguments even if they emanate from government itself. Thus the essential limitations on foreign policy lie within the executive branch. Seldom will any policy reasonable enough to win inside approval fail to achieve public acceptance. The lack of internal conviction is as much a barrier to action as is the challenge of gaining and sustaining the needed public support.

If foreign policies are generated internally, the task of government is less to accommodate itself to opposing opinions than to capture and maintain the necessary public approval for its policy choices. "The support of the American people for our foreign relations," wrote former State Department official Andrew Berding, "can be obtained only if they are kept adequately informed of our foreign policy thinking and developments. If they understand what our foreign policy makers have in mind, they are far more likely to give their approval."[12] With its command of the news and its dominance of the media in all their forms, the government faces no difficulty in sustaining its educative role. Much of the State Department's effort is devoted to public relations. Official speeches, hearings, news releases, and press conferences are designed to impart information, not to gather it. Merely by dispensing official policy statements the press and television serve the interests of government admirably.

Essentially the power of the executive branch to control opinion rests on its capacity to define any problem in terms that will establish the minimum objective of policy and simultaneously to define the means that will promise success at the least possible cost to the American people. Those who would attack such a policy, once it has been established, by arguing for reduced commitments face the charge that they endanger the country in the face of the superior knowledge of the executive branch. Those who would increase the means will stand accused of impatience, unnecessary risk taking, or a willingness to waste human and material resources needlessly. It is not strange that presidents generally manage to outmaneuver their critics. The widespread lack of intellectual sophistication among the American people simply enhances the power of the executive to control them. It is often the absence of critical judgment that enables officials, as representatives of government authority, to sustain the approval of the majority against those who cite the unachievable goals or the absence of adequate means in official policy formulations. The better informed the public, the more threatening it becomes. No important policy is so flawless that it can stand close scrutiny through time; eventually even the most successful become subject to telling criticism. When pressed, officials often dismiss contrary opinions with the charge that only those in government have access to the relevant facts, usually secret. At issue in the perennial contest between government and its critics is not the obligation of the former to defend its decisions, but the quality of the decisions that it defends.

16

NORMAN A. GRAEBNER

The Interwar Years: A Public Misled

Seldom after Versailles was the public influential or troublesome. The major foreign policies of the interwar years reflected a broad consensus that included both government officials and the public. Republican and Democratic leaders, sharing the post-Versailles euphoria with its central assumption that the Great War had eliminated power politics from international life, logically denied that conditions abroad necessitated any costly American responsibility for the maintenance of order. Their denial merely reinforced the country's distrust of traditional diplomacy, its assumptions of moral superiority, its lack of interest in foreign commitments (especially toward Europe), and its preference for avoiding rather than confronting the challenges to international stability that were bound to recur. Successive policy proposals, all emanating from the government, assured the public that the nation could achieve a peaceful future without cost, commitment, or responsibility. The universal emphasis on peace encouraged opinion makers inside and outside the government to exaggerate the importance, even the unique morality, of the status quo. It was true that any serious disturbance of the Versailles treaty structure could endanger regional stability if not world stability. Still the appealing conviction, common in official thought, that only peaceful change could be legitimate burdened diplomacy, not with the traditional management of change, but with its total elimination. The only defense against such varied forms of official over-expectation lay in the nonexistent capacity of the public to recognize and resist them.

Isolationists argued fundamentally that Europe would not involve the United States in another continental conflict. Internationalists insisted not only that the United States would not escape another European war but also that it carried a moral obligation to lead the world toward the further institutionalization of the peace. Both isolationists and internationalists were strangers to the conservative tradition of American diplomacy. Both denied that the United States need be concerned with any specific political or military configuration in Europe or Asia. Whereas isolationists limited the nation's interests to the Western Hemisphere, internationalists assumed that American interests were universal—wherever mankind was oppressed or threatened by aggression. In practice, however, the internationalists would control the world environment, not with the traditional devices of diplomacy or force, but by confronting aggressors with a combination of international law, signed agreements, and world opinion. Behind such undemanding assurances the American foreign policy consensus became almost unshakable. Internationalists offered their four major

17

causes of the 1920s—membership in the League of Nations, membership in the World Court, the Four Power Pact for the Far East, and the Kellogg-Briand Peace Pact—as devices to maintain the status quo without cost or obligation. What mattered in world politics was the limitation of change to peaceful means. In the hands of the internationalists the concepts of peace and peaceful change thus became the bulwark of the status quo, for change limited to general agreement could alter the international order little if at all.

Clearly Franklin D. Roosevelt, after 1933, faced a country addicted to a combination of isolationism and utopian internationalism, either of which would impede the creation of a strategic concept based on interests and power. If his efforts to redirect American policy before the Nazi invasion of Poland in September 1939 were futile, the explanation lies no more in the crippling influence of public opinion than in his own adherence to the utopian formula of peaceful change that he inherited from his Republican predecessors. Roosevelt and his advisers did little to counter the isolationism of the decade. A *Christian Century* poll of 1935 revealed that 91 percent of all Americans agreed that they "would regard as an imbecile anyone who might suggest that, in the event of another European war, the United States should again participate in it." This antiwar sentiment fueled the popular support for the neutrality legislation of 1935–1937. But many of the decisions of the Roosevelt years were no measure of either the strength of American isolationism or Roosevelt's concern with public opinion. Isolationist sentiment embraced only the imperative that the United States avoid another European war; it did not curtail Roosevelt's initiatives elsewhere, especially in Latin America and the Far East. Public opinion favored the recognition of Russia in 1933 by a margin of two to one. Still the decision to end Russia's diplomatic isolation from the United States probably evolved within the administration itself, with executive officials and the press succumbing to parallel arguments.[13]

Roosevelt's Quarantine Speech of October 1937 constituted a cautious assault on isolationist opinion. The reaction to the speech was complex, but it was not an isolationist triumph. Actually there was little in Roosevelt's proposal from which the public could demand a retreat. Even the president's mail conveyed an overwhelming expression of approval. Roosevelt's references to a quarantine defined no program of action, nor did they require much of the American people. They did propose some form of action; that was too much for his critics. Roosevelt admitted to newsmen that his speech constituted less a program than an attitude and a search for a program.[14] What remained was the chasm between the suggestion of a quarantine and the negotiation of a firm alliance against Hitler. Nothing in the American experience prepared Roosevelt to embark on that venture. In the 1930s even the study of international relations, Louis J. Halle has written, "applied to the world as the professors thought it ought to be, rather than to the world as it was. In this dream world, power politics was a thing of the past, power no longer counted, international organization sufficed for the maintenance of international security."[15]

Long before the fall of France in June 1940 isolationism was on the wane, the victim more of Nazi aggressions than of Roosevelt's anti-Nazi preachments. Britain, standing alone, became the central object of American opinion. As early as February 1939 some 69 percent of all Americans polled favored aid to Britain short of war; by April, 66 percent were prepared to send arms and ammunition to Britain in case of war. The battle for Britain, the election of 1940, and lend-lease reaffirmed the commitment of the United States to Britain. When on May 27, 1941, Roosevelt declared in a national radio address that the United States faced the task of ensuring the delivery of American goods in Britain, his mail was overwhelming in its approval. But the president informed newsmen that he had no intention of instituting a system of convoys. Already extreme isolationists who opposed aid to Britain had dwindled to a small minority. Some had become vulnerable to charges of un-Americanism. Still, Roosevelt would not defy the country's isolationists by asking Congress for a declaration of war against Germany. He had anchored his appeal for congressional support to the argument that aid to Britain would keep the United States out of war. Those who favored aid to Britain on the president's terms had carried the interventionist legislation. Roosevelt could not ask such congressmen for war until the Japanese attack on Pearl Harbor destroyed what remained of isolationist influence in Congress.

Executive Leadership and the Creation of the Cold War Consensus: The Truman Years

Americans in 1945 shared a deep respect for the Soviet Union because of that country's special contribution to Germany's destruction. Unfortunately the mutual interests that underwrote the wartime cooperation could not survive the disagreements over the postwar reconstruction of Europe. Polish and other Slavic minorities in the United States, supported by the Catholic press, revealed a deep dissatisfaction with the Yalta agreements, but most Americans regarded the Soviet occupation of Eastern Europe with profound detachment. Even amid the burgeoning evidences of conflict, public attitudes toward the Soviet Union remained ambivalent. Indeed, there was a strong current of pro-Soviet sentiment in the United States as late as the autumn of 1945. Facing a divided and largely unconcerned public, President Harry S. Truman and his advisers were in complete control of American policy. The decision to elevate Eastern Europe into a major issue in United States–Soviet relations emanated from the administration itself. Stalin's belligerent speech of February 1, 1946, and the subsequent Iranian crisis produced a sharp increase in anti-Soviet sentiment, although the bitter reaction to Winston Churchill's Iron Curtain speech in March revealed a still divided opinion toward the emergence of a divided Europe. Throughout 1946 public anti-Soviet opinion lagged behind that of the State Department. The doubts regarding Soviet intentions that dominated the pages of the diaries of James Forrestal, George Kennan's "long telegram" of February 1946, and Clark Clifford's report to the president belonged largely to government insiders.

Britain's plea for aid in the eastern Mediterranean in February 1947 confronted Washington with the opportunity to rally public and congressional support for its burgeoning anti-Soviet convictions. The president's Truman Doctrine speech of March was directed at the American public. Clifford termed it "the opening gun in a campaign to bring people up to [the] realization that the war isn't over by any means."[16] Initially the new program of aid for Greece and Turkey faced a revival of isolationist sentiment in Congress and a still divided public that questioned an anti-Soviet involvement in the eastern Mediterranean. Still, the Truman Doctrine was essential for the evolution of postwar American policy. It not only committed the United States to a global program of resistance to Communist influence but also inaugurated a successful presidential effort to create a broad American consensus on the need for such a program. The Marshall Plan, like the Truman Doctrine, originated totally within the government. For the public, however, it was logical and reassuring; neither in cost nor in obligation did it exceed the capabilities of the United States. Most regarded the massive effort to reconstruct the European economy as a program whose time had come. The Communist coup in Czechoslovakia in February 1948, followed by the Berlin blockade, merely solidified American anti-Soviet sentiment. The emerging consensus toward Europe freed the government to complete the course of containment with the creation of the North Atlantic Treaty Organization (NATO) and the military assistance program.[17]

America's Cold War policies, responding to official perceptions of danger more than visible Soviet demonstrations of hostility, had no precedent in the country's peacetime history. The innovative character of the decisions reinforced the government's control of the national mood. Actually Truman had little interest in public opinion. "Our government," he informed news analysts in May 1947, "is not a democracy, thank God. It's a republic. We elect men to use their best judgment for the public interest." Acheson added bluntly, "If you truly had a democracy and did what the people wanted, you'd go wrong every time."[18] Writers who lauded the new American Cold War policies agreed overwhelmingly that the power to determine policy belonged in the executive branch, not in Congress or with the public. Congress had performed its proper function by approving the measures that the president had offered. The public underwrote those policies by recording, in a succession of opinion polls, its growing distrust of Russia.

Government officials defined the dangers and designed the responses that continued to emerge as national policy. Essentially the Soviet Union gave the United States two realistic choices in Europe. Either this country, supported by its European allies, could attempt to force Soviet compliance with the earlier agreements regarding self-determination, probably at the price of war, or it could recognize the Soviet hegemony in Eastern Europe and accept its existence as the basis of future negotiations. By avoiding both alternatives, containment appealed to all segments of the American people. Acheson bridged the gap between the American determination to avoid war and yet achieve self-determination for east-central Europe by assuming that Europe's very stability, reinforced by NATO, would ultimately force a Soviet retreat and permit a settlement on Western terms.[19] The National Security Council's noted planning document, NSC-68, submitted to the president on April 7, 1950, described a highly dangerous world and advocated larger military expenditures. Facing no public constraints, its creators argued that the United States could arrange the disintegration of Soviet authority without war. They contemplated no less than Soviet acceptance of "an international environment in which free institutions can flourish, and in which the Russian peoples will have a new chance to work out their own destiny. If we can make the Russian people our allies in this enterprise we will obviously have made our task easier and victory more certain." To achieve this goal the United States had no alternative but "to demonstrate the superiority of freedom . . . and to attempt to change the world situation by means short of war in such a way as to frustrate the Kremlin design and hasten the decay of the Soviet system." For NSC-68 the means lay in military strength, readily mobilizable, which would render containment an effective policy "of calculated and gradual coercion." Such containment, by avoiding any direct challenge to Soviet prestige, would sustain "the possibility for the U.S.S.R. to retreat before pressure with a minimum loss of face."[20]

Toward the Far East as well the Truman administration shielded its assumptions from public constraints. Unlike the Cold War policies in Europe, those toward the Orient required little congressional support. To maintain their freedom of action the Democratic leaders sought neither the advice nor the approval of congressional leaders. At no time did they compel their potential critics, whether Republican or Democratic, to acknowledge publicly the nation's limited policy choices in China, the overwhelming prospects of failure, and the possibly exorbitant price of protecting the interests of Chiang Kai-shek militarily. That American policy toward China after 1949 appeared uniquely the result of public and partisan pressure, exerted against a reluctant administration, was in part a measure of the success of the Truman administration in hoarding responsibility for American policy in China before the final collapse of the Nationalist regime in December 1949. China offered Republican leaders only limited partisan advantage until they could demonstrate, first, that the Nationalist collapse endangered American security and, second, that alternative policies available to the Truman administration could have prevented the catastrophe in China and thereby have protected the security of the United States. The Truman administration, under no public pressure, filled the first requirement by transforming China into a key element in the overarching struggle with Russia. It was the spokesmen of the administration who, after 1950, developed the notion that Asian communism was less a vertical movement, lodged essentially in indigenous conditions, than a horizontal movement, an international force directed from Moscow, skimming the Asian landscape in search of nations to conquer and add to the international Communist bloc. When China appeared to be achieving true independence, said Acheson in March 1950, its Communist leaders forced it into the Soviet orbit. The danger to Asia, he said, lay in Soviet-Communist imperialism.[21]

Within that context the North Korean invasion of South Korea in June 1950 was merely another demonstration of Soviet imperialism in Asia. As Truman explained to the American people in January 1951, "Our men are fighting . . . because they know, as we do, that the aggression in Korea is part of the attempt of the Russian communist dictatorship to take over the world, step by step."[22] John Foster Dulles, in his capacity as State Department adviser, informed a New York audience in May 1951, "By the test of conception, birth, nurture, and obedience, the Mao Tse-tung regime [of China] is a creature of the Moscow Politburo, and it is in behalf of Moscow, not of China, that it is destroying the friendship of the Chinese people toward the United States."[23] It was left for Senator Joseph McCarthy of Wisconsin and other Republican leaders to create the required partisan rationale that the Truman administration had alternative policy choices but rejected them because of internal Communist sympathies. Subsequent Republican campaigning reinforced the twin conclusions that communism in Asia was a danger to Asian and Western security and that a spectrum of anti-Communist policies in Asia, centered largely in U.S. recognition and support of the exiled Nationalist regime on Formosa, would contain Communist power in Asia and eventually send it into retreat. Such assumptions of policy in Asia became an essential element in the American consensus on the Cold War.

By midcentury the American foreign policy elite, almost synonymous with the New York Council on Foreign Relations, came into its own as a group of immense influence, thoroughly united internally and truly representative of the American consensus on the Cold War. Yet the very completeness of the consensus from the beginning was an indication that its spokesmen, in power and out, would tend to eliminate from their considerations questions of real complexity. The assumption that the United States possessed the power to render its policies effective eliminated for them the need to examine with sophistication such matters as Soviet intentions or the nature of communism in Asia. It was enough that American policies of containment recognized the presence of danger and prepared to limit that danger through various forms of military expansion and collective security. The consensus on the Cold War had the effect of identifying American conservatism with anticommunism. This deprived conservatism of its historic emphasis on means and bound it to ends that defied the creation of policy. What was lacking in the spectrum of opinion was an organized opposition that could analyze and criticize American policy in conservative terms. Mainline Democratic liberals, represented by the Americans for Democratic Action, had joined the Cold War consensus. Henry Wallace's more radical strain of American liberalism rejected the consensus, as did a minority of Republican isolationists, led by Robert A. Taft and Herbert Hoover.[24] Those who commanded the consensus managed to discredit the objections of both political factions. What remained in potentially effective opposition was a small group of critics from journalism and the universities, led by George Kennan, Walter Lippmann, and Hans J. Morgenthau.

The Eisenhower Consensus: Executive Power in a Divided Nation

Long before Dwight D. Eisenhower entered the White House in January 1953, the nation's foreign policy elites had formulated two distinct approaches to the challenge of Soviet power and ideology. One group, among them leading public officials, such as Dean Acheson, saw the European situation as one in flux, with the Soviets, having taken possession of Slavic Europe, determined to extend their influence, if not their military power, over portions of Western Europe. Soviet power, alleged to be in control of China and the Communist-led forces of Indochina, had converted these traditionally friendly and nonaggressive regions into enemies of peace and stability in Asia. To meet this global challenge, by definition centered in the Kremlin, the United States sustained its commitment both to NATO and to the anti-Communist elements in China, Indochina, and Korea. American officials and those who supported them were determined to accept no change in world politics that flowed from the Soviet victory over Germany or from the triumph of Mao Tse-tung in China. The greater their perceptions of danger, the greater was their insistence that the United States eliminate Soviet control from Eastern Europe and the Peking regime from China. For official Washington the achievement of such purposes presented no problem. Successful containment, they predicted, would aggravate the inconsistencies within the Communist world and assure an ultimate victory without war.

Those who questioned this official view of the Cold War—and they were not numerous—argued that Europe, if divided, was stable and that the Soviet intention was less to conquer Western Europe than to legitimize the Russian hegemony in Eastern Europe. Such assumptions dictated two realistic courses of action for the United States and its allies in Europe: the maintenance of NATO at a reduced level of military expenditure and the ultimate diplomatic recognition of the military-political division of Europe as the best settlement available without another war. Such recognition might achieve a reduction in United States–Soviet tensions and permit a broader range of agreements. The critics of official American policy in Asia argued that the power that propelled both Mao Tse-tung and Ho Chi Minh, Indochina's Communist leader, into positions of leadership and established their goals was not a monolithic communism centered in the Kremlin, but a radical, indigenous nationalism that sought above all the creation of two successful, thoroughly independent nations in East Asia. Since the Peking regime, they warned, rested on the foundation of a massive internal revolution, not the power and influence of the Soviet Union, it would survive any American effort to return Chiang

Kai-shek to power over the mainland. Ultimately, therefore, the United States had no choice but to recognize Peking. Similarly, this minority argued, the United States would be no more successful in resisting Ho Chi Minh in his crusade to free Indochina of French rule and unite its people into one independent nation. Thus the United States had no realistic alternative to that of coming to terms with the Communist leaders of Indochina.[25]

Whatever the responsibility of John Foster Dulles for the foreign policy decisions of the Eisenhower years, American policy after January 1953 received its tone from the words and personality of the noted secretary of state.[26] His reliance on dramatic phrases such as "liberation," "massive retaliation," "unleashing Chiang Kai-shek," "agonizing reappraisal," and "united action" suggested that his policies were grander in purpose and more successful in performance than were those he inherited from the Truman administration. In every case the words and the intentions reflected the will of the administration, not the public. Still, the specific goals that Dulles sought—the liberation of Eastern Europe, China, and Indochina from Communist rule—appealed to powerful, organized minorities. Unfortunately, Dulles's objectives exceeded the possibilities of American policies and thereby rendered them insolvent. Many questioned the rhetoric and the objectives; the administration, free to maneuver, remained firm. Dulles confronted his critics with a consensus so overwhelming that the goals he advocated remained untouchable long after his death in 1959.

Dulles shared Acheson's expectations of success in Europe, but with less patience. His article "A Policy of Boldness," published in Life (May 19, 1952), expressed his determination to give the Truman policies of containment, combined with nonrecognition of the Soviet hegemony, a more positive content to speed up the processes of Soviet decay. The United States, he wrote, possessed moral resources that could topple the Russian imperial structure and ultimately establish a universal dominion of freedom. The time had come to develop a dynamic foreign policy that conformed to moral principles. American policy, he charged, must move beyond "containment" and contemplate the "liberation" of those who lived under compulsion behind the Iron Curtain. This new concept of liberation demanded, as its initial step, that the United States shun any settlement which would recognize Soviet control of alien peoples. As secretary of state, Dulles embodied the twin goals of liberation and German unification in American purpose. So attractive were both goals that Dulles quickly embodied them in the American consensus. Always, however, the means of achieving the triumph of self-determination in Europe lay not in Western power but in the intrinsic weakness of the Soviet system. "If we persist in the course I outline," he assured the nation in January 1954,

> we shall confront dictatorship with a task that is, in the long run, beyond its strength. For unless it changes, it must suppress the human desires that freedom satisfies. . . . If the dictators persist in their present course, then it is they who will be limited to superficial successes, while their foundations crumble under the tread of their iron boots.[27]

Unfortunately, Dulles's goal of liberation, like all broad objectives based on principle, either meant nothing or meant war. Time would demonstrate that liberation meant nothing and that the Eisenhower administration, like that of Truman, would emphasize preparedness and containment.

Following the Korean truce of July 1953, the Committee of One Million, headed by Marvin Liebman of New York, organized and directed the national effort to keep the Peking regime of China out of the United Nations and prevent Washington's recognition of that government. Much of the committee's activity centered on the Congress, where large majorities endorsed its support of Chiang Kai-shek. In many respects the operation of the Committee of One Million was an example of congressional initiative in postwar American foreign policy. When Congress, under periodic prodding from the committee, endorsed the anti-Peking posture of nonrecognition, it generally did so with unanimous votes. From the beginning, however, the committee used Secretary Dulles's uncompromising arguments for nonrecognition to further its cause and saw itself as the necessary source of support for the Eisenhower administration in Far Eastern matters. The progression of events in 1954 and 1955—the formation of the Southeast Asia Treaty Organization (SEATO), the negotiation of the United States–Nationalist China security pact, and the crisis over the offshore islands—enabled the committee, as Liebman phrased it, to strengthen the hand of the Eisenhower administration on China policy.[28]

Whatever the committee's influence on public opinion, it was Dulles himself who led the crusade against mainland China and perfected the rationale for nonrecognition. It was Dulles who assured the country that nonrecognition ultimately would achieve the destruction of the Peking regime. "We can confidently assume," he informed the nation in June 1957, "that international communism's rule of strict conformity is, in China, as elsewhere, a passing and not a perpetual phase. We owe it to ourselves, our allies, and the Chinese people to do all that we can to contribute to that passing."[29] Supported by such predictions of success, the government turned on its critics with a ferocity that suggested grave internal doubts. Few dared dissent from the thesis that China had become part of the Soviet empire and that nonrecognition could determine China's political future. Not even the press chose to offer a more objective and balanced portrayal; it shared responsibility for sustaining the premises that involved the country in China's internal affairs for more than two decades. After 1961 the Committee of One Million accepted the task of holding Congress in line behind the nonrecognition policies of the Kennedy and Johnson administrations. But the committee's influence on Congress and the public never transcended that of the government itself.

Unlike Eastern Europe and China, Indochina had no American constituency at all. Except for the presumption that Ho Chi Minh's North Vietnam had become the Asian spearhead of a Moscow-based international Communist conspiracy, the United States would have avoided its long and humiliating engagement in Indochina. By predicting disaster for the globe should South Vietnam fall, successive administrations transformed a small jungle country into a critical area in the struggle against world communism. Dulles informed the Overseas Press Club of New York on March 29, 1954: "Under the conditions of today the imposition on Southeast Asia of the political system of Communist Russia and its Chinese Communist ally . . . would be a grave threat to the whole free community."[30] After that warning Dulles had no choice but to revise downward the official American estimation of the region's strategic importance or commit the United States to the defense of the province. By escaping this fundamental decision, the Eisenhower administration succeeded in bringing the defense of South Vietnam into the American foreign policy consensus. Whatever the magnitude of the danger, the administration insisted that its support of the new Saigon regime of Ngo Dinh Diem assured Ho's destruction.

Replacing the French in 1954 after the forces of Ho Chi Minh had put them to rout, the administration recognized no lesson in the French defeat at Dienbienphu and ignored the existence of Indochinese nationalism and Ho's relationship to it. Logically, therefore, it would always place too much reliance on Saigon and underestimate the power of Ho Chi Minh. By 1957 American officials spoke freely of Diem's "miracle" in South Vietnam and predicted the unification of that country under free elections.[31] Should the Saigon regime fail to destroy Ho Chi Minh politically, the newly created Southeast Asia Treaty Organization, supported by American air and naval power, would assure Ho's destruction militarily. When after 1961 it was apparent that neither program carried any assurance of success, the Kennedy administration, without any review of the Eisenhower policies, reaffirmed the commitment of the United States to Saigon and began the process of increasing the American presence in Southeast Asia. Determined to avoid a hard decision, Kennedy committed the nation to victory, but with increments of military and economic aid sufficient only to sustain the administration's options, not large enough to require formal national approval. The United States drifted into the war, fought it, and left it without the benefit of a national decision. It was not strange that the involvement ended in disaster.

Kennedy to Kissinger: The Changing Consensus

For more than a decade the Eisenhower-Dulles consensus toward Europe, China, and Indochina was almost complete. The fears of Russian-based communism, combined with the absence of war, rendered the nation's approval even more profound. Right-wing groups, with strong minority support, urged the government to avoid accommodation with Moscow or Peking, convinced that firmness would ultimately produce victory. Senator Barry Goldwater of Arizona emerged as the country's leading spokesman for such foreign policy views. He argued his case for victory in two books, *The Conscience of a Conservative* (1960) and *Why Not Victory?* (1961). Still, the ease with which Eisenhower and his successors defended their anti-Communist foreign policies never eliminated the critics, led by Senator J. William Fulbright of Arkansas and a number of scholars, who argued that the United States lacked both the interests and the means to render its basic policies effective.[32] As early as the Kennedy years, U.S. policy toward China began to waver and with it the influence of the Committee of One Million. State Department official Roger Hilsman's noted speech on China in 1963 suggested no dramatic changes in American policy, but it assumed the persistence of the Peking regime and anticipated the time when the United States would seek accommodation with a less hostile Chinese government.[33] As late as 1965 the committee could still muster majorities in both houses of Congress, but it could no longer maintain much interest outside government or in the United Nations. In December 1966 several senators, including Paul Douglas of Illinois, formally severed their ties with the committee. By 1968 the committee had fewer than one hundred supporters in the House and failed that year in its effort to extract a hard anti-Chinese statement from Republican candidate

Richard Nixon. Indeed, by 1968 much of the Congress and the nation's intellectual community demanded a new approach to China.

Still, any changes in policy would come hard and reflect internal conviction far more than external pressure. That power which enabled the government to create policy with little regard for public opinion provided it with ample capacity to resist its critics. The internal impediments to change were prodigious. Once officials have generated the necessary fears and expectations, have perfected their arguments, and have honed their phrases to achieve the desired public response, they have no desire to desert what has required so much time and energy to create. Ongoing policies, whatever their promises of success, encourage bureaucratic inertia by establishing individual interests in those policies. It is not difficult for officials to become convinced that the policies they defend are indeed the best available. Those in power have no desire to admit error; they face no compulsion to change what is merely extravagant or pointless.[34]

Finally, no government cares to downgrade its commitments to allies. For twenty years Washington resisted every pressure to curtail its obligations to Peking, Saigon, and Berlin. To maintain its cordial relations with West Germany, Washington sustained an uncompromising mood within NATO on the question of unification. George Kennan noted the price of such inflexibility in an interview with J. Robert Moskin, which appeared in *Look* on November 19, 1963:

> This coalition is incapable of agreeing on any negotiated solutions except unconditional capitulation and the satisfaction of the maximum demands of each of our allies. It is easier for a coalition to agree to ask for everything but the kitchen sink, rather than take a real negotiating position. This worries me because there is not going to be any capitulation. Our adversaries are not weak. If we cannot find any negotiating position, the Cold War will continue, and the dangers will not decrease.[35]

After the mid-1960s, world events increasingly demonstrated the limitations of established policies toward Russia and China. The old assumptions that containment would lead to the disintegration of both powers no longer held any promise. By January 1969, when Nixon entered the White House, the times seemed to call for some significant reversals of policy. Henry A. Kissinger, the new president's national security adviser and, after 1973, the secretary of state, explained:

> When I came into office with the Nixon Administration, we were really at the end of a period of American foreign policy in which a redesign would have been necessary to do no

matter who took over. . . . First, Western Europe and Japan had regained economic vitality and some political constancy. Secondly, the simplicities of the cold war began to evaporate. The domestic pressures in all countries for putting an end to tension became greater and greater, and within the Communist world it was self-evident that we were no longer confronting a monolith. . . . So our problem was how to orient America in this world and how to do it in such a way that we could avoid these oscillations between excessive moralism and excessive pragmatism, with excessive concern with power and total rejection of power, which have been fairly characteristic of American policy.[36]

During 1969 President Nixon announced the resumption of ambassadorial talks with China in Warsaw; soon thereafter the State Department published a three-phased relaxation of trade restrictions with China. Early that year Liebman moved to London. In his preparations for the Peking and Moscow summits of 1972 Nixon recognized the new circumstances on the world scene and the opportunities afforded by the Sino-Soviet conflict for improved East-West relations. Both the American people and Congress regarded Nixon's summit conferences and the SALT agreements as important achievements in foreign policy. Nixon was the first president in twenty years to recognize the legitimacy of the Peking regime and to exorcise liberation from American purposes in Europe. Kissinger was the first secretary of state in three generations to judge countries and deal with them on the basis of interest and power, not their alleged moral qualities. It was precisely his political approach to diplomacy, and the arrangements that it permitted, that brought such widespread approval of his activities. What was astonishing in this acceptance of Kissinger's basically pragmatic approach was the fact that it won the plaudits of the same groups that had lauded the largely moralistic and legalistic policies of his predecessors from Cordell Hull to Dean Rusk. The public, Kissinger again demonstrated, is inclined to follow the government.

Vietnam, an American concern, ran its separate course. Lyndon Johnson sustained the necessary majorities in Congress and among the people to escalate the American involvement. By 1968 critics of the war dominated the press, the television networks, the colleges and universities, and the public declarations of congressmen. That year, the Vietnam War broke the consensus of the establishment on American Cold War policy for the first time as the administration now faced the opposition of such establishment figures as Clark Clifford and Dean Acheson. What had rendered the struggle for

Vietnam critical for Western security was not the expansionism of North Vietnam but the global force of international communism, supposedly centered in Russia and China. The recognition of the Sino-Soviet split and the assumption that both Communist giants either were or could be enticed to become status quo powers eliminated the significance of Vietnam as a danger to world security. Still, the Nixon administration sustained the direct American involvement another four years with ample public endorsement. By offering the country the alternative of immediate withdrawal, leading, said Nixon, to global disaster, or Vietnamization of the war with its promise of victory and American withdrawal, the president maintained the necessary public and congressional support until the truce of January 1973 enabled him to withdraw all remaining American ground forces.[37] Polls revealed a steady decline in the number of Americans who favored the initial intervention from 61 percent in August 1965 to 35 percent in August 1968 and 28 percent in May 1971. What supported the war to the end was the majority who hoped that the country could still avoid defeat or at least manage a graceful escape. As Saigon fell in April 1975, bringing the American effort to its long-predicted conclusion, the administration assumed no responsibility for what it and its predecessors had done. The time had come, Kissinger informed newsmen, to put Vietnam behind us and to concentrate on the problems of the future.

Conclusion

In the long run foreign policy is self-corrective. Whatever the governmental or bureaucratic resistance to change, the perennial dichotomy between declared purpose and actual performance will take its toll on national decisions. Experience will test the validity of official evaluations of interest and power embodied in national purposes. The political realities of Eastern Europe, China, and Indochina were no less detectable in 1950 than they were twenty years later. Ultimately the United States would come to terms with them. That the American people supported the full spectrum of the country's foreign policies from the Truman Doctrine to the Vietnam War, including those that would never achieve their designated goals, measured the influence of government over public opinion. Throughout the Cold War, no less than during the interwar years, the American people were no more right or wrong than the policies themselves. Every external cause that failed did so because of errors in official judgment.

Unfortunately, when policies fail, it is not always obvious why they do so. The public can learn from experience only to the extent that government leaders evaluate past decisions openly and offer the nation that education which alone can compensate it for the costs of mistaken policy. In practice, even those who preside at moments of change or failure seldom acknowledge the existence of error in previous decisions. Perhaps this explains why public opinion never reached the level of sophistication that Elihu Root predicted for it almost sixty years ago.

Notes

1. Quoted in Gordon A. Craig, "The Professional Diplomat and His Problems," *World Politics*, vol. 4 (January 1952), p. 147.

2. Lord Strang, quoted in Lester B. Pearson, *Diplomacy in the Nuclear Age* (Cambridge, Mass.: Harvard University Press, 1959; reprint ed., Westport, Conn.: Greenwood Press, 1969), p. 5. Pearson argued that the public had the right to pass judgment on every foreign commitment; see ibid., p. 36.

3. Elihu Root, "A Requisite for the Success of Popular Diplomacy," *Foreign Affairs*, vol. 1 (September 1922), p. 5.

4. For Borah's statement see the Scrapbooks of William E. Borah, 1907–1937, Reel 4, May 10, 1927, Library of Congress.

5. Lester Markel, "Opinion—A Neglected Instrument," in *Public Opinion and Foreign Policy*, ed. Lester Markel (New York: published for the Council on Foreign Relations by Harper, 1949; reprint ed., New York: Arno Press, 1972), p. 23; Martin Kriesberg, "Dark Areas of Ignorance," ibid., p. 49.

6. Dean Rusk, "The Anatomy of Foreign Policy Decisions," *Department of State Bulletin*, vol. 53 (September 27, 1965), pp. 506–7.

7. Alexis de Tocqueville, *Democracy in America*, trans. Henry Reeve (New York, 1899; reprint ed., New York: Simon & Schuster, Washington Square Press, 1971), vol. 1, pp. 237–38.

8. Walter Lippmann, *The Public Philosophy* (Boston: Little, Brown and Company, Atlantic Monthly Press, 1955; paperback ed., New York: New American Library, 1956), pp. 23–24. George Kennan, on occasion, was equally critical of democratic restraints on foreign policy. He wrote in 1978: "Nowhere is the conflict between the requirements of a farseeing, intelligent and effective diplomacy and the shortsighted confusion of the democratic process more flagrant—nowhere does it appear in sharper outline, and nowhere does it have more serious consequences—than in the case of my country." See Kennan, "Foreign Policy and the Professional Diplomat," in *Foreign Policy and the Democratic Process: The Geneva Papers*, ed. Louis J. Halle and Kenneth W. Thompson (Washington, D.C.: University Press of America, 1978), p. 14. In assaying the influence of democratic processes on foreign policy, it is essential that analysts

distinguish between mass or group pressures and the initiatives of government designed to create and sustain a body of popular approval.

9. Dean Acheson, *Present at the Creation: My Years in the State Department* (New York: W. W. Norton & Company, 1969), p. 377.

10. No president accepted his role as the shaper of public opinion more fully than did Harry Truman. He viewed himself essentially as a public relations man. See Manfred Landecker, *The President and Public Opinion* (Washington, D.C.: Public Affairs Press, 1968), p. 64.

11. This view is shared by many students of public opinion. See, for example, Lee Benson, "An Approach to the Scientific Study of Past Public Opinion," *Public Opinion Quarterly*, vol. 31 (Winter 1967–1968), pp. 522–67; Ralph B. Levering, *The Public and American Foreign Policy, 1918–1978* (New York: William Morrow & Company, 1978), pp. 150–51; Bernard C. Cohen, *The Public's Impact on Foreign Policy* (Boston: Little, Brown and Company, 1973).

12. Andrew H. Berding, *Foreign Affairs and You* (Garden City, N.Y.: Doubleday, 1962), p. 168.

13. Robert Browder argues that Roosevelt's decision to recognize the Soviet Union was the result of the pressures of public opinion. Browder, *The Origins of Soviet-American Diplomacy* (Princeton, N.J.: Princeton University Press, 1953), p. 119. Bernard Cohen disagrees. See Cohen, *The Public's Impact on Foreign Policy*, p. 10.

14. Dorothy Borg, *The United States and the Far Eastern Crisis of 1933–1938* (Cambridge, Mass.: Harvard University Press, 1964), pp. 383–86.

15. Louis J. Halle, "The Conduct versus the Teaching of International Relations," *Virginia Quarterly Review*, vol. 53 (Spring 1977), p. 212.

16. Clifford, quoted in John Lewis Gaddis, *The United States and the Origins of the Cold War, 1941–1947* (New York: Columbia University Press, 1972), p. 350.

17. Joseph Marion Jones, *The Fifteen Weeks* (New York: Harcourt, Brace, 1964), pp. 262–63.

18. For a full discussion of Truman's leadership role, see Thomas G. Paterson, "Presidential Foreign Policy, Public Opinion, and Congress: The Truman Years," *Diplomatic History*, vol. 3 (Winter 1979), pp. 1–18. George Elsey, a chief adviser, commented: "The President's job is to *lead* public opinion, not to be a blind follower. You can't sit around and wait for public opinion to tell you what to do. . . . there isn't any public opinion." Ibid., p. 1.

19. For Acheson's assumptions of Russia's decline see David S. McLellan, *Dean Acheson: The State Department Years* (New York: Dodd, Mead & Company, 1976), p. 163.

20. For the passages quoted from NSC-68 see Thomas H. Etzold and John Lewis Gaddis, eds., *Containment: Documents on American Policy and Strategy, 1945–1950* (New York: Columbia University Press, 1978), pp. 390–91, 392, 402.

21. *Department of State Bulletin,* vol. 22 (March 27, 1950), pp. 469–72.

22. Ibid., vol. 24 (January 22, 1951), p. 123.

23. Ibid., vol. 24 (May 28, 1951), p. 844.

24. For Taft's views see Robert A. Taft, *A Foreign Policy for Americans* (Garden City, N.Y.: Doubleday, 1951), pp. 14, 68–69; W. Reed West, "Senator Taft's Foreign Policy," *The Atlantic,* vol. 189 (June 1952), pp. 50–52. For a contemporary criticism of Taft's proposals from the viewpoint of the liberal consensus, see Arthur M. Schlesinger, Jr., "The New Isolationism," ibid., vol. 189 (May 1952), pp. 34–38.

25. This minority consensus found expression in many books and articles in the 1950s. The full spectrum of this criticism of official policy appears in Norman A. Graebner, *The New Isolationism* (New York: Ronald Press, 1956).

26. Richard H. Immerman argues that Eisenhower exercised considerable responsibility in the formulation of foreign policy, despite Dulles's dominant personality. See Immerman, "Eisenhower and Dulles: Who Made the Decisions?" *Political Psychology,* vol. 1 (Autumn 1979), pp. 3–20.

27. *Department of State Bulletin,* vol. 30 (January 25, 1954), pp. 109–10.

28. For this material on the Committee of One Million I am indebted to Stanley D. Bachrack's paper on the committee delivered at the Duquesne History Forum, October 30, 1974.

29. *Department of State Bulletin,* vol. 37 (July 15, 1957), pp. 91–95.

30. Department of State, *American Foreign Policy, 1950–1955: Basic Documents* (Washington, D.C., 1957), vol. 2, p. 2376.

31. See *Department of State Bulletin,* vol. 36 (May 27, 1957), pp. 851–54.

32. Senator J. William Fulbright stated his views in several books and articles. One signal effort was his speech in the Senate on March 25, 1964, in which he developed the theme of "Old Myths and New Realities." The speech was quoted in full in the *New York Times,* March 26, 1964.

33. *Department of State Bulletin,* vol. 50 (January 6, 1964), pp. 11–17.

34. Henry A. Kissinger noted the pressures against change in "The Policymaker and the Intellectual," *The Reporter,* vol. 20 (March 5, 1959), pp. 30–35.

35. J. Robert Moskin, "Our Foreign Policy Is Paralyzed," *Look,* vol. 27 (November 19, 1963), p. 26.

36. Interview with Pierre Salinger of *L'Express,* News Release, April 12, 1975, Bureau of Public Affairs, Department of State.

37. The classic example of Nixon's appeal to the American people for support on the Vietnam war was his television address of November 3, 1969. *Department of State Bulletin,* vol. 61 (November 24, 1969), pp. 437–43.

2

Congressional Response to Presidential Vetoes in Foreign and Defense Policy: Truman to Ford

Frank B. Feigert

Presidential leadership in foreign affairs and defense policy is generally recognized both by members of Congress and by scholars of the presidency and Congress. Rarely is it disputed that the president can and must be in command of certain instruments of foreign and defense policy and the resources with which to make these policies function. Because of this command of resources, it is understood that he, and only he, can react both institutionally and behaviorally to developments within a larger policy framework.

However much the president may be conceded the ability to take the initiative, either in situational responses or in those involving development of policy, it is a simple fact that the president will not go unchallenged very often. Leadership is not to be confused with omnipotence.

Congressional critics have opposed the preeminence of the president in foreign policy in a variety of ways. Congressional investigations and confirmation hearings have been used to embarrass the executive branch and send signals to the president about intense congressional concern. Amendments to foreign and national defense legislation have also been employed to alter and sometimes even reverse the foreign policy of the administration. The necessity for the president to maintain cordial relations with the Congress is indicated by continuing White House liaison and frequent testimony before Congress by ranking members of the administration. Further, the wide array of informal but regular meetings and briefings between congressional leaders and the president and his cabinet and staff have served to alert each side to potentially conflicting positions about foreign policy. Out of the network of give and take, compromises are frequently constructed that make foreign policy issues at least tolerable to the executive branch and a majority of Congress. But efforts at accommodation sometimes fail and the two branches of government stand as adversaries. After compromise and accommodation have failed and a majority of each chamber has passed bills opposed by the president, the prospect of a presidential veto comes into play. In this chapter, I am concerned with the way Congress responds to presidential vetoes that affect foreign and defense policy. In a sense, the veto is one of the most potent legislative weapons at the president's disposal, often carrying a potential for political costs to the president as well. Conversely, the processes involved in attempting to override a veto are complex and cumbersome, and they may be costly to members of Congress.

The process innately favors the president when he vetoes a bill, whether through the so-called pocket veto or through a regular or message veto—the latter so called because the president routinely sends a message to Congress explaining his reasons for the veto.[1] This message can also suggest ways of remedying the legislation so that the president might consider it acceptable, thus providing a cue as to the shape and substance of a substitute bill. Indeed, there are so many potential obstacles as to make it seem remarkable that any bills at all are successful in the override attempt.

There were 2,361 vetoes in the period from Washington to Ford and only ninety-two overrides, a rate of 3.9 percent. Closer examination, however, shows that the president is not always such a clear victor. For one thing, 993 were pocket vetoes, to which the Congress, having adjourned, could not respond. Second, of the remaining 1,368, 823, or more than 60 percent, dealt with private bills, of the sort that Congress would be least likely to attempt to override or to propose a substitute for.[2] As Bertram Gross pointed out in a classic work:

> A large number of vetoed bills are either private relief bills or other minor bills on which it is almost impossible to muster a two-third vote. On bills of a truly major character, it has been harder for a President to make his veto stick.[3]

Four of the ninety-two overrides were of these relatively trivial bills, leaving eight-eighty overrides for the 544 public bills that have been vetoed. This constitutes about 16 percent of the real potential for such action.[4]

36

Thus it can be seen that the process clearly favors the president in most instances. This can be attributed not only to the structural and procedural obstacles in the legislative process but to several other factors as well. One of these, clearly, is the political capital that must be risked by members of Congress who would attempt an override. To try and to fail has costs that members of Congress may be unwilling to assume. Congressional leaders will be especially loath to attempt to override vetoes of bills that are relatively insignificant. Even if the bill should involve a significant change in national policy, the likelihood of an attempt to override the veto is somewhat reduced if the bill finally passed Congress with a margin somewhat less than the requisite two-thirds needed in each chamber for an override. In some instances, therefore, a substitute bill or no attempt might be more desirable.

It might be expected, rather, that override attempts would be more likely to be made when there are some significant issues involved *and* when the issues can also be framed in the context of a challenge to congressional authority. In this case, where the prerogatives of the Congress may be seen as in need of assertion over those of the president, Congress may be more likely to act.

The Foreign and Defense Policy Context

Occasionally certain issues arise that may provoke a confrontation between the president and the Congress. I have analyzed congressional reaction to all foreign and defense policy vetoes by Presidents Truman to Ford. It is important to note that foreign policy and defense have been given the broadest possible definition in this tabulation. Included, for instance, are a number of tariff bills, questions of benefits for veterans, and various bills that could scarcely be considered of major import, such as a bill, vetoed by Truman in 1946, that would have established an optometry corps in the Army Medical Department.

Even with such a broad definition of the term "foreign policy vetoes," fewer than 13 percent of all regular vetoes fall into this category. This could be accounted for in several ways. First, it is conceivable, if not demonstrable, that legislation having to do with foreign and defense policy accounts for roughly 13 percent of all legislation; hence, the veto rate of 13 percent would be more or less appropriate. This may be a moot point, for the simple reason that it is not possible to test this hypothesis with the data now available.

A second hypothesis, also not testable, is that congressional actions in foreign and defense policy rarely elicit legislation that might evoke a presidential veto. This line of argument would be

37

based on the supposition that Congress typically gives the president what he wants, which means that the legislation is not likely to be vetoed in the first place. A basic problem with such a hypothesis is that it ignores certain important constituency-related variables which might affect legislators in the writing, amending, and passage of bills. For instance, a presidential request for military construction funds could be happily amended by any number of congressmen seeking more dollars for their districts. The net result could be a bill that thoroughly distorted the president's priorities or was "inflationary," a reason cited often by Presidents Nixon and Ford in their many veto messages.

A third hypothesis deals with the crux of my argument, reinterpreting the preceding discussion. Although Congress may typically concede leadership to the president in foreign and defense policy, situations may arise that test the relative status or prerogatives of the two branches of government severely. In such instances, Congress may attempt to emerge as an initiator, perhaps even the primary determiner, of policy. It might be expected, then, that Congress would attempt to override vetoes of such legislation more often than not. Some indication of this is given in table 1.

TABLE 1

SUMMARY OF FOREIGN AND DEFENSE POLICY VETOES, BY PRESIDENT, 1945–1976

President	All Regular Public Bill Vetoes	Foreign and Defense Policy Action			
		Vetoes	Overridden vetoes	Sustained vetoes	No Action
Truman	56	8	2	2	4
Eisenhower	36	1	0	0	1
Kennedy	4	0	0	0	0
Johnson	11	1	0	0	1
Nixon	24	3	1	2	0
Ford	45	9	1	4	4
Total	176	22	4	8	10

SOURCES: J. S. Kimmitt, comp., *Presidential Vetoes, 1789–1976*, Office of the Secretary of the Senate (Washington, D.C., 1978), p. ix; R. D. Hupman, comp., *Presidential Vetoes, 1789–1961*, Office of the Secretary of the Senate (Washington, D.C., 1961), p. iv. Data for public vetoes of Presidents Kennedy through Ford are drawn from the *Congressional Quarterly Almanacs, 1962–1976* (Washington, D.C.: Congressional Quarterly, Inc., 1963–1977).

No Congressional Response. Of the twenty-two foreign and defense policy vetoes, no action was taken on ten bills, which, for the most part, were noncontentious. Although they may have had sufficient importance to sponsoring legislators and the Congress, most of the bills were not of a kind to invoke congressional responses that might be costly to the leaders in the event of failure. Included in these "no attempt" at override bills were the bulk of the relatively trivial bills, such as the correction of naval records for members of two revenue cutters and the establishment of an army optometry corps.

Other bills for which there was no attempt made at overriding the president are more problematical, inasmuch as they might have involved a question of prerogatives, such as two military construction bills (H.R. 9893, 1956; H.R. 8439, 1965).

We are therefore left with two bills that were vetoed by the president and for which no override was attempted. In 1975, Congress had passed H.R. 1767, regulating oil import fees, a matter of some importance in relation not only to foreign policy but to domestic policy as well. Passage had been fairly strong, inasmuch as the vote in the House exceeded by twenty-seven the requisite two-thirds required for an override and that in the Senate exceeded it by three. Granted that a few switched votes could have condemned the bill to the dust heap, congressional leaders may have been unwilling to undertake a challenge and be defeated.[5] Perhaps for that reason, congressional leaders expressed themselves as feeling that a compromise with President Ford was desirable, and they therefore took no action to override.[6]

On the last bill for which there was no attempt, there was a clear case of potential conflict between the two institutions, one that the president was able to win simply because the requisite two-thirds majority could not have been achieved. This particular bill, S. 2662 (Foreign Military Aid and Arms Sales), was vetoed in 1976. President Ford's reason for his veto was based on a provision in the bill that would have required the executive to submit for congressional review contracts for foreign arms sales.[7] Interestingly, this had also been the reason behind President Johnson's 1965 veto of H.R. 8439, which dealt with military construction. In that instance, President Johnson had objected to a requirement for advance congressional review of decisions to close military installations.[8]

Clearly, the so-called congressional or legislative veto is a question of interinstitutional prerogatives.[9] Initial passage of S. 2662 showed that there were not enough votes to attempt an override, inasmuch as the Senate had voted 51–35 (7 short of two-thirds) and the House had passed the bill by a 215–185 margin (52 votes short).

In this case a successful override attempt was clearly unlikely, but Congress did not capitulate cleanly. Rather, it passed a substitute bill, reluctantly signed by President Ford, requiring congressional review of sales of arms amounting to more than $7 million, or sales totaling $25 million for all equipment. In this instance, neither institution could claim a clear-cut victory, but Congress was able to gain for itself a voice in a critical aspect of U.S. foreign policy.

To summarize the findings to this point, there were only twenty-two bills vetoed by Presidents Truman through Ford that might be linked to questions of foreign and defense policy. Of these, there was no attempt to override in ten instances; six were essentially trivial or frivolous when considered in the larger context of policy making; two involved the congressional veto (and on one of these a substitute bill was passed); and one clearly had the potential for an override, since there were apparently enough votes for the requisite two-thirds majority, barring any defections on the override vote. On the last-mentioned bill, however, Congress worked out a compromise with the president. In short, for most of those bills for which no override was attempted, Congress acted in a fairly responsible manner, perhaps because the issues were not substantial enough or because effective compromises could be worked out.

We must turn to the remaining categories of congressional action —successful and unsuccessful attempts to override—in order to elicit some understanding of the reasons Congress may choose to challenge the president on certain substantive matters of foreign and defense policy.

Unsuccessful Override Attempts. Override attempts on eight bills failed, thereby sustaining the presidential veto. As might be expected, these were substantively more important, inasmuch as they carried with them the potential stigma of failure by congressional leaders. Five times—four times in the House, once in the Senate—override attempts were defeated in the chamber of origin. Of the remaining three bills, the veto was effectively sustained twice when the other chamber failed to take an override vote. A summary of the unsuccessful overrides can be seen in table 2.

A methodological problem of some importance should be noted here—that is, the designation of bills by their short titles does not always make clear their true nature or the possible reasons for vetoing them. Take, for instance, the third bill listed in table 2. On the surface of it, it could possibly be concluded that President Nixon, ever budget-conscious, vetoed that bill because it was "inflationary," a reason cited quite often both by Mr. Nixon and by his successor,

TABLE 2

Vetoes Sustained, 1945–1976

Bill Number	Date Vetoed	Title of Bill	Action
H.J.R. 106	May 3, 1945	Amend Selective Service Act	Sustained by House, May 3, 1945, 186–177
H.J.R. 238	September 9, 1950	Amend Nationality Act of 1940	Overridden by House, September 14, 1950, 307–14
H.R. 7447	June 6, 1973	Supplemental Appropriations	Sustained by House, June 27, 1973, 241–173
S. 1317	October 23, 1973	USIA Appropriations	Sustained by Senate, October 30, 1973, 54–42
H.J.R. 1131	October 14, 1974	Military Assistance to Turkey	Sustained by House, October 15, 1974, 223–135
H.J.R. 1163	October 17, 1974	Military Assistance to Turkey	Sustained by House, October 17, 1974, 161–83
S. 2350	December 31, 1975	Amend National Security Act of 1947	Overridden by Senate, January 22, 1976, 72–16 No action in House
H.R. 12334	July 2, 1976	Military Construction	Overridden by House, July 22, 1976, 270–131 Sustained by Senate, July 22, 1976, 51–42

Gerald Ford. As we know only too well, however, amendments can more often than not completely distort the intent of legislation.

In this particular case, the title obscures an important conflict that had erupted between Congress and President Nixon over the bombing in Cambodia. Specifically, the amendment forbade the use of appropriated funds for continued bombing in Cambodia. This bill is an example of several facets of legislative behavior in the attempt to override a veto. First, the votes simply were not present when the House passed the bill initially. This vote was 235–172, some thirty-seven votes short of the number that would have been needed for an override. Second, it is evident that Democratic leaders in the House considered the bill important enough to warrant an attempt to override the veto, despite the odds against its success. In other words, the gesture was important enough to justify the attempt. Third, there was substantial vote switching on both sides of the aisle in the override attempt. On the latter vote, 241–173, thirty-five short of the needed two-thirds, the lineup showed some shifts that indicate the difficulty of achieving an override:

> Initial passage: Democrats, 172–52; Republicans, 63–120
> Override vote: Democrats, 188–40; Republicans, 53–133

Clearly, just as the Democratic leaders had exerted pressure to override the veto, Republican leaders had countered in order to sustain the position of the president. Had the bill actually cleared the House, it is likely that an override would have succeeded. The Senate's initial vote was 81–11, the Democrats voting unanimously, 51–0, for passage of the bill with its limit on the president.

Another attempted override that year concerned the U.S. Information Agency (now the U.S. International Communication Agency). This bill (S. 1317) also illustrates the pitfalls of reading too much, or too little, into the title of a bill. Nominally an appropriations bill, it contained a provision that would have required access by members of Congress to certain documents of the agency. This was opposed by President Nixon on the grounds that the confidentiality of internal documents was an executive privilege. Cast in this light, it might appear that an override attempt would have been successful, inasmuch as it posed a conflict over institutional prerogatives. On initial passage by the Senate, the necessary two-thirds majority was present, 62–26. Substantial vote switching by Republicans—from 16–22 to 7–35—between the two votes, however, provided an ample margin of 54–42 on the override attempt, while Democrats remained firm—46–4; 47–7.

Inheriting the same Democratic Congress with which his predecessor had to contend, President Ford also vetoed two bills having to do with foreign policy in 1974, within three days of each other. These dealt with the same issue, in slightly different ways. Ostensibly continuing appropriations bills, each contained a provision regarding sales of arms to Turkey. In the first case (H.J.R. 1131), the House had passed the bill by a vote of 330–25, with a prohibition on funding military assistance to Turkey unless certain conditions were met by the president. One of these was that he certify Turkey's compliance with the Foreign Assistance Act of 1961 and the Foreign Military Sales Act. But more telling was the provision that the president certify to Congress that significant progress had been made in negotiations with Turkey regarding the presence of Turkish military forces on Cyprus. In effect, this interposed a congressional veto on President Ford, and he would have none of it. The next day, the override attempt failed, falling seventeen short, by a vote of 223–135. Even though there had been an overwhelming majority of members of both parties in favor of the bill on initial passage, wholesale Republican vote-switching—from 131–16 to 59–93—defeated the override.

Two days after the defeat of the override attempt, President Ford vetoed a similar resolution, H.J.R. 1163. In this version, the president was authorized to delay a ban on military aid if he felt that this would be of assistance in negotiations dealing with the Cyprus situation. While not a congressional veto, it was evidently seen as a gratuitous congressional interference in the president's power to make foreign policy, as well as injecting another variable into the process of negotiation. This bill had also had substantial support—287–30—on initial passage, but fell two votes short on the attempt to override the veto—161–83. Interestingly, although there was the expected switching of votes by members of the president's party—from 109–22 to 38–50—the failure to override can primarily be attributed to a substantially smaller vote from members of both parties; seventy-three fewer representatives participated in the override attempt.

It might appear that members of both parties were backing away from a fight with the president, but it is hard to reach this conclusion. Rather, the Congress shortly thereafter passed what can only loosely be called a compromise or substitute bill, incorporating specific language on the Turkish-Cypriot situation. Perhaps fearful of a further confrontation, President Ford accepted the bill, restrictions and all.

Hence in the situations in which Congress has attempted to override but failed, we see that the bills have tended to be substantively more important than those on which no attempts at all have been made. Further, they may typically have enjoyed more bipartisan support when passed initially. Members of the president's own party, however, could frequently be counted on in sufficient numbers to support the president, even though the opposition more or less held firm.

Successful Attempts to Override. Only four vetoes were overriden in the subjects we are considering; a summary of vetoes overridden appears in table 3. As can be seen, President Truman was overridden in two instances, and Presidents Nixon and Ford were each overridden once.

At first glance, it might be concluded that the party balance in Congress is the principal variable that accounts for successful overrides, but such a conclusion presents certain problems. For one thing, this might have been a factor only in the third and fourth vetoes. In these, Presidents Nixon and Ford were opposed by congresses under opposition control, but this certainly was not true in the case of the first two vetoes. Second, the sheer weight of some of the balloting suggests that party was not the only variable that affected the override vote. Clearly, members of the president's party were not opposed outright by members of the opposition. In short, there is little reason to believe that vote-switching took place in a manner at all like that which was found in the unsuccessful override attempts. Finally, it is necessary to examine the substance of the bills to see what other pressures might have come to bear on members of Congress in this confrontation.

It must be borne in mind that I have used an extremely broad definition of foreign and defense policy in arriving at my list of vetoed bills. Included are some that fit only loosely under the purview of the president as commander in chief.[10] Two of the overridden bills deal with benefits for veterans—persons who have already served under the president's command. Quite obviously, these two can be seen as having greater relevance to domestic affairs than to defense, inasmuch as veterans' benefits have a significant place in the budget and have to do more generally with domestic policy, but also, and perhaps most significantly, are of concern to incumbent members of Congress who are seeking reelection. Such bills are often regarded as "sacred cows," and votes against them can be perceived, rightly or not, as affecting members' chances for reelection.

An example of the domestic content of many foreign policy bills is given in our immigration laws. Such laws can affect our relations with other countries, but they can also have broad domestic effects. Hence, H.R. 5678, vetoed in 1952 but rather quickly overridden, might properly be construed not as a challenge to President Truman's power to make foreign policy, but as a bill having strong domestic

TABLE 3
VETOES OVERRIDDEN, 1950–1974

Bill Number	Date Vetoed	Title of Bill	Votes to Override
H.R. 6217	September 6, 1950	VA Care for Spanish-American War Veterans	House, September 14, 1950, 321–12 Senate, September 19, 1950, 58–3
H.R. 5678	June 25, 1952	Revise Immigration Laws	House, June 25, 1952, 278–112 Senate, June 27, 1952, 57–26
H.J.R. 542	October 24, 1973	War Powers of Congress	House, November 7, 1973, 284–135 Senate, November 7, 1973, 75–18
H.R. 12628	November 26, 1974	Veterans' Educational Benefits	House, December 3, 1974, 394–10 Senate, December 3, 1974, 90–1

implications. More widely known as the McCarran-Walter Act, this bill had been vetoed by President Truman on the grounds that parts of it were "worse than the infamous Alien Act of 1798."[11] Race was ostensibly eliminated as a criterion for immigration, but national origins were to be considered in allocation of immigration quotas. Further, in the intense atmosphere of rabid postwar concern with communism and subversion, the law made special provision for the exclusion and deportation of aliens. In short, the bill was judged by Congress primarily for its domestic implications rather than as an attempt to override the president's prerogatives in foreign policy.

Finally, a rare example of the potential for major confrontation between Congress and president is presented by the War Powers Act of 1973. Congress had become disenchanted with continued U.S. involvement in the bombing of Cambodia after the Vietnam peace settlement had been signed. The act as passed by Congress imposed stringent controls on the war-making powers of the president. Without exploring the details of the bill, it clearly offered members of Congress a choice between executive power and congressional power. President Nixon rejected the bill as dangerous and unconstitutional.[12] In the override of his veto, there was virtually no shifting of votes:

	House	Senate
Initial passage:	283–123	75–20
Override vote:	284–135	75–18

Clearly, then, this was that extraordinarily rare instance in which there were both a clear confrontation between the two branches and the possibility of judging the issue according to the criterion of executive prerogative versus congressional prerogative alone. In this unusual situation, given great enough disenchantment with presidential behavior, Congress was able to muster sufficient votes to override the presidential veto and to place limits on the president. Whether these are indeed real and effective limits is another story, inasmuch as the law requires, in part, presidential consultation with Congress "in every possible instance" prior to the commitment of U.S. forces either to hostilities or to a situation in which hostilities may be imminent.

Conclusions

We have seen that Congress rarely challenges presidential leadership in foreign and defense policy when faced with a presidential veto. Using a broad approach to the president's prerogative, I have found very few instances of vetoes of bills that concern such matters in the first place and a notable tendency on the part of Congress not even to attempt an override. Part of the reason may be that the bills were for the most part essentially trivial, not worthy of a confrontation in which congressional leaders could lose face in an unsuccessful attempt to override a veto. Another reason that Congress has so seldom overridden presidential vetoes in these two broad areas of policy is that it has shown a tendency to be conciliatory and to pass substitute bills that tend to be in keeping with presidential objections to the original legislation. Even when passing substitute legislation, however, Congress has, on at least one occasion in the recent past (the ban on sales of arms to Turkey), developed legislation that was not at all in line with the president's wishes, legislation that the president was forced to accept if he was not to lose face.

In substantively important situations in which there is a genuine test of presidential prerogatives versus congressional prerogatives, there is no clear rule. In the two situations that emerged from the bombing of Cambodia in 1973, Congress was unable to muster the two-thirds vote necessary to override in one instance. Yet in another, more sweeping in its implications, Congress stood firm, with hardly a switched vote, and imposed limits on the president's ability to commit forces to hostile situations. In retrospect, though the latter legislation appears to become standard textbook fare for the future, it is only fitting to suggest that Congress may, wittingly or not, have provided the president with an "escape clause."

This clause requires that the president consult with Congress "in every possible instance." We have since seen several instances, however, in which such consultation has not taken place, and each represents a unique way in which the applicable restrictions on the president may be interpreted. In the first, the Mayaguez incident of May 1975, President Ford committed U.S. forces in order to free an American-flag merchant vessel. The argument can be made that prior consultation was simply not possible, given the time constraints and the necessity for maintaining security in conducting the operation. The security requirement can also be applied to President Carter's April 1980 use of American forces in Iran, in the attempt to free our hostages there. Indeed, President Carter, in a message to the House and Senate required by the War Powers Resolution, *invoked* that resolution in defending his actions, claiming that this authority was "expressly recognized in Section 8 (d)(1) of the War Powers Resolution."[13]

Further, a question can be raised about the effectiveness of the resolution when the United States is not necessarily facing hostile forces. President Reagan's use of marines as a "peacekeeping" force in Lebanon, during the 1982 withdrawal of Palestinian forces, has raised some serious questions about the extent to which the president may be responsible for committing U.S. forces when blatant hostilities are not expected. When Americans were killed by land mines, for instance, and were not under direct fire, did this constitute an unknowing violation of the intent of the resolution? In short, Congress may have had a "victory" in overriding President Nixon's veto, but three commanders in chief have thus far not been unduly restrained by the effect of that act. One might suggest that the legislative branch won on stylistic prerogative on this issue, but the executive branch has not lost substantively.

Several of the vetoes analyzed were not concerned exclusively with foreign policy. Domestic interests and domestic constituencies were involved with veterans' benefits, tariff questions, immigration policy, local military construction, oil import fees, and Greek ethnic politics (in regard to military aid to Turkey). To the extent that domestic policy impinges on matters of foreign policy, we might expect to find less legislative accommodation with the president, more confrontation, and more frequent use of the veto.

One reason for a greater legislative challenge to the executive can be traced to the way each branch tends to define its responsibilities. Members of Congress see themselves as representatives of their districts or states and find it theoretically justifiable and politically wise to protect and advance the interests of their local constituencies. The president, with a national constituency and international pressures, sees his responsibilities as spokesman and guardian of the national interest. So long as politically potent domestic interests are not threatened by the president's foreign policy, the legislative branch is apt to prove deferential and follow the president's lead in foreign policy. But when foreign policy proposals jeopardize domestic interests, particularly well-organized interests scattered in several congressional districts and states, legislative deference is apt to decline and confrontation increase.

Given the ineffectiveness of clear challenges, I would suggest that Congress is seldom given an advantage by attempting to override a veto on matters of foreign and defense policy. Even if the attempt should succeed, there is some question left as to the function of Congress in these policy areas. As I have shown, the passage of the War Powers Act was a Pyrrhic victory at best, even though the override attempt was successful. It may well be that the veto override is an inadequate tool for achieving accountability. Rather, the normal legislative process, seeking accommodation rather than confrontation, may best fulfill this need. By formulating legislation that is generally acceptable to the executive branch, but incorporating congressional desires and the notion of accountability, Congress may yet achieve more of a coequal status in the areas of foreign and defense policy.

Harmony between the president and Congress is more likely if one party controls both branches of government. This is by no means a certainty, however, as President Carter discovered in numerous instances. The prospects at this writing, with a divided Congress, are even less clear. President Reagan has already been challenged successfully on the nomination of Ernest Lefever in a Senate controlled by his own party. Opposition developed to the sale of Airborne Warning and Control System (AWACS) aircraft to Saudi Arabia and to potential suspension of sales of the F-16 to Israel. In these instances, whether out of conviction or because of appeals of clientele groups seen as essential to the reelection chances of some members, it is evident that Congress has tools at its disposal to challenge the president even before legislation has been passed and is susceptible to veto. Thus, the veto and decisions regarding override attempts represent the acid test of relations between the president and Congress. The issues that will confront President Reagan and the Congress during the next several years have yet to be clearly determined. It is unlikely, however, that either this president or his successors will go unchallenged on issues of foreign and defense policy or that the Congress will often develop clear and successful alternatives through the veto override process.

Notes

1. Clement E. Vose, "The Memorandum Pocket Veto," *Journal of Politics*, vol. 26 (May 1964), pp. 397–405.

2. Clarence A. Berdahl, "The President's Veto of Private Bills," *Political Science Quarterly*, vol. 52 (December 1937), pp. 505–31; Robert Luce, "Petty Business in Congress," *American Political Science Review*, vol. 30 (October 1942), pp. 815–27.

3. Bertram Gross, *The Legislative Struggle* (New York: McGraw-Hill Book Company, 1953), p. 410.

4. Jong R. Lee, "Presidential Vetoes from Washington to Nixon," *Journal of Politics*, vol. 37 (May 1975), p. 523, reports overrides of 6 percent. Lee includes private bills, however, which are rarely the subject of override attempts, because they do not involve questions of substantial public interest.

5. Frank B. Feigert, "Congress and Presidential Vetoes: The Nixon-Ford Years," *American Studies* (Taipei), vol. 7 (December 1977), pp. 77–107;

Feigert and Robert S. Getz, "Congress and the Nixon Vetoes: A Test of Burns' Four-Party Thesis" (Paper prepared for delivery at the annual meeting of the American Political Science Association, San Francisco, September 2–5, 1975).

6. *Congressional Quarterly Weekly Report*, vol. 32 (March 8, 1975), p. 472.

7. *Public Papers of the Presidents of the United States: Gerald R. Ford, 1976–1977* (Washington, D.C.: National Archives and Records Service, 1979), pp. 1481–85.

8. *Public Papers of the Presidents: Lyndon B. Johnson, 1965* (Washington, D.C., 1966), pp. 907–9.

9. See John R. Bolton, *The Legislative Veto: Unseparating the Powers* (Washington, D.C.: American Enterprise Institute, 1977).

10. Clinton Rossiter, *The American Presidency*, 2d ed. (New York: Time, Inc., 1966), especially pp. 10–13.

11. *Public Papers of the Presidents: Harry S. Truman, 1952–1953* (Washington, D.C., 1966), pp. 441–47.

12. *Public Papers of the Presidents: Richard Nixon, 1973* (Washington, D.C., 1975), pp. 893–95.

13. *Congressional Quarterly Weekly Report*, vol. 38 (May 3, 1980), p. 1195.

3

Foreign and Domestic Policy Linkages: Constraints and Challenges to the Foreign Policy Process

RONALD J. TERCHEK

Foreign and domestic policies have frequently been seen as distinct processes, with active political participation on the domestic side and considerably less public attention and energy devoted to international relations. Concentrating on issues of distribution and status, the domestic sector has attracted well-organized interest groups that have made domestic public policy a process of bargaining and compromise. The foreign policy process has occasionally dealt with economic concerns and status, thereby attracting public attention, but, for the most part, high levels of indifference and deference have enabled the makers of foreign policy decisions to proceed with independence and flexibility.

This insulation of the foreign policy process from intense public scrutiny and debate has been thought to enhance the prospects for a coherent national policy, free from the pushes and shoves that help shape much domestic policy. Accordingly, foreign policy is expected to be steadier and more resilient than domestic policy, which must respond not merely to domestic needs but also to the power configurations of domestic politics.

Although the line separating the foreign and domestic policy processes has not always been as sharp as pure models would sometimes have it, the distinction has been valid enough for most policies most of the time. Today, however, the differences between the two processes are becoming blurred, because many foreign policy issues have become intimately linked to domestic political issues. The change is important, not because this is the first time domestic interests have been tied to foreign policy matters, but because of the magnitude of the present-day linkage between foreign and domestic politics and the institutionalization of much of that linkage. The kinds of policies resulting from the new foreign policy process can be expected to differ from policies made by a more or less isolated decision-making elite, untroubled by competing power centers. Nevertheless, before proceeding with a discussion of the growing linkage between foreign and domestic policies and its consequences for foreign policy, it is necessary to stress that not all aspects of the foreign policy process will come to resemble pluralist politics, with such areas as crisis decision making remaining largely exempt from the scrutiny and influence of groups until after the policy has been implemented.

The traditional immunity of the foreign policy process to the turbulence and contention of domestic politics stemmed from several normative and constitutional assumptions that have been stable throughout much of American history. The structure and motivations of the participants, moreover, have been substantially different in the areas of foreign policy and domestic policy. In the next two sections the theoretical, legal, and empirical background that promoted differences between foreign and domestic policy will be considered. In the several succeeding sections I will take up the linkage between domestic interests and foreign policy, following that with a discussion of the relation between foreign policy and national character.

Constitutional and Normative Background

The place to begin an analysis of the making of American foreign policy is the Constitution and the people who fashioned it. The Constitution provided a novel form of representative government that rested on the consent of the governed but was also immune from the temporary turbulences of shifting majorities. The founders were particularly suspicious of concentrated power and built an intricate system of checks and balances and apportioned power throughout the new government. The sharing of power that characterized the making of domestic policy at the federal level is well known, with each legislative chamber, the president, and the courts given important roles. This pattern was not consistently applied to foreign policy, however. With the specific exceptions of tariffs and wars, the most representative body of the new government was excluded from the foreign policy of the day.

The framers of the Constitution did not expect the new government to pursue an active foreign policy. They believed, moreover, that foreign and domestic policies, except for tariffs and wars, were largely separable. In the 1780s, foreign policy seemed remote from the concerns and routines of everyday life, and in a country with expansive growth before it, the intricacies of diplomacy seemed little related to the pressing problems of internal debts, banking, canals, and other domestic issues. The exclusion from the foreign policy process of the popularly elected branch of the new government could be justified on three grounds: (1) foreign policy was generally unimportant; (2) when it was important, as in the case of taxes and war, the House of Representatives was given a vital function; and (3) the inclusion of the House of Representatives, the legislative chamber most likely to follow swift and sharp shifts in public opinion, would contribute to an unstable foreign policy.

The foreign policy assumptions of the framers of the Constitution had a long legacy in liberal and classical republican thought. John Locke, for one, thought there were three powers of government: legislative, executive, and federative. According to Locke, the last of these "contains the power of war and peace, leagues and alliance, and all the transactions with all persons and communities outside the commonwealth."[1] Locke reasoned that "though in a commonwealth the members of it are distinct persons still in reference to one another, and as such are governed by the law of the society," which is made by the legislative and executive powers, the nations of the world are "still in the state of war" and each nation requires a single federative power to speak and act for it.[2] Locke recognized that there were distinctions between his federative and executive powers, but he placed the two powers in the same hands because it was not practical to have one agency entrusted with domestic matters and another with foreign matters.

Classical republican theory also had a profound influence on the framers, who were especially attracted to the republican idea of civic virtue.[3] Cicero and the Roman republicans as well as the English and Florentine republicans despaired of the dangers of self-interest in the body politic. According to the republicans, when each individual or group pursued its own best interests, without regard for the common good, other individuals or groups would feel threatened, lose their earlier self-restraint, and work energetically to protect or expand their own interests. In such an environment, public policy would be a function of the distribution of power among groups rather than a reflection of what was assumed to be best for the entire community. The classical republicans were particularly concerned about the effects of a weakened civic virtue on foreign policy. This is seen in the persistent republican call for a citizen militia rather than mercenaries or a professional army. According to the classical republicans, citizens should be prepared to suspend their private interests during periods of great consequence to the community, rather than allowing narrow interests to dictate policy.

The founding fathers were troubled by many of the problems raised by the republicans, and the writings of Madison and Adams, in particular, point to their considerable concern about the effects of narrow self-interests. Madison relied on competing factions within a continental setting to serve as a check on any single faction's gaining control of national policy. But the danger that factions might dominate the foreign policy process was too great to leave foreign policy to the internal checks that Madison predicted would control domestic factions, and the founders relied on constitutional solutions for control of those dangers.

Empirical Considerations

Political scientists generally rely on two models to explain policy making in America: the pluralist model, replete with interest groups, competition, and compromise, that has been applied to domestic politics, and an elite model that has been applied to foreign policy. The foreign policy model is focused on a small group who generally agree about the substance and direction of foreign policy and have relatively free rein in determining its course. According to this elite model, decisions in the foreign policy area are generally met with popular support or indifference, and widespread controversy is the exception rather than the rule. In contrast, the domestic model is populated with contending interest groups that have developed points of access to the bureaucracy and legislative bodies and can mobilize their members to become politically active. There have traditionally been significantly fewer groups concerned with foreign policy issues, however, and they have tended to be poorly organized and small and to have fewer points of access to the political system. The foreign policy area, moreover, is seen as reflecting a broad national consensus rather than the contentiousness that often accompanies many issues of domestic policy. Controversies such as the debates over the League of Nations after World War I, lend-lease before World War II, and American intervention in Vietnam have frequently been considered anomalies in the overall pattern of elite consensus and elite control of foreign policy.

The distinction between foreign and domestic policy making was based on considerations of both structure and behavior. Generally, people become active over those issues that affect them directly, or what Anthony Downs called producer interests, and are indifferent about issues that touch them only indirectly, or what he called consumer interests.[4] Working with assumptions of this sort about political motivation, writers such as James Rosenau have seen domestic politics as devoted to issues of resources and status, and foreign policy as largely devoid of these concerns. Accordingly, the motivation to participate in domestic politics was appreciably greater than the motivation to participate in foreign policy. In other words, distributive and redistributive issues were structurally confined to domestic policy, in which interest groups contended to influence public policy in ways congenial to their members. In foreign policy, however, public indifference was usually greater than in the domestic arena, group activity correspondingly less, and decision makers less constrained.[5]

Because the sharp distinctions between the foreign and domestic policy models rested on the types of issues processed in the two sectors, there was always a possibility that differences between the models would fade if issues of distribution and income became an important part of the foreign policy agenda or if decisions about foreign policy were tied to the allocation of domestic resources and status. Rosenau recognized this possibility when he observed that if the content of foreign policy issues appreciably changed to encompass "a society's resources and relationships," the foreign policy process would resemble the domestic policy process.[6] That condition is now with us in several foreign policy sectors.

Foreign Policy Sectors and Group Activity

Domestic political issues are frequently sorted into discrete policy sectors, such as transportation, education, or agriculture. The assumption behind sectors is that certain issues, programs, and policies within a sector share some common properties and tend to be distinct from programs and policies outside the sector. It is within issue sectors that interest groups, government advocates, and members of Congress operate, committing their resources, forming alliances, and attempting to influence policy outcomes.

Policy sectors do not necessarily become issue sectors. By their very nature, issues signal disagreements among the parties, and much foreign policy is formulated and implemented without the controversies that are at the heart of issue politics, which is characteristic of domestic politics. Nevertheless, many foreign policy sectors are becoming issue sectors, replete with groups, bargaining, and compromise and not seeming to be much different from domestic issue sectors.

Foreign policies tend to become issues when there are disputes about their morality or their effects on domestic interests. While these features have always been present in one aspect or another of American foreign policy, today more foreign policies affect domestic interests and more domestic interests affect foreign policy. In such a setting, the neat conceptual dividing line between domestic policies and foreign policies begins to fade. Food policy, for example, has become a complex nexus of domestic and international trade-offs, with acreage controls that affect export potential, exports that affect domestic supplies and consumer prices, and grain embargoes that serve foreign policy goals but penalize domestic farmers. What is true of foreign food policy is no less applicable to other economic policies, prompting one recent observer to find the interrelations between foreign economic policy and related domestic policy "so close that one cannot even distinguish on technical grounds what is foreign economic policy and what is not."[7]

Not only have more domestic policy sectors been affected by foreign policy decisions, more and more groups of the population are effectively organized today and in a position to advance their claims in the political process. Since the period immediately following World War II, there has been an explosion in the number and diversity of interest groups, each primarily concerned with the welfare of its own members and quick to act when it believes that its members' interests are threatened. The potential of groups that influence the foreign policy process can be seen in a State Department estimate that more than 3,000 national organizations have an interest in foreign policy.[8]

As important as organized interest groups are in formulating and pressing their interests, the mere presence of such groups does not assure their effectiveness in contemporary pluralist politics. Most of the groups that emphasize foreign policy have not been notably effective. Although some have been on the winning side of various foreign policy issues, few have yet to be decisive participants in formulating policy or in securing its approval. Part of their weakness is to be found in the absence of any strong congressional or bureaucratic constituency that is willing to advocate their position consistently.

One important change in much present-day foreign policy making is that the groups now participating are established organizations primarily concerned with domestic policies. Through the years, these groups, such as manufacturing associations, trade unions, and ethnic groups, have developed their credit with politicians, have cultivated friendly contacts in Congress, have worked hard to create and strengthen federal agencies that protect and advance their interests, and have formed alliances with other groups in policy areas of mutual interest. They are experienced, well-organized, well-financed organizations with access to decision makers in matters of importance to their members. When such groups find that international policies affect their members, they bring to bear on the foreign policy process the politically potent resources they have cultivated in the domestic arena.

Groups are more likely to be important in the policy process when they have institutional advocates in government. Farmers with their ties to the Department of Agriculture, businesses with their ties to the Department of Commerce, unions with their ties to the Department of Labor, and each with important allies on congressional committees not only monitor policies that affect their interests but rely on strategically located advocates to advance their interests when new policies are proposed or old ones are revised. As organized groups and their bureaucratic and congressional allies discover that their policy interests have spilled over into international relations, the traditional foreign policy decision-making process has to contend with new participants whose primary interest is not foreign policy per se but the effects of a segment of foreign policy on their immediate interests. With the expansion of the number of issues and participants in the foreign policy process, protracted interagency bargaining has made decision making more complicated. For example, during the 1974 debate on United States trade policy, the shoe industry drew considerable support from Congress as well as from Commerce, Labor, and the Office of Management and Budget, while State, Treasury, and the Council of Economic Advisers opposed the industry.[9]

With growing international interdependence and complexity, foreign policy is no longer a distant enterprise, remote from the lives of citizens. On the contrary, one or another aspect of international relations now affects some segment of the population.[10] To the extent that they are able, those affected will attempt to influence foreign policy in ways that are favorable to them. The linkage beween the domestic and foreign policy processes has been most noticeable in foreign economic policy, although ethnic politics has been and promises to remain another important area of policy in which domestic groups become important participants in the formulation of policy.[11] In addition, environment, ecology, transportation, communication, and related areas are not merely domestic concerns but overlap with foreign policy to a growing extent.

Economic Groups and Foreign Policy

Domestic economic interests have historically been central to many issues in American foreign policy. What is novel about the present role of economic interests is that the domestic economy is undergoing important changes that promise to bring even closer relations between domestic and foreign policy issues.

Probably the most important reason that domestic economic considerations will drive foreign policy much more frequently in the coming decades is the sluggish rate of domestic economic growth. The economic history of America had been one of unrivaled growth, which caused standards of living to rise, accommodated a growing population with jobs and rising real income, and fulfilled the promise of equality of opportunity for many. At a time of increased expectations, growing foreign competition and mounting inflation, along with a reduced rate of growth, threaten these goals.[12] They threaten not only those who fear they will lose their jobs and markets but also those who fear they will be unable to advance in a constricted economy. Slow domestic growth, intense foreign competition, and other factors provide an incentive for American industry and unions to protect their jobs and earnings—that is, to enter the field of foreign economic policy. Foreign policy considerations—from the most-favored-nation status to tariffs on specific goods to import-quota agreements—can have profound effects both on the domestic economy and on foreign affairs, and domestic economic interest groups have an incentive to increase their activity in both these areas.

The extent of the change in the economic position of the United States in world trade can be seen in the import and export position of the country in relation to that of the rest of the world in 1948 and in 1977. In 1948 the United States accounted for 22 percent of world export trade and 11 percent of imports, but thirty years later, the American share of imports remained stable while its share of exports had fallen more than 50 percent, accounting for only 10 percent of international export trade.[13]

Changes in exports and imports have not been uniform, and some sectors of the economy today show considerable pressure from imports without gaining compensating strong foreign markets. Manufactured goods such as iron ore and clothing registered a trade deficit of $20 billion in 1979. In the transportation sector, almost $30 billion worth of automobiles, parts, and engines were imported, but only $7.5 billion worth were exported, causing declining domestic sales of American cars and a shrinking employment base for American auto workers.[14] Not surprisingly, the leaders of the United Automobile

Workers and executives of Ford and Chrysler have called for relief from foreign competition, particularly from Japanese imports.[15] While domestic interests are primarily concerned with protecting their markets and jobs in the United States, the president and the secretary of state have been fearful lest wide-scale import relief for other hard-pressed industries lead to foreign retribution against other American goods, touch off a destabilizing tariff war, threaten international currency exchanges, and weaken the Western alliance.

Tariff policy has long bridged foreign and domestic policies, and the present situation is no exception. Industries fearful of foreign competition demur from free-trade policies, while industries heavily dependent on exports favor free trade. In the period following World War II, when the United States was a heavy exporter, trade policy, while sometimes controversial, was not a matter of protracted conflict. A broad bipartisan coalition of opinion makers and decision makers generally favored a liberal trade policy, tariffs were reduced, and the most-favored-nation status was generously extended to more and more countries. But as various segments of the American economy became more vulnerable to foreign competition, several organized interests exempted themselves from their earlier endorsement of free trade. Organized labor and many businesses, once strong opponents of protectionism, have recently called for selective trade barriers to protect American jobs. In such a setting, foreign economic policy has come to resemble a pluralist bargaining sector.

There are, of course, many factors that explain the price advantage of imported goods, such as new and more efficient plants and equipment or cheaper labor. Interestingly, however, some of the most intense price competition has come from countries that have standards of living approximately the same as or only marginally lower than that of the United States—that is, most goods competing with American goods in the domestic market cannot be traced to countries with exceedingly low wage rates except in a few selected markets, such as textiles.

Many American-made goods carry a higher cost premium because of increasing wages unaccompanied by greater productivity. In the period between 1973 and 1979, hourly compensation in the United States increased annually between 8.0 percent and 9.9 percent, while annual productivity ranged between −3.0 percent and 3.5 percent during the same six years.[16] During this period of strong domestic demand, much American industry found it profitable to avoid strikes, pay higher wages, and pass the increased costs to consumers in the form of higher prices. Indeed, corporate profits, which might be expected to fall when wages far outdistance gains in productivity, generally increased during the period. Because the stakes in foreign economic policy are so high, it is no wonder that when people's incomes were directly affected by foreign policy, interest groups became more and more active in trying to influence foreign policy. Endowed with organizational strength and allied with bureaucratic and congressional support, economic interests have been critical in shaping important parts of American foreign policy. Indeed, the process favors "immediate domestic concerns over broader foreign policy objectives."[17] In such a policy-making framework the traditional foreign policy elite not only shares its power with other influential, institutionalized actors, it frequently plays a subordinate role in policy formation.

Ethnic Issues and Foreign Policy

In many critical ways, ethnic interest groups are similar to other interest groups, held together by some common interest, which, when threatened, mobilizes their members politically.[18] Ethnic values generally rank low on the scale of preferences of most Americans, however, issues of distribution and status claiming more of their attention and resources. Even so, ethnic issues have spilled over into foreign policy from time to time. One historic set of ethnic issues centers on immigration—the exclusion of Orientals at the turn of the nineteenth century and the immigration acts of the early 1920s, for example. Exclusionary migration acts frequently combine concerns about status and distribution of citizens who fear that the new immigrants would somehow weaken American institutions and culture or would work for lower wages and either force citizens out of work or force them to accept lower wages.

Another set of ethnic issues revolves around ethnically self-conscious groups that have clear foreign policy goals tied to their ethnicity. In the conventional wisdom, they have been credited with an extraordinary amount of influence and with moving administrations and congresses in directions they would not otherwise have taken. Actually the record of ethnic lobbies is mixed. American Irish Catholics were long opposed to any U.S. policy that might favor Britain so long as Ireland was not a free, independent, and united country. And early in this century American politicians frequently, but to a large extent symbolically, accommodated the Irish Catholics with appropriate slurs on the British. When the issue involved American national security, however, the president sided with Britain.

The best-known ethnic group active in foreign policy today is the pro-Israel lobby, which has a record of some notable successes and some notable failures. With American Jews among the politically most attentive and active of any group in the country, with electoral leverage supplied by the concentration of Jews in certain states, and with a salient issue in the security of Israel, the group has the resources and motivation for political involvement. In addition, their cause has traditionally elicited the support of the overwhelming majority of the American people, and the pro-Israel lobby has sought policies that generally did not conflict with the strategic plans of successive administrations in Washington. Although it has developed points of access within the executive branch, the lobby has concentrated its attention on Congress, where it has cultivated sufficient support to veto, if not always to compel, action.[19] When American decision makers saw interests of the United States diverging from those of Israel on key points, however, the pro-Israel lobby sometimes lost. President Eisenhower's decision to oppose the British-French-Israeli attack on Egypt in 1956 was clearly a loss for the pro-Israel lobby. This might be taken to show that when an administration's foreign policy has differed from what the lobbies were seeking, the administration's will has prevailed. But another set of examples can be mustered to show a different picture. In 1972, President Nixon negotiated a trade agreement with the Soviet Union, promising broad trade concessions to Moscow as part of his policy of détente. When the agreement finally reached Congress in 1974, however, the Jackson-Vanik amendment was added, prohibiting most-favored-nation status for the Soviet Union unless emigration of Russian Jews was freely permitted. A year later, the Soviets repudiated the agreement, citing the amendment as a show of bad faith.

Interest groups are important not because they invariably win every contest they enter, but because they are politically important and must be taken seriously when policies are made. As labor, business, and agriculture have found, to establish a credible record it is sufficient to win some of the hard fights. Interest groups do not have to win every contest to demonstrate their importance in the policy-making process. And so it is with the pro-Israel lobby: not powerful enough to dictate American foreign policy in the Middle East, but influential enough to become an important factor in the decision-making process.

The factors that prompted the pro-Israel lobby to political mobilization are unlikely to disappear soon. Threats to the security of Israel will continue to pose a problem. The problems in the region are becoming more complex, moreover, with the growth of economic power among the oil-producing Arab states, and the cross-pressures on the administration and Congress are likely to intensify. Pressure from the Arab states will mount to sell more sophisticated arms to selected Arab states, to keep the United States embassy out of Jerusalem, and to open relations with the Palestine Liberation Organization, and each will fuel political controversy in American foreign policy and generate greater participation by the pro-Israel lobby.

The combination of a salient issue, group cohesiveness, and active mobilization also helps to explain the effectiveness of Greek-Americans in influencing American foreign policy toward Turkey. The overthrow of the democratic regime in Athens was not sufficient to mobilize Greek-Americans, but Turkish military operations in Cyprus, causing forced displacement of thousands of Greeks in territory occupied by the Turkish army for ethnic Turkish Cypriots, brought a quick, unified, and effective response from Greek-Americans that brought about an embargo of American arms to Turkey for several years, in spite of repeated opposition by the administration in Washington.

Not every political disturbance abroad will excite an American ethnic reaction, as witness the indifference of Greek-Americans to the military coup in Greece, and not every salient political issue will give rise to intense ethnic lobbying in the United States, because the groups are either too weak or too divided in their political goals. In addition to the pro-Israel lobby concerning Middle East questions, however, there appear to be several potentially volatile areas of increasing ethnic activity in American foreign policy, and two seem likely to be particularly important: the immigration of illegal aliens from Latin America, and U.S.-African relations.

1. The trade-offs between domestic and foreign policy that revolve around the issue of illegal aliens will probably intensify. Greater ethnic demands can be expected to accompany the growing size of the Spanish-speaking population in the United States. Efforts to satisfy these demands, such as educational programs in Spanish, increased services with expanded tax requirements, and employment protection, will undoubtedly excite considerable opposition in the Anglo and black communities. In the midst of local and regional controversies and pressures, the foreign policy elite must consider the ramifications of foreign policy toward Mexico, not only a close and strategic neighbor but also an important source of imported petroleum. Just as President Kennedy considered American race relations as affecting the image of the United States abroad and therefore the relations between the United States and the newly independent countries of Africa, so leaders today will be encouraged to recognize the

importance of Spanish-speaking ethnic groups for American foreign policy toward Latin America.

2. Although most American blacks are not preoccupied with U.S.-African relations, many members of the black political elite are. Frequently troubled about the unfavorable ratio of American aid to Africa to aid to other parts of the world, and angered by tacit U.S. support for South Africa, various leaders of the black community have given increasing attention to foreign policy.[20] Although it is highly improbable that U.S.-African foreign policy will soon replace issues of domestic distribution for American blacks, it is likely that black leaders will respond to crises on the continent and attempt to influence U.S. foreign policy there. In doing so, black leaders can count on some modest support from the black community and little overt opposition.

What makes the issues of illegal immigration and African relations potentially so important is not that the ethnic constituencies involved—Hispanics and blacks—are cohesive, quickly mobilized groups; their importance lies rather in their sheer numbers and their concentration and strategic location in some key electoral states that may be seen by decision makers as politically important for reasons of domestic politics. In any event, ethnic-based efforts to influence foreign policy will resemble economic-based group efforts, reflecting the transference of pluralist politics into foreign policy issue sectors.

The elite model of foreign policy holds that the public is generally indifferent to most foreign policy, giving decision makers considerable flexibility in constructing and implementing policy. But that virtual isolation of foreign policy from domestic politics has been seriously eroded because of the increasing concern of much foreign policy with matters of income, ethnicity, and distribution.

When the boundaries between the concerns of domestic policy and foreign policy are relatively clear, the foreign policy elite can generally pursue its options without either fearing public opposition or requiring much public support. Most international monetary agreements, for example, require no more than public indifference or deference, but questions that impinge directly on the lives of citizens, such as war and the draft, require concrete support.

Even in issues such as war, the public has more often than not supported the decisions of the elite on these matters. Today a set of issues that calls for considerable sacrifice and is related both to national security and to personal interests, but does not carry the same urgency as war, is developing. The solutions to these issues require a substantial reordering of the habits, expectations, and gratifications of Americans, and the way the domestic side of the issues is resolved will affect the future course of foreign policy as well. Among the many examples of this growing linkage is the recent relationship between domestic economic policies and foreign policy options and between domestic and defense expenditures in the budget.

National Character and Foreign Policy

Students of American foreign policy have assumed that national character provides the foundation and limits of concrete decisions in democratic regimes.[21] Most of the treatments of the American character seem to emphasize one trait or another and in the process ignore much in the national character. What probably needs to be emphasized is that the American character embodies many values, some of which are incompatible. To understand national character, it is helpful to remember that countries, like individuals, sometimes have divergent goals. What helps to define both nations and persons is not merely a list of their characteristics but an understanding of the way those characteristics are assembled, how various potentially conflicting values are arranged in an often uneasy tension, and how one set of values may be important at one time but discounted in favor of other values later. This is not to say that core values cannot be identified; having identified them, however, we need to consider the difference in importance that certain values have at various times.

Today there is a feeling in many quarters that the American character has changed. The concern is generally not that Americans are more militant or more pacifist but rather that they are more self-centered. According to this view, the earlier sense of community, civic virtue, restraint, and patriotism has given way to an introverted citizen body, preoccupied with its own materialism, comforts, entitlements, and privacy. Indeed, the critique is so widespread that it is sometimes difficult to distinguish liberal and conservative assessments about the lack of community and the ascendancy of private interests in contemporary society. Christopher Lasch's quasi-radical concern about the narcissistic personality is matched by Daniel Bell's more conservative critique of the entitlement society.[22] Or consider, for example, the titles of two commentaries about the present moral state of the country, one by the liberal writer John Schaar, "The Case for Patriotism," and the other by the neoconservative Irving Kristol, " 'When virtue loses all her loveliness'—Some Reflections on Capitalism and the Free Society."[23] We would not generally expect liberals to complain that patriotism and duty are dangerously discounted or conservatives to fear that material success has failed to provide us a virtuous life in a just society.

What emerges from the contemporary critique of the American character is not merely its materialism and individualism, which were, after all, features in Tocqueville's treatment of the American character. What must be observed is that individualism was formerly seen as tempered by other values; the American of the past was presented as more civic-minded, and community and patriotism were taken seriously rather than ritualistically or nostalgically.

The values that appear to have been discounted are those the classical republicans feared were especially vulnerable to material self-interest. For them, materialism weakened the social bond. The classical republicans would accept Schaar's observation that people are defined by the way they identify their duties. Because duty often interferes with our private goals, it is frequently impossible to fulfill one's duty and gratify one's personal desires simultaneously. In order for duty to remain viable, people must believe that they are involved in a common enterprise, and the costs they must pay do not relieve someone else of his obligations or enable someone else to profit at their expense. The sense that public policies are considered fair, however, is weak in contemporary America. The rich believe that they are overtaxed and the poor that they are neglected; blacks and women see the continuing legacies of discrimination, while white males fear that their jobs are jeopardized by affirmative action. Indeed, many Americans believe that they are asked to make way for others who, they believe, are no more deserving than they are. When this occurs, the incentive to civic duty and restraint diminishes. As a result, there is a tendency for each individual to wait for others to fulfill their obligations first. Such a strategy, however, has a predictable consequence: each waits for the other, no one moves, and nothing is done. When everyone becomes a free rider, no one rides.

This kind of self-interest differs from the self-interest discussed earlier, in the section on pluralist interest groups. In the latter case, interest provided a motivation to work to influence public policy. With the free rider, there is an incentive to do nothing regarding collective goods and allow someone else to do the work. The free-rider problem has become important regarding two issues that are related to foreign policy: the draft and energy.

For most people in most places during most periods, conscription is a burden, interrupting routines, enforcing separation, and portending danger. That Americans in the 1980s are not enthusiastic about military service is not surprising: in few historical periods have people been. Present-day reluctance about the military draft probably stems from several factors. The political cynicism following the Vietnam War and Watergate and the general lack of political efficacy reduce political commitments and trust. Threats to American security often seem remote and removed, moreover, and the incentive to accept conscription is reduced, particularly when foreign policy is ambiguous. A clear threat to American security would probably serve to unite the country behind conscription, but to wait for such an international crisis might be costly.

Cynicism, suspicion, and confusion are not unique to American society. What is novel and troubling in the national debate about the draft today is the absence of any tension between service and liberty. There is little sense that a civic responsibility might be necessary to secure the rights and prosperity that constitute an important part of the nation's goals.

Tension between rights and duties was always present in classical republicanism: a free people would not submerge its liberties to work for someone or something else constantly. But the impetus to think about oneself was tempered with a sense of civic virtue and restraint. Whatever can be said about present-day America, it cannot be said to possess a strong civic virtue. Nor can it be said to have a vital tension between civic duty and personal entitlements.

The decline in the sense of fairness, civic duty, and service is not a matter that can be traced primarily to foreign policy. We must look rather to domestic policy to find the sources of our present moral and psychological state. Nevertheless, the character of America will have an important effect on the substance and conduct of future foreign policy. A reversal of present attitudes will require transformation of the debate that accompanies national domestic policy. Only when political leaders are unafraid to itemize the costs of policy and to speak of national sacrifice will the prospects of reintroducing civic duty return. But such admonitions will ring hollow unless people believe that the substance of domestic policy is fair.

Defining domestic policies that are fair is not merely beyond the scope of this chapter, it is the beginning of another debate. But surely one aspect of fairness is that politics must increasingly deemphasize interests and begin to concentrate on national policies that emphasize common problems, common costs, and common solutions. This is true of both domestic and foreign policy. One obstacle to a sense of fairness in foreign policy will be the growing influence of interest groups in the foreign policy process. There is the danger that foreign policy decisions may increasingly be seen as reflecting narrow interests and as requiring the rest of the community to tolerate or pay for those interests. Ultimately large segments of the public may condemn the foreign policy process and its decisions as unfair.

Conclusions

The broadening of the foreign policy process has introduced new interests, new actors, and new restraints into the traditional foreign policy model. What this means for foreign policy is not entirely clear, but some of the possible consequences are apparent. First, issues have arisen in recent decades that excite group activity in foreign politics. In the second place, the groups that count in the expanded foreign policy process have an institutional presence in domestic issue sectors. These are the organizations with leverage, influence, and resources, not necessarily the groups with a primary interest in foreign policy. This suggests that policy will reflect either compromises, when opposing sides are roughly paired in foreign policy sectors, or organizational dominance, when there is little institutional competition in the issue sector. Third, there is likely to be less flexibility in a growing number of foreign policy sectors for the foreign policy elite.

Foreign policies that depend on the support of several disparate and often competing interest groups—or at least on the absence of a veto from them—may be policies that are unfocused and that change, not with international events or new administrations, but rather with the strength or weakness of domestic interest groups. Indeed, there is a real possibility that groups heavily involved in both domestic and foreign policy issues may trade benefits on some domestic policies in return for working their will on international issues, or they may reduce their foreign policy goals in exchange for advantages in the domestic arena. There is a danger that as bargaining intensifies, with trade-offs between various foreign and domestic policy issues, foreign policy will become even less coherent than it is now, resembling a heavily amended tax bill rather than reflecting national interests.

The penetration of domestic groups into foreign policy has reduced the ability of traditional foreign policy elite groups to develop timely policy, and the prospects for further delay or even paralysis may increase. Foreign policy often requires clear and timely responses, however, and policy lag can be highly injurious to American interests. The lag problem is particularly important because groups are adept in delaying the implementation of policies far beyond their most effective dates.

Even in those areas in which the influence of domestic interest groups has not been felt, the foreign policy elite frequently finds itself constrained. It has not been able to mobilize an apathetic public in many areas. But public indifference, once important to the foreign policy elite, may become a liability for certain issues. New priorities in the national character that exaggerate individualism and comfort and depreciate service and duty reduce the likelihood of public commitment and service. To reintroduce the tension between rights and duties is the preeminent task of domestic policy, and until that task is accomplished, American foreign policy runs the risk of verging on incoherence, indecision, and stalemate.

Notes

1. John Locke, *Second Treatise of Government*, ed. Peter Laslett (New York: Cambridge University Press, 1960), p. 411.

2. Ibid., pp. 410–11.

3. Cf. Bernard Bailyn, *The Ideological Origins of the American Revolution* (Cambridge: Harvard University Press, 1967), and Gordon S. Wood, *The Creation of the American Republic, 1776–1787* (New York: W. W. Norton & Company, 1969).

4. Anthony Downs, *An Economic Theory of Democracy* (New York: Harper & Row, 1957), p. 9.

5. James Rosenau, *The Scientific Study of Foreign Policy* (New York: Free Press, 1971), pp. 423–39. Cf. Ronald J. Terchek, *The Making of the Test Ban Treaty* (The Hague: Martinus Nijhoff, 1970), chap. 9.

6. Rosenau, *Scientific Study of Foreign Policy*, p. 439.

7. I. M. Destler, *Making Foreign Economic Policy* (Washington, D.C.: Brookings Institution, 1980), p. 212.

8. Barry Hughes, *Domestic Context of American Foreign Policy* (San Francisco: W. H. Freeman, 1978), p. 156. Cf. John Spanier and Eric Uslaner, *How American Foreign Policy Is Made*, 2d ed. (New York: Holt, Rinehart and Winston, 1978), pp. 83–91.

9. Destler, *Making Foreign Economic Policy*, p. 203.

10. Bailyn, *Ideological Origins of the American Revolution*; Wood, *Creation of the American Republic*.

11. Rosenau, *Scientific Study of Foreign Policy*.

12. Cf. Daniel Bell, "The Revolution of Rising Entitlements," *Fortune*, vol. 91, no. 4 (April 1975); and Ronald Terchek, "The Liberal Theory of Entitlements and the Conflict of Good Causes," Midwestern Political Science Association, Chicago, April 20, 1979.

13. Department of International Economic and Social Affairs, Statistical Office, *Yearbook of International Trade Statistics, 1977* (New York: United Nations, 1978), pp. 22–23.

14. Ibid., p. 69.

15. *Wall Street Journal*, February 15, 1980; and *Washington Post*, February 13, 1980.

16. *Washington Post*, May 18, 1980.

17. Graham Allison and Peter Szanton, *Remaking Foreign Policy: The Organizational Connection* (New York: Basic Books, 1976), p. 151.

18. Clifford Hackett, "Ethnic Politics in Congress: The Turkish Embargo Experience," in *Ethnicity and U.S. Foreign Policy*, ed. Abdul A. Said (New York: Praeger Publishers, 1977), p. 40.

19. Robert H. Trice, *Interest Groups and the Foreign Policy Process: U.S. Policy in the Middle East*, Professional Papers in International Studies, vol. 4 (Beverly Hills: Sage Publications, 1977), pp. 57–58.

20. For a discussion of black ethnic foreign policy interests, see Herschelle S. Challenor, "The Influence of Black Americans on U.S. Foreign Policy toward Africa," in *Ethnicity and U.S. Foreign Policy*, ed. Said, pp. 139–75.

21. Gabriel Almond, *The American People and Foreign Policy* (New York: Praeger Publishers, 1960), chap. 2.

22. Christopher Lasch, *The Culture of Narcissism* (New York: W. W. Norton & Company, 1978); Bell, "Revolution of Rising Entitlements."

23. John Schaar, "The Case for Patriotism," *New American Review*, vol. 17 (May 1973); Irving Kristol, " 'When virtue loses all her loveliness'— Some Reflections on Capitalism and the Free Society," *Public Interest*, no. 21 (Fall 1970).

4

Strategic Intelligence and the Formulation of Public Policy

HARRY HOWE RANSOM

Strategic intelligence will be a pivotal influence in foreign and defense policy as the great debates over national security continue into the 1980s. The purpose of this essay is to analyze the nature, performance, and problems of that most mysterious of all elements in foreign policy: information packaged in a variety of forms and labeled "intelligence." The focus will be on intelligence as organization, as process, and as product. The primary focus will be on the Central Intelligence Agency (CIA), although it is but first among equals of half a dozen intelligence units of the United States government.

I assume that public policy cannot be understood without knowledge of the way it is made. Often the crucial ingredient in policy is the information that serves as its base. But even if perfect information were available—which is rarely the case—this would not make decisions predictable or guarantee their effectiveness. Effective policy making is unlikely to take place, however—barring fortuitous good luck—from a base of erroneous information. My hope here is to dispel some of the mystery surrounding the functions of intelligence so that we can better understand how foreign policy is made or how to recognize the failure or success of intelligence and how this relates to the success or failure of policy.

Many obstacles confront the scholar who attempts to deal with this subject. One, perhaps the most obvious, is the government secrecy enveloping most activities labeled "intelligence." A second problem is the definitional jungle one enters when addressing this subject, where widespread confusion characterizes the use, and misuse, of terms that denote such disparate activities as intelligence, espionage, and covert action. Indeed, a conceptual confusion abounds with regard to these functions, and it is compounded by structural ambiguity.

First, let us define these terms as they will be used here. "Intelligence," in its simplest meaning, refers to evaluated information. "Strategic intelligence," accordingly, is information collected, analyzed, evaluated, interpreted, and communicated to leaders who must make decisions at the highest government levels involving U.S. goals, interests, and program actions relating to the external—that is, the foreign-international—environment. "Counterintelligence" is a police and security function to protect state secrets and to detect and deter the efforts of foreign intelligence agents to discover such secrets or to penetrate national intelligence operations. Counterintelligence sometimes produces positive intelligence, but that is not its primary purpose. "Espionage" is a sharply distinct term that should be understood to denote *one* of the many methods of gathering intelligence, specifically the illegal gathering of information that other nations wish to protect from disclosure. In other words, "spying" should not, as is commonly the case, be viewed as synonymous with "intelligence" but simply as one way, perhaps the most notorious and glamorous, of collecting raw data for processing into intelligence. "Covert action," sometimes referred to as "covert intervention," "covert operations," or "special activity," is primarily political action. Covert action is not directly related to the intelligence function. It is designed to influence the course of politics in a foreign nation while concealing the U.S. role. The overthrow of an unfriendly government by assassination or by secret support of opposition elements is an example, if an extreme one, of covert action. Covert actions may require intelligence, or they may bring about the collection of some elements of information, but they constitute a function sharply distinct from intelligence.

I labor over these definitions because of the widespread confusion that characterizes the use of intelligence terminology. Terminological and conceptual confusion is compounded by organizational arrangements that associate the disparate intelligence, espionage, counterintelligence, and covert action functions under the administrative roof of the CIA. Conceptual confusion has characterized the modern American intelligence system and may be responsible for some of its deficiencies. The focus of this chapter is on the intelligence ingredient in the making of foreign policy. But the conceptual chaos and the organizational arrangements, and their effect on policy, cannot be ignored.

Origins, Organization, Evolution

More than any other event in modern history, the surprise Japanese attack on Pearl Harbor in December 1941 left an indelible imprint on the United States intelligence system. Pearl Harbor was seen in retrospect as primarily a failure of organization. Forewarning of the attack was hypothetically possible. Japanese organization for the attack and the launching of it were "knowable" information, and the essential American failure was perceived as a systematic failure to collect, interpret, and, most important, to *communicate* intelligence that was available in advance. Better organization, and therefore better intelligence, may not have been able to prevent the attack on Pearl Harbor, but could have blunted it and sharply reduced U.S. losses.

At any rate, the Pearl Harbor experience was the dominant influence, indeed the determining element, in the establishment of a central intelligence system in 1947. For the principal lesson of Pearl Harbor was seen to be the need for a central guiding hand in the collection, coordination, and analysis of information required by national decision makers and, most important, the timely communication of that information to decision makers. Whether or not a "Pearl Harbor syndrome" has dominated intelligence behavior remains a matter of dispute.

In addition, the World War II experience with the hastily organized Office of Strategic Services (OSS) left its imprint on the postwar intelligence system. Many of the OSS concepts—some borrowed from the British—and a significant number of OSS personnel provided the foundation for the CIA. An *esprit de guerre* was an important element of the OSS heritage; Stalin replaced Hitler as the enemy.

And so the CIA was created in 1947 to avoid the overlapping and potential biases that characterized the existing prewar system for intelligence production in the armed services and the State Department. By analyzing and interpreting the information collected by these agencies, the CIA was to provide the president and his principal advisers with the best possible, unbiased national intelligence. In reality, however, the CIA within a few years after its founding was deeply involved on its own in the collection of intelligence data, thereby becoming an additional operational agency competing with the other departments. This was a consequence, in part, of the reluctance of the other departments to supply their data to the CIA, thus preventing it from fulfilling its original function as intelligence coordinator at the top of the system for the president.

Furthermore, within a year of its founding, the CIA came to be assigned the separate function of covert political action abroad, and this captured the fancy of the agency's early directors, particularly Allen Dulles. A principal consequence of this was a rearrangement of administrative priorities in which the intelligence function was assigned second place behind covert action. According to the Church committee report, "individual Directors of Central Intelligence have not been consistent advocates of the Agency's intelligence production function."[1] Senate investigators found that only three directors of the CIA had attempted to address primary attention to the quality of intelligence production. As a specific example of what happened to the original function of the CIA, by 1952 clandestine collection and covert action accounted for 74 percent of the agency's budget.[2]

One consequence of the scandals and investigations of the mid-1970s was the alteration of the priorities within the intelligence system, particularly the CIA, giving the collection, analysis, interpretation, and timely communication of information to decision makers first priority. But this has not produced any visible miracles in forecasting performance.

The Process and Production of Intelligence

The ultimate test of an intelligence agency is the quality of its product, which is its ability to tell decision makers what they need to know in time to shape effective foreign policy decisions. Judging this quality is difficult for a number of reasons. First, there is no clearly defined theory of intelligence to provide evaluative criteria. Second, intelligence estimates for the most part remain secret long after events. A third difficulty is the intangible element of the process, which involves perception of information and final interpretation of its meaning by decision makers. This is very difficult evidence to uncover. Few measures have been developed for judging the weight of intelligence in the process, and secrecy tends to inform us of failures and to conceal successes. Indeed, a glaring deficiency in the open literature on intelligence is a list of examples of spectacular intelligence successes. Absent this, one must wonder whether such examples are few. Patently, the problem of demonstrating the success of intelligence is far greater than that of demonstrating failure. Successes can be expected more often when hard data about foreign capabilities are involved than when political intentions are to be predicted.

Before examining several specific cases that illustrate intelligence performance, let us analyze, briefly, the intelligence process by considering separate discrete functions for intelligence and specific tasks for the intelligence officer.

Following the categories set forth by William J. Barnds, four separate intelligence functions can be identified.[3] The first is the monitoring of foreign events in order to point out significant developments so that policy makers are alerted to impending problems and opportunities. A second function is the making of periodic estimates of situations around the world that impinge on strategic interests of the United States in the hope of reducing uncertainties and avoiding pitfalls. A third is a more specific kind of estimating, directed toward prediction of foreign reactions to alternative options in current U.S. policies that are under consideration. The fourth activity is a general monitoring of worldwide conditions that are relevant to the success of policies or operations under way.

To fulfill these assignments, the intelligence professional must perform four distinct tasks. First must be guidance of the collection process, making as sure as possible that the policy maker will have the necessary information. Second is to be alert to policy concerns so that the facts will be at hand for forthcoming policy decisions. The third and perhaps most demanding task is the production of accurate, objective, and pertinent intelligence reports and estimates. Finally comes the task of making sure the relevant intelligence product is communicated in a timely, clear, and unambiguous form. These, then, are the demanding functions of the intelligence professional.

But since the intelligence process succeeds or fails in the context of policy, what of the corresponding tasks of the policy maker? Often overlooked in evaluating the performance of an intelligence system is the crucial role of the policy maker. It is also a delicate, sensitive role, for the policy maker must always be aware of the danger of prejudicing the intelligence process by signaling his *preferred* view of the world. The cost of this posture can be the failure of intelligence, about which more later.

Policy makers have three intelligence tasks. First, the policy maker must inform intelligence officers about the kinds of information needed, so that the collection and analysis efforts will be relevant. When policy makers conceal their intentions and plans, the task of intelligence professionals becomes impossible. A second requirement is that policy makers keep intelligence professionals informed not only of policy options under consideration but of significant actions and operations already under way. Intelligence professionals who are attempting to predict the behavior of other states cannot be expected to perform well if they are ignorant of the full range of U.S. decisions, promises, or actions that will affect those foreign states. Finally, intelligence professionals need to know how useful their product is to decision makers. Are they reading the reports? Do the reports provide informative guidance in the choice of options? In sum, intelligence professionals need to know whether their product is serving the needs of policy makers. Obviously these tasks place a heavy communications burden on busy policy makers, particularly because the process is continuous. The point is that an intelligence system cannot operate in a policy vacuum.

The role and functional model described above, of course, cannot describe the reality. But it suggests a frame of reference against which to compare the process as it appears to have worked in recent history. It is important to understand that the intelligence process is always part of an encompassing political process that incorporates personalities, bureaucratic politics, and varying contexts shaped by contemporary events.

A classic debate surrounds the question of the appropriate distance between intelligence professional and policy maker: how to guarantee that intelligence tells policy makers what they need to know rather than what they want to hear. Intelligence doctrine calls for an arm's-length relationship to ensure that intelligence reports remain objective and uncolored by subjective policy preferences. The problem derives from the reality that the "distance" stance of the intelligence professional can produce intelligence work in splendid isolation, unrelated to the policy maker's real world and to the information that is needed. As Barnds has phrased it, the danger exists that "intelligence work becomes the pursuit of knowledge for its own sake rather than a carefully focused input to the policy-maker's thinking and decision-making process."[4] For the policy maker, however, intelligence is but one ingredient in the making of a foreign policy decision. The intelligence report must compete with domestic political pressures, including those from both Congress and public opinion.

Intelligence doctrine teaches that "we give facts only, not opinions or advice." But obviously intelligence workers must decide which facts are relevant and when and how to present them to policy makers. And the normal, human intelligence professional will have developed views on world affairs and will have at least a hidden policy agenda that encompasses an ideology. The predictable intelligence officer is likely to lose his audience. Remaining objective and clear-eyed is a constant challenge.

Another problem derives from the tendency of policy makers to demand that intelligence professionals supply the facts, selectively, to support predetermined policy positions. A leader committed to balancing the budget, say, is strongly inclined to seek intelligence judgments that support such an aim. It is not unusual, furthermore, in our complex government when there are interdepartmental disputes, as between the State Department and the Pentagon on arms-control agreements, to see leaders using intelligence reports selectively to justify one position or another. Those who advocate the arm's-length doctrine argue that intelligence objectivity can be protected only by isolating intelligence professionals. If this is done at the cost of making the intelligence product irrelevant, it is obviously self-defeating. This issue has been at the heart of the organizational evolution and tinkering through the years. Achieving a balance between objectivity and relevance will never be easy. But an imbalanced structure can be a primary cause of inadequacy or failure of intelligence. Keep in mind that knowledge is potential power, and the American way is to provide for checks and balances for all forms of power.

Some policy makers, an aggressive, self-confident president or secretary of defense, for example, exhibit what is perhaps the most central problem of intelligence: the tendency to feel that, regardless of the intelligence reports or estimates, they "know best." Keep in mind that high-level policy makers normally have access to a variety of sources of information not labeled formally as "intelligence." Examples are diplomatic exchanges, private conversations with respected advisers, hunches, and even hot-line communications with foreign leaders. Intelligence reports and estimates, consequently, always have competitors. So the decision maker may have a tendency to pick and choose, particularly if his intelligence experience has not always been positive with respect to accuracy. Old-hand intelligence professionals commonly complain about the policy maker's fascination with current, hot-off-the-wire intelligence, the lack of attention to long-range estimates, and, indeed, resistance to policy planning.

An ideal construct for an intelligence service is one that functions with complete objectivity, untouched by the biases of partisan politics and competing ideologies, and one that keeps the decision maker both currently informed and forewarned of impending events of significance. In this model, the decision maker is a rational actor, eager to receive unvarnished information, even if it conveys negative implications for preferred policies. He proceeds toward decisions in logical steps, immune to subjective cross pressures and the tides of bureaucratic policies. Reality is likely to be somewhat different, with decision makers beset by the conflicting pressures of a pluralist political process, with intelligence reports often ambiguous or hedged in such a way as to allow the decision maker to find justification for the most politically convenient policy. Capping the system in reality is the practice in recent times that assumes that each new president is entitled to choose "his" new director of central intelligence, which in turn may mean a substantial turnover in the higher echelons of the CIA. In sum, then, the intelligence process is inescapably a part of the political process.

Consider as an illustrative example Henry Kissinger's description of Nixon's attitude toward the leaders of the CIA when he became president in 1969. "Nixon considered the CIA a refuge of Ivy League intellectuals opposed to him. And he felt ill at ease with [CIA Director] Helms personally since he suspected that Helms was well liked by the liberal Georgetown social set to which Nixon ascribed many of his difficulties."[5] Kissinger goes on to describe how Nixon initially attempted without success to exclude Helms from the deliberations of the National Security Council. In other words, Nixon took a highly political view of the CIA. One astute observer has written, "No government institution elicited Nixon's sullen suspicion more than the CIA. . . . He often complained about CIA failures to warn him of something in advance, saying the Agency couldn't even keep up with the wire services. He once said to John Ehrlichman, 'what use are they? They've got forty thousand people over there reading newspapers.' "[6] Nixon can be found saying elsewhere, however, that "the quality of intelligence received during my Administration was relatively adequate."[7] President Kennedy became disillusioned with the CIA at the Bay of Pigs in 1961. President Johnson appears to have ignored some CIA estimates, particularly when they challenged his Vietnam policy. President Carter, surprised by developments in Iran in 1978, expressed his dissatisfaction with the quality of the political intelligence he was receiving. It may be that all presidents, recognizing that knowledge is potential power, come to recognize that intelligence agencies exist within a political context. Recognition of this may have prompted President Reagan to appoint a political ally, William J. Casey, to head the CIA in 1981.

The Nixon administration was nonetheless aware of the inadequacies of the intelligence system, and in 1971 James R. Schlesinger headed a study group of the Office of Management and Budget to evaluate the system. Perhaps of most importance was the study's conclusion that no policy-level guidance was being given to the "intelligence community" on substantive intelligence. No steady monitoring or assessment was being made of the quality, scope, and timeliness of the product of the intelligence system. The president had created a variety of high-level committees, most of them headed by Kissinger, but they rarely met. And the president's wish for a continuing evaluation of intelligence estimates and reports went unfulfilled. Perhaps the basic problem was that, without a theory of intelligence, evaluative criteria were not easily visible.

Another fundamental challenge to efforts at understanding intelligence and foreign policy is the fact that U.S. intelligence operations today involve hundreds of thousands of individuals expending billions of dollars. Operations go forward under a variety of units organized into a complex intelligence "community," which remains more of an aspiration than a reality. Five major institutions make up this community, with a variety of subunits: the National Security Council, which directs the intelligence system and is its main and ultimate consumer; the director of central intelligence, who both heads the CIA and in theory is the president's principal intelligence adviser; the Central Intelligence Agency, created in 1947 to institutionalize the "lessons of Pearl Harbor"; the Department of State, which is the primary source of nonclandestine information on political and economic affairs; and the Department of Defense, which commands by far the largest amount of intelligence resources and encompasses the National Security Agency (code making and breaking), the National Reconnaissance Office, the National Photo Interpretation Center, the Defense Intelligence Agency, and the various intelligence organizations of the armed services. A variety of other intelligence organizations participate on the periphery of the "community."

The intelligence process and organization described above are designed to operate on the basis of a few simple propositions: First, decision makers, as principal users of intelligence, make known the kinds of information needed. Second, needs are converted into intelligence requirements or "key questions" by the intelligence leaders. Third, requirements, once established, guide the allocation of resources to the "collection" units and mobilize their efforts in the field. Fourth, collectors gather the information, as assigned, in the form of "raw" intelligence. Fifth, such information is collated, analyzed and interpreted, and converted into "finished" intelligence (in a variety of formats) by analysts. Sixth, the finished product is communicated to decision makers and intelligence managers, producing a feedback that generates new requirements and begins the cycle anew. Finally, the ultimate step in the process is the use of intelligence in the making of decisions.

This hypothetical pattern is a model of a process that may be barely recognizable in reality, for, in the words of the report of the Church committee of the U.S. Senate:

> There are many different consumers, from the President to
> the weapons designer. Their needs can conflict. Consumers

rarely take the time to define their intelligence needs and even if they do so there is no effective and systematic mechanism for translating them into intelligence requirements.

Therefore, intelligence requirements reflect what intelligence managers think the consumers need, and equally important, what they think the organization can produce. Since there are many managers and little central control, each is relatively free to set his own requirements.[8]

Given the size, scope, and decentralized nature of intelligence operations today—and the innate self-serving tendencies of separate intelligence bureaucracies—the reality is that the decision maker often finds that his immediate needs for information are not served by the system. And so intelligence "failures" tend to be commonplace—a consequence of faulty conceptions, elaborate organization, bureaucratic tendencies, and, perhaps most important, the fact that there are sometimes questions, particularly about the future intentions of others, which cannot be answered. In the words of a Senate report: "The world of intelligence is dominated by uncertainty and chance, and those in the intelligence bureaucracy, as elsewhere in the Government, try to defend themselves against uncertainties in ways which militate against efficient management and accountability."[9] Another debilitating factor is that "the organizations of the intelligence community must operate in peace but be prepared for war. This has an enormous impact on the kind of intelligence that is sought, the way resources are allocated, and the way the intelligence community is organized and managed."[10] Furthermore, under the administrative roof of the CIA have gone forward a variety of secret operations not directly related to the intelligence function, including psychological, political, and paramilitary warfare. This has had the effect of compromising some intelligence functions, confusing the picture, and diverting intelligence leaders from the informational function. All these factors tend to undermine and distort the intelligence process with a significant effect upon its performance. These influences must be recognized if we are to understand the intelligence function in foreign policy decision making. Let us turn now to examples in some important cases in modern history that will illustrate the problems of intelligence.

The Case of Pearl Harbor

Conventional wisdom advises that the surprise attack on Pearl Harbor by the Japanese in December 1941 could have been avoided had the United States had a central intelligence system. Like most conventional assumptions, this one is subject to challenge. Indeed, in 1975

U.S. Representative Otis Pike, as head of a yearlong House investigation of the U.S. intelligence system, asserted that the United States could suffer a surprise military attack "today" even with the existence of a multibillion-dollar, highly organized intelligence warning network.

What are the intelligence lessons of Pearl Harbor? How was it possible for the United States, which had been reading Japan's most secret "Magic" code for more than a year, to have been caught asleep? How was it possible to have intercepted a lengthy, secret message to Japan's foreign ambassadors warning of impending war and still to have been surprised in the early morning of December 7 at Pearl Harbor? The answers to these and related questions remain embedded in historical controversy, but they highlight the difficulties that confront intelligence agencies as they attempt to carry out the forecasting or forewarning function.

Contrary to some popular beliefs, the United States had a variety of intelligence capabilities before the attack on Pearl Harbor, and intelligence supplied decision makers with large quantities of data on the impending crisis. The U.S. Navy had an extensive system that included aerial surveillance for spotting the location of Japanese naval vessels; the Japanese diplomatic code—Magic—had been broken by Americans; ground observers watched from ports along the Chinese and Southeast Asian coasts; U.S. foreign service officers in Tokyo under Ambassador Joseph Grew were closely observing Japan's policy; and British intelligence was helpful. In retrospect, much evidence can be found pointing to an attack on Pearl Harbor. But, in Roberta Wohlstetter's careful analysis, "the data were ambiguous and incomplete. There was never a single, definite signal that said, 'Get ready, get set, go!' but rather a number of signals which, when put together, tended to crystallize suspicion."[11] As William Corson has observed, "for every positive item pointing toward the attack at Pearl Harbor there is an equally compelling one to suggest either no attack or one much more likely to take place elsewhere in Asia."[12] In fact, naval intelligence in November 1941 lost track of a good part of the Japanese battle fleet. The reason that this crucial event did not produce a serious warning was that those who controlled such information thought an attack on Pearl Harbor improbable.

The problem, then as now, is that "true" signals are often mixed in with the noise and irrelevance of false ones. It can be expected that in any planned surprise attack the enemy will deliberately send out false signals of intentions for the purpose of deception. In complex intelligence warning systems, delays in time can also be expected; indeed careful analysis often takes time because of the awful consequences of impetuous decisions. Also to be anticipated is the likelihood that Murphy's law will be in effect: "if anything can go wrong in the system, it will."

The Pearl Harbor attack, which has been analyzed from an enormous variety of perspectives, is commonly regarded today as a case in which signals warning of the attack were clear but were ignored. Conspiracy theorists argue that signals were deliberately ignored by decision makers who wanted war. But close and objective analysis demonstrates the difficulty of hearing signals against the prevailing noise, or countersignals, particularly when ears are tuned to what in hindsight turn out to be the wrong signals. The United States government was expecting a Japanese attack, but not at Pearl Harbor. And so the signals of a Pearl Harbor attack that can be ferreted out of the historical record and that stand out in bold relief today did not so stand out at the time because eyes were focused elsewhere. Deliberate deception combined with unconscious self-deception dominated the scene.

Correct interpretation of intelligence signals, particularly in the realm of impending military events, depends upon the estimate of one's enemy and *his* estimate of the situation, coupled with one's own calculus of *his* calculus of risks and his willingness to take risks. This delicate interactive process suggests the difficulty any intelligence service might have in predicting a surprise attack. As Wohlstetter writes: "The problem of warning . . . is inseparable from the problem of decision. The more drastic our reply, the greater the certainty we need."[13] The problem is, of course, that such certainty is often lacking. We are all inclined to selective perception, perhaps innately so; we will normally estimate what our adversary will do both on the basis of our guesses about his capabilities and about his (selective) perceptions and especially on the basis of what *we* would do if we were he. Invitations to self-fulfilling prophecies abound; and so intelligence failures abound.

Although a vast and ever-growing bibliography exists on the Pearl Harbor attack and some of the "facts" will always be in dispute, two facts seem to be widely accepted: first, that the Japanese achieved surprise in the attack; and second, that the U.S. intelligence system provided many significant clues in advance of the attack, but these were inadequately interpreted and even more poorly communicated to those who "needed to know." In sum, warnings at every level were ambiguous and incomplete. Whether one must assume that this will always be so in foreign policy decisions will be discussed later.

The Pearl Harbor example is instructive in a number of ways, but we must understand its importance in the creation of the CIA after World War II. In the words of the 1955 Hoover Commission Report: "The CIA may well attribute its existence to the surprise attack on Pearl Harbor and to the postwar investigation into the part Intelligence or lack of Intelligence played in the failure of our military forces to receive adequate and prompt warning of an impending attack."[14]

Intelligence Failures and the Korean War

Some three years after the creation of the CIA, in the early morning of June 25, 1950, North Korean armed forces launched a major air and ground attack across the thirty-eighth parallel. The attack came as a surprise to Washington, D.C., and to the American military command in Tokyo and in South Korea. Within a few days the United States had become deeply involved in the Korean War—an unexpected event for which we were neither forewarned nor prepared. The three-year-old intelligence system, designed to prevent such surprises, had failed to do so.

After the event, intelligence officials at all levels could produce documentation of advance warnings about the possibility of war. But a close examination of such reports would probably reveal that they contained hedges and qualifications, leaving to the decision maker the judgment of true probabilities and risks. Indeed, Secretary of State Dean Acheson later testified to a Senate committee investigating the advent and conduct of the Korean War as follows:

> Intelligence was available to the [State] Department prior to the 25th of June, made available by the Far East Command, the CIA, the Department of the Army, and by the State Department representatives here and overseas, and [it] shows that all these agencies were in agreement that the possibility for an attack on the Korean Republic existed at that time, but all were in agreement that its launching in the summer of 1950 did not appear imminent.[15]

During the period 1948–1950, intelligence organization in the field, as it was in Washington, was in organizational transition—some would say chaos. In the Far East, the CIA and General MacArthur's headquarters were in jealous jurisdictional conflict. Indeed, the term "internecine warfare" well describes relations between MacArthur's military intelligence and the civilian CIA. Community spirit was lacking, to say the least. To complicate matters, within the CIA itself a chaotic struggle was under way between the intelligence analysts and the covert operators, who were in the process of being incorporated into the CIA. According to one informed observer:

> In the final months before the North Korean invasion, the OPC-OSO [Office of Policy Coordination–Office of Special Operations] feud had reached major proportions, the other elements of the intelligence community had been affected by it, and the state of national intelligence—the intelligence derived from all sources and supposedly synthesized by the CIA—was chaotic. Intelligence community organizations held on to information acquired by their sources, or used it to discredit the actions, estimates, and analyses of one or more of the other community members. It was intelligence competition at its worst, and Hillenkoetter [director of central intelligence] was caught between the rock and the hard place.[16]

Since mid-1949, a plethora of units within the American intelligence system had been assigned the duty of monitoring the potential for military action in Korea. Some fifteen separate "watch committees" were assigned the duty of sounding an alarm if hostile military action in Korea seemed imminent. These were capped by an interdepartmental committee assigned to consolidate and evaluate reports of various field committees. Such reports appear to have been dominated by reports from MacArthur's headquarters in Tokyo that all was quiet and well in Korea. In fact there were hit-and-run attacks by North Korean raiding units for almost a year before the invasion. There were many indicators of a North Korean buildup, including a sizable flow of Soviet war materiel into North Korea. Indeed a considerable mobilization of forces was seen to be under way for a year before the attack in force across the thirty-eighth parallel.

Clearly, American intelligence had a detailed view of the capability for attack—or was it for defense? Here, again, the critical problem was the reading of *intentions*. In fact, there was a special CIA report on June 14, estimating that North Korea had by then developed the capability to invade South Korea at any time and to capture the capital city of Seoul within ten to twelve days. This CIA estimate was sent to the State Department, the Pentagon, and the White House. But the report centered on capabilities, not intentions, and policy makers ignored it. President Truman was occupied with other policy concerns, such as holding the lid on the military budget, and Congress was reassured by government officials that all was well in Korea. Furthermore, the CIA estimate did not reach those in the field in Korea who can be said to have had the greatest "need to know" of CIA's latest and disturbing estimate. Those in the field might have taken action to prevent the total surprise achieved by the North Koreans on June 25, but this is not certain.

And so on June 20—five days before the attack—Assistant Secretary of State for Far Eastern Affairs Dean Rusk could be heard assuring a congressional committee, "We see no present indication that the people across the border [North Koreans] have any intention of fighting a major war [for taking over South Korea]."[17]

President Truman was said to be enraged that the CIA had not forewarned him of the June 25 attack, which was followed by a successful drive on Seoul. In a post-mortem, it was discovered that analysts had discounted information from secret sources pointing to the attack and, perhaps most significantly, had not properly interpreted what was a crucial North Korean deception plan with regard to its communications, which went virtually silent to disguise the inevitable activity preceding mobilization for attack. In the perfect vision of hindsight it is clear that intentions were not aggressively pursued in setting intelligence requirements. Indeed, the basic problem, in retrospect, was that no intelligence "community" in fact existed.

The outbreak of the Korean War precipitated fundamental changes in the organization, size, and management of the intelligence system. The compromises that characterized the structure of central intelligence in the 1947 legislation had not worked well. Yet one fundamental fault in the system was not changed, and the second great intelligence failure of the Korean War was the result. This was the surprise in Washington at the full-scale Chinese intervention in Korea in November 1950. Here again there had developed a serious imbalance between reading capabilities and reading intentions. And here again we see manifestations of organizational problems arising from MacArthur's apparent distrust of any intelligence other than that gathered by organizations that he controlled. The records are replete with warnings from the CIA of large-scale movements of Chinese troops in the direction of Korea, and indeed the capture of Chinese soldiers confirmed the existence of Chinese combat units already in Korea by September. MacArthur refused to accept the significance of such information, and President Truman seemed unconvinced by warnings from the CIA that MacArthur's "drive to the Yalu" River separating North Korea from China might precipitate large-scale intervention by the Chinese. Rather than fire MacArthur, Truman in fact sacked CIA Director Hillenkoetter.

On November 24 the CIA estimated categorically that the

Chinese possessed sufficient military strength in Korea to force the withdrawal of UN-U.S. forces to defensive positions. On the very same day MacArthur announced the start of his "end the war" offensive. Four days later he was to declare, "We face an entirely new war," for his troops had been marched into a trap. Red Chinese struck not from north of the Yalu River but from concealed positions in the mountain *behind* MacArthur's forces.

The Korean War intelligence performance is summed up in this exchange:

"Senator Saltonstall: They really fooled us when it comes right down to it; didn't they?

"Secretary Acheson: Yes, Sir."[18]

In generalizing about this example, the point is that the failure was primarily in predicting intentions; capabilities were well charted. Four other points can also be noted: First, there was a failure to comprehend a foreign power's definition of its own self-interest, in the case of both North Korea and China. Second, political leaders seem to have expected greater certainty than is reasonable from the strategic warning system. Too much, rather than too little, reliance was placed on the intelligence system. Third, intelligence failures of the type described are in part failures of national policy. Our adversaries could see, as we could not, fundamental contradictions between our declared policies and our capabilities. Fourth, the American leaders became prisoners of a plan. MacArthur's plan to drive north to the Yalu was not to be deterred by information suggesting that it would fail. And since MacArthur was the planner, the operator, and a major supplier of information to justify the feasibility of the plan, failure was invited—as would be the case in later events such as the Bay of Pigs, the Vietnam War, and the unexpected revolution in Iran.

The Intelligence Failure in Iran

The fall from power and exile of the shah of Iran in early 1979 came as a shock to American policy makers. Barely a year earlier President Carter had personally toasted the shah as representing a stable island in the deeply troubled Middle East.

An event that had wide-ranging foreign policy implications for the United States occurred in the face of predictions by the U.S. intelligence community that it would not happen. American oil policy and defense strategy for the Persian Gulf rested upon the assumption that the shah would remain a bulwark of Western security for the indefinite future.

In late 1977 and early 1978 Iran witnessed massive demonstrations of protest against the shah, who had been assisted to power in the first place by the CIA in 1953. Violent demonstrations continued during the summer and fall of 1978. Reviewing policy options toward Iran in early November, the president declared U.S. support for the shah's efforts to restore order. Within a few weeks the shah had been overthrown.

Here was yet another example of intelligence failure. But like Pearl Harbor and the Korean War, it was not simply a failure of the system, but rather an intelligence failure wrapped in a bureaucratic failure wrapped in a policy failure. That is to say that what happened in Iran was not simply a case of inadequate information, inexpertly interpreted and ineptly communicated. It may have been all that, but clearly, thirty-seven years after Pearl Harbor, the intelligence system was still capable of monumental failure. Why?

To answer this question with only limited access to the record is difficult, but it is made easier because the staff of the U.S. House of Representatives Select Committee on Intelligence undertook an evaluative study in late 1978 and issued a report in January 1979. The report is based upon presumably full access to the secret record and upon interviews with managers and analysts of the CIA and officials in the Department of State, the Defense Intelligence Agency, and the National Security Agency as well as an extensive review of current intelligence archives and public sources. What emerge are some classic weaknesses of intelligence, including the following:

First, the collection and analysis of information from Iran were weak. Reports of massive anti-shah demonstrations were greeted with analytic complacency in Washington. The power of the religious opposition, which later came to be the ruling group, was seriously underestimated. Also misinterpreted were the breadth and depth of popular, even middle-class, opposition to the shah and the desire for radical change. The intelligence collection effort, both in the U.S. embassy in Tehran and by CIA agents in the field, proved to be misleading to analysts. Put simply, intelligence agents were not observing, or talking with, politically significant persons.

Second, U.S. foreign policy in the Persian Gulf region was anchored to the survival of the shah, in whom the American leaders apparently had great confidence. It is evident that a deliberate policy of no contact with elements in opposition to the shah was in force, out of fear of antagonizing the shah, who himself feared covert action by CIA within his realm. Embassy political reporting on the shah's opponents was seen as "rare and sometimes contemptuous."[19] It seems clear that policy makers were not asking the intelligence system to assess the strength of the shah; they simply assumed that the shah would prevail over his opposition indefinitely. In sum, policy makers were not seeking clear-eyed assessments; indeed, they seemed to be implicitly forbidding them out of fear of displeasing the shah. The CIA feared that should the shah be antagonized, he would deny them use of the highly valued electronic monitoring sites in northern Iran thought to be of great importance for strategic surveillance of activities within the Soviet Union.

One striking example of the inefficiency of the intelligence reporting from Iran is that the *New York Times* and the *Washington Post* clearly "scooped" the intelligence agencies by several weeks in reporting on a crucial alliance between Islamic traditionalists and other opponents of the shah. A congressional study also revealed the almost tragicomic efforts of the intelligence "community" to produce a "National Intelligence Estimate" for the president in 1978: "The process bogged down in differences over the product's length and focus as well as over substantive differences. Ultimately, no NIE was produced."[20] One wonders why the president did not demand a national estimate. Failure to do so may be an important part of the story.

The quality of intelligence performance and the depth of the failure may be further illustrated by the following snippets:

• In September 1978 the Defense Intelligence Agency made the prognosis that the shah "is expected to remain actively in power over the next ten years."[21]

• The preface to an August 1978 twenty-three-page CIA assessment entitled "Iran after the Shah" declared, "Iran is not in a revolutionary or even a 'prerevolutionary' situation."[22]

Yet in fairness to the intelligence establishment it must be noted that one could sift through the vast amount of intelligence paper constantly available to decision makers and discover a number of warning signals. State Department *Morning Summaries,* for example, early noted the seriousness of the disturbances in Iran, and these were received daily at the White House for the president's eyes. White House reaction to such signals was not to ask for more detailed analysis of the shah's stability. No attention was given to the question of removing restrictions that had been placed on clandestine collection of intelligence by the CIA in Iran, out of fear of displeasing the shah. Ultimately the intelligence analysis of the Iranian situation seems to have been superficial. Put more simply, political leaders seemed to want only good news from Iran. And intelligence agencies are prone to report what they think—or know— that leaders want to hear. Yet the intelligence system was quick to feel the sting of presidential displeasure after the event. President Carter in November 1978 penned a handwritten note to his national security advisers, including the director of the CIA. With pointed reference to his surprise at events in Iran, he let them know of his dissatisfaction with the quality of intelligence being supplied him.

It would be easy to conclude simply that here was another case of intelligence failure, carrying with it—like Pearl Harbor in 1941 and Korea in 1950—world-shaking consequences. Such an assessment would be simplistic because it would ignore the share of policy and political leadership in responsibility for the failure, and it would also ignore the organizational implications of the failure. One must agree with the conclusion of the House Select Committee on Intelligence in its finding that "in the case of Iran, long-standing U.S. attitudes toward the Shah inhibited intelligence collection, dampened policymakers' appetite for analysis of the Shah's position, and deafened policymakers to the warning implicit in available current intelligence."[23] Furthermore, the left hand of the CIA—the covert action branch—had put the shah in power and he was the CIA's man; the CIA was a principal booster of the shah. Meanwhile, the right hand of the CIA—the intelligence collection and analysis branch—was supposed to provide clear-eyed and objective information about the shah's position. Here, obviously, was a situation lacking in incentives to challenge the conventional wisdom or to replace commitments or preferences with facts. And so an old issue is raised again about the wisdom of combining under one CIA roof the functions of intelligence analysis and covert action or other clandestine operations in the field. The intelligence system so far has remained resistant to radical structural change. "Lessons" from failures through the years have produced patchwork reforms, yet failures of the system continue. But we should note that they are not always *intelligence* failures, but broadly failures of policy, organization, and perception, and, most important, failures in the *use* of intelligence in the making of foreign policy.[24]

Conclusions

Failures in strategic warning are the result of a complex set of variables, the interactions and influence of which are very difficult to discern and measure. To understand the causes of intelligence failure, one must measure cognitive or perceptual factors against institutional factors. Substantive policy must be considered within the context of intelligence organization, doctrine, and process. And the ideal of rational choice must be modified by the realism of bureaucratic politics.

The incidence of intelligence failure in significant foreign policy events since 1947 is high. Understanding of these failures, if it is fair to call them that, remains low. Yet if we are to understand how the decision-making system in American foreign policy works, we must confront the analytical challenge, made all the more difficult by official secrecy. The following three elements of the problem are of greatest significance:

One, the policy context in which intelligence judgments are made is usually the dominant influence. Even complete information, which is rare, normally requires human—and thus fallible—choice. Policy is the outcome of human values, preferences, and cognitive, perceptual, and psychological elements. Once an organization has made a strong commitment to a policy, later information that calls the viability of the policy into question is likely to be received skeptically. A second element is the problem of historical analyses and interpretation. In the language of intelligence professionals, the term "post-mortem" is used for the study of failures. Patently, we always study failures after the event and from the privileged position of hindsight. The tendency from the vantage point of policy autopsy is to impose expectations of foresight that would have been impossible.

A third crucial element is organization. The U.S. intelligence system on which attention is here focused is a confederation with many separate competing parts. Is this a strength or a weakness? The answer must be both. But organizational pluralism surely compounds the intelligence problem and certainly interacts with the policy and with the human and after-the-fact elements referred to above.

Theoretical understanding of the interaction of information, public policy choice, action, and power remains elusive. But the policy consequences of intelligence failure in today's world include Armageddon. And so we must continue to search for a clearer understanding of the relation between information and policy choice. Are there identifiable common elements in intelligence performance in crucial events as disparate as the surprise attack on Pearl Harbor, the Korean War, and Iran in 1978–1979? Is it possible to generalize about these and numerous other intelligence failures in the past four decades that could be cited? I suggest that what we need to know may be contained in the following tentative hypotheses:

• First, intelligence agencies tend to report what decision makers want to hear, not so much in the sense of conscious catering to their views but in often unconscious acceptance of common assumptions. And there are striking tendencies of policy makers to ignore information that challenges preexisting beliefs or policy commitments and to select information that supports beliefs, commitments, or plans. This may ultimately discourage candor in the reporting of intelligence.

• Second, leaders often make decisions without regard to, or contrary to evidence in, intelligence reports, even when the reports are highly accurate. Accuracy, of course, can often be determined only after the event.

Assuming that these generalizations have some validity, how is public policy thereby affected? To what extent does the policy maker's tendency to ignore intelligence and the intelligence system's tendency to share preconceptions with policy makers have consequences for public policy? Several examples from recent history are illuminating.

First, although it is a complex issue not discussed in this essay, one policy impact of these hypothesized tendencies can be said to be a U.S. military defense posture that is ill designed for the realities of future Soviet military power. Estimates by the intelligence community of Soviet strategic military forces have rarely been accurate since the end of World War II. The policy consequences of improperly designed U.S. military defense systems are potentially catastrophic, both economically and strategically.[25]

A second broad policy effect from the tendencies just suggested is illustrated by the Vietnam War. As a consequence of combined intelligence failures and the illusions of decision makers—such as the existence of a Sino-Soviet "bloc" and the domino theory—the United States engaged in a decade of tragic, unsuccessful war in Southeast Asia. This monumental intelligence failure has had a profound effect on past, present, and future public policy.

A third example of intelligence failure is the earlier analyzed collapse of the shah of Iran and the subsequent taking of the American embassy staff as hostages. The fall of the shah was a surprise in Washington; the warnings that special precautions needed to be taken for the safety of embassy personnel in Tehran were ignored. The public policy impact of these events reverberated widely into the 1980s, altering basic national security assumptions.

While no simple relation between good, timely information and effective policy can be postulated, it is clear that public policy is likely to fail if it is based upon erroneous information, and decision-making systems are highly vulnerable to information pathologies.

No easy doctrinal or organizational solutions to these problems are available. Given the importance of accurate information to effective public policy, political decision makers and intelligence professionals, despite the severe turbulence of the past decade, remain inadequately sensitive to information pathologies and insufficiently innovative in the search for cures. The most promising ways to avoid future failures would include the following: (1) reorganization, and perhaps renaming, of the CIA to make foreign intelligence its only function; (2) achievement of a better balance between objectivity and policy relevance, to make intelligence serve the information requirements of policy makers without compromising objectivity; (3) more careful identification of intelligence requirements or key questions, and in the process elimination of unwarranted duplication and collection overkill; (4) more vigorous recruitment of talented analysts and the subcontracting of some intelligence analyses to academic institutions or "think tanks"; and (5) constant monitoring, assessment, and tough-minded evaluation of intelligence performance, both by presidential boards and commissions and by independent, well-staffed congressional watchdog committees. Finally, nongovernmental scholars should be encouraged to assemble the building blocks for a more precise conceptualization of the intelligence function and for a foundation on which a theory of strategic intelligence might be built.

Notes

1. U.S. Senate, 94th Cong., 2d sess., Select Committee on Intelligence (Church Committee) Final Report, "Foreign and Military Intelligence," Book 1, Washington, D.C., April 26, 1976, p. 258.

2. Ibid., Book 4, p. 41.

3. "Intelligence and Policymaking in the Institutional Context" (Murphy) Commission on the Organization of the Government for the Conduct of Foreign Policy, Appendix, vol. 7, Washington, D.C., 1975, p. 29.

4. Ibid., p. 30.

5. Kissinger, The White House Years (Boston: Little, Brown & Company, 1979), p. 36.

6. Thomas Powers, The Man Who Kept the Secrets (New York: Alfred A. Knopf, 1979), p. 201.

7. Written and sworn interrogatory no. 73, Church Committee Final Report, Book 4, p. 167.

8. Church Committee, Book 1, p. 18.

9. Ibid., pp. 18–19.

10. Ibid., p. 19. For alternative interpretations see Robert L. Pfaltz-graff, Jr., Uri Ra'anan, and Warren H. Milberg, *Intelligence Policy and National Security* (Hamden, Conn.: Archon Books, 1981).

11. Roberta Wohlstetter, "Cuba and Pearl Harbor: Hindsight and Fore-sight," Memorandum RM-4328-ISA (Santa Monica, Calif.: Rand Corporation, April 1965), p. v.

12. William R. Corson, *The Armies of Ignorance* (New York: Dial Press/James Wade, 1977), p. 155. The most exhaustive review of the Pearl Harbor case is found in Gordon W. Prange, *At Dawn We Slept* (New York: McGraw-Hill, 1981). For a "conspiracy thesis" view, see John Toland, *Infamy: Pearl Harbor and Its Aftermath* (New York: Doubleday, 1982). For a more general treatment of strategic surprise, see Klaus Knorr and Patrick Morgan, *Strategic Military Surprise* (New Brunswick, N.J.: Transaction Books, 1983).

13. Wohlstetter, "Cuba and Pearl Harbor," p. 41.

14. Commission on the Organization of the Executive Branch of the Government, "Intelligence Activities," Report to Congress (Washington, D.C., June 1955), pp. 29–30.

15. U.S. Senate, 82d Cong., 1st sess., Committee on Armed Services and Foreign Relations, "Military Situation in the Far East" (MacArthur Hearings), 1951, pp. 1990–91.

16. Corson, *Armies of Ignorance*, p. 315.

17. U.S. House of Representatives, Committee on International Relations, Selected Executive Session Hearings, 1943–50, vol. 7, "U.S. Policy in the Far East, Part 2" (Washington, D.C., 1976), p. 464.

18. "MacArthur Hearings," p. 1835. A good account is found in Joseph C. Goulden, *Korea: The Untold Story of the War* (New York: Times Books, 1982), especially chap. 11.

19. U.S. House of Representatives, Select Committee on Intelligence, "Iran: Evaluation of U.S. Intelligence Performance prior to November 1978," Staff Report (Washington, D.C., 1979), p. 2. For alternative views, see Barry Rubin, *Paved with Good Intentions* (New York: Oxford University Press, 1980), and William H. Sullivan, *Mission to Iran* (New York: Norton, 1981), especially chaps. 15–25.

20. House, Select Committee on Intelligence, "Iran," p. 5.

21. Ibid., p. 6.

22. Ibid., p. 7.

23. Ibid.

24. Among the relevant discussions of this problem are Richard K. Betts, "Analysis, War, and Decision: Why Intelligence Failures Are Inevitable," *World Politics*, vol. 31, no. 1 (October 1978), pp. 61–89; Steve Chan, "The Intelligence of Stupidity: Understanding Failures in Strategic Warning," *American Political Science Review*, vol. 73 (March 1979), pp. 171–80; Roy Godson, ed., *Intelligence Requirements for the 1980's: Analysis and Estimates* (Washington, D.C.: Consortium for the Study of Intelligence,

National Strategy Information Center, 1980); Richards J. Heuer, Jr., "Improving Intelligence Analysis," *The Bureaucrat*, Winter 1979–80, pp. 2–11; Thomas L. Hughes, "The Fate of Facts in a World of Men—Foreign Policy and Intelligence-Making," *Foreign Policy Headline Series*, no. 233 (December 1976), p. 80; Charles Maechling, Jr., "Improving the Intelligence System," *Foreign Service Journal*, June 1980, pp. 10–13, 41–42; Harry Howe Ransom, "Strategic Intelligence and Foreign Policy," *World Politics*, vol. 27 (October 1974), pp. 131–46; and U.S. Congress, House Foreign Affairs Subcommittee on Intelligence and Security Affairs, *Hearings*, "The Role of Intelligence in the Policy Process," 96th Cong., 1st sess. (1980).

25. See John Prados, *The Soviet Estimate* (New York: Dial Press, 1982), and Steven Rosefielde, *False Science: Underestimating the Soviet Military Buildup* (New Brunswick, N.J.: Transaction Books, 1982).

PART TWO

Substantive Issues

5

United States Immigration Policy at the Crossroads

Demetrios G. Papademetriou

International migration in search of work has been an enduring component of the international economic, social, and political milieu. Millions of people, in response to a variety of domestic and international pressures, have left their home countries to undertake uncertain journeys to various advanced industrial societies. Although such migration has traditionally been expected to be an unmitigated benefit both to the sending and to the receiving societies, its almost uncontrolled growth during the last twenty-five years has prompted a fundamental reassessment of the process. The early results of this reassessment, albeit incomplete, have had a sobering effect on all of the principals in the migration chain.[1]

From the perspective of the labor-receiving, advanced industrial societies, migration of labor may actually contribute to maintaining and aggravating the structural conditions that originally necessitated importing labor. Furthermore, it now appears that, except for the obvious economic benefit accruing to the worker himself and his significant contribution to the short-term profit of certain industrial sectors, importing labor has given rise to severe economic, political, and social problems. The issue has profound implications, both global and domestic. Many nontraditional social scientists offer a structural analysis of international migration as a process fundamentally central to both sending and receiving societies that operates in a "world economy which simultaneously depends on and recreates conditions for economic inequality world-wide."[2]

From this point of view, the flow of labor benefits two centers: private capital in the receiving economy and the political and economic elites of the sending country, who are relieved of some political pressures, such as a high rate of unemployment. Naturally in this harmony of interests between the two centers, the receiving country benefits more than the sending country, while the workers find themselves in an essentially discordant relationship, both with their respective centers and with one another. Furthermore, since what the sender and the receiver get out of the migration of labor is cumulatively unequal, international migration becomes an integral part of the present global relationship of dominance, an element in a "vertically integrated system of control and accumulation, production and distribution on a global scale."[3]

This theoretical perspective is useful principally for its emphasis on the structural components of international labor migration—in terms of both the state-specific internal division of labor and the international political-economic hierarchy of nations that limits state independence of action in both the production and the distribution of commodities. Accordingly, in addressing the structural problems of international migration, U.S. policy makers must first adopt a more comprehensive perspective in their study of international politics and economics.

Such a perspective should include a more thorough grasp of the domestic impact of international migration, the economic, demographic, social, and political factors involved, and the myriad individual motives that shape the profile of specific migration flows. It is the background for a domestic perspective that I will try to sketch in this paper. I will attempt to identify and assess the complex forces that have shaped U.S. immigration policy during the last century and to offer some guidelines for the future course of action in this arena. In addition, I will try to identify the policy that takes these factors into account.

There is, in fact, a substantial consensus that it is necessary to rethink our immigration policies and make them an integral component of both domestic and foreign policy. Yet, as U.S. policy makers stumble toward that goal, the confusion generated by masses of contradictory "evidence" about every possible effect of legal and illegal immigrants on American society and its economy is heightened. Simultaneously, the public is becoming increasingly active, and many are demanding that they be consulted on this matter. The growing politicization of the issues and potential polarization of the attitudes of both opinion makers and the public contribute toward increasing popular uncertainties and insecurity among the working class and minority groups. These factors also deprive policy makers of some of the options they might otherwise have wished to consider in both the domestic and international arenas.

If the experience of other advanced industrial democracies, as well as our own history with immigration, is relevant to the making of policies for the future, we can expect myths and rumors about immigrants to challenge the legitimacy of virtually any government action in this matter and to interfere both with the improvement of the conditions of legal and illegal immigrants and with the amelioration of some of the negative consequences attendant upon the problem. In fact, the appearance of elite ambivalence and confusion encourages negative racial and ethnic stereotyping, supplants the real population and labor issues, and may compel the government to respond to the former challenges rather than the latter. It is helpful, therefore, to examine our history for its lessons.

The History of U.S. Immigration Policy

U.S. immigration policy has usually reflected the preoccupation of a particular period with its immediate past, rather than its future. Its dimensions, at least until very recently, have been influenced by a host of often inadequately understood and contradictory forces, such as the demographic composition of the population, economics, and foreign and domestic politics. As a result, U.S. policy makers have been unable to formulate an immigration policy that complements our long-term goals in the increasingly interdependent foreign and domestic political and economic realms.

As Zolberg points out, U.S. immigration policies, though considered to be domestic matters with only an incidental relationship to diplomacy, have always had global consequences in the way they have encouraged or discouraged emigration and the effects of such emigration on global economies.[4] Even under the so-called laissez-faire policies that prevailed before 1882, a whole host of seemingly unrelated legislation helped shape the composition of the U.S. population, the direction of the American society, and the development of sending nations. For example, the various passenger acts influenced the cost and pattern of ocean crossing, land policies controlled the incentive for immigration, and naturalization laws controlled the composition of the U.S. body politic.

Despite the effects of immigration, certain groups in the United States have not always taken their proper historical role in influencing immigration policy. Organized labor, for example, has been traditionally suspicious of or hostile to immigration and, for the most part, with good reason. Throughout the nineteenth century, industry prevailed on both executive and legislative branches and won legislation that responded to contrived labor shortages as well as real ones.

Some industries, in fact, such as the transportation industry in the confusing days following the Civil War, have actually on occasion secured legislation that included incentives and indirect public subsidies for procurement of labor.

By the end of the century, however, in its struggle to restrict immigration, labor had gained some important allies. These groups questioned the moral, physical, and political fitness of certain immigrant groups. After the conclusion of World War I this coalition was successful in imposing literacy requirements on new immigrants and then in imposing quotas on each country while basically banning immigration from the "Asian-Pacific triangle," that is, all Asian countries except Russia, Persia, and parts of Afghanistan.

In spite of these de jure limitations, capital has usually been able to exploit even genuine labor shortages to its advantage. Labor is often the loser. Zolberg distinguishes between the "main gate," or legal entry for immigrants, and the "back door," or exceptional entry for immigrants through temporary programs. The main gate–back door system emerged from a "specifically American configuration and has structured our immigration policy from approximately 1880 to the present."[5] What is more, de facto open immigration policies of recent years have allowed vast numbers of illegal foreign workers to enter the country and perform critical economic functions with only a small risk of detection and apprehension. Within this framework, immigration policies, particularly in the Southwest, have been the result of "conscientious human efforts . . . to keep wages low, to keep incomes depressed, and to keep unionism to a minimum by using waves of legal immigrants [from China, Japan, Mexico, and from Europe as well], braceros [from Mexico], border commuters [from Mexico], and now illegal aliens [mainly from Mexico, but by no means exclusively so]."[6]

By the early 1920s, both of Zolberg's avenues for immigration—the main gate and the back door—had been restricted, the former with the requirements outlined above, the latter with the termination of what some students of U.S. immigration have called the "first bracero program." This program was the result of the first significant exception to the immigration law when Congress, under pressure from agricultural interests in the Southwest, authorized a temporary-worker program that exempted recruits from both the literacy requirement and the head tax required of each immigrant. With the termination of that program and the uncertain economic times of the 1920s and 1930s, the illegal and explicitly temporary immigration of labor to the United States became less significant, while at the same time the pressure for both voluntary and involuntary return of immigrants increased.

Substantial pressure for immigration was renewed in 1942 during World War II, when there were once more severe labor shortages in the United States. In response to these shortages, the United States instituted the second bracero program, which, after its official reconfirmation by P.L. 78 (1951) during the height of U.S. involvement in the Korean War, lasted until 1964. P.L. 78 was the result of an unexpected alliance of American special interests, such as agribusiness and organized labor and the Mexican government, while most of the opposition to it came from the Mexican-American community in the Southwest. During the later stages of the bracero program this odd alliance became even more of an oddity. By 1964, when the program was discontinued, the climate of opinion among the various special interests had shifted considerably: U.S. agriculture had come to resent the increasingly interventionist policies of the Department of Labor with regard to wages and working conditions and was willing to acquiesce in the termination of the program. A growing outcry from many quarters about the conditions of life and employment of the braceros created an antibracero program alliance between the Mexican government and the liberal voices in the United States. Finally, an ever more vocal and politically important coalition of the Mexican-American and black communities actively opposed the program. Characteristically, this shifting of opinion occurred in the midst of increasing official and unofficial confusion over the precise effect of the braceros on local and regional labor markets, over the relation between the bracero program and illegal immigration, and over the effect of the program on the social and economic well-being of the most disadvantaged and politically powerless group in the region.

Beginning in the early 1950s, the main gate was also moving toward reform. Although immigration policy was reviewed in Senate Report 1515 (1950) and few legislative changes were recommended, there was an undercurrent of change in the mood of both the executive branch and the multitude of interest groups involved in the review process. In spite of evolving attitudes about immigration, however, Congress symbolically maintained the restrictionist status quo by overriding President Truman's veto of the McCarran-Walter Immigration and Nationality Act in 1952.[7]

The McCarran-Walter Act continued the racial focus of the 1920s legislation, which had reflected the doctrine that quotas were necessary to preserve the existing standard and character of American life. The 1952 legislation maintained a quota system already heavily skewed toward advanced European societies while making some nominal concessions to the rest of the world. Greece, for instance, was awarded a ceiling of 308 entries, while most Asian countries were given 100. In all fairness to the system, the anachronistic nature of the legislation was recognized and adjusted to take into account U.S. needs for certain skills and for population and our responsibilities to Eastern European refugees by allowing almost two-thirds of all those admitted in the 1950s to enter as exceptions to the law. The 1952 act, however, is equally instructive by virtue of what it did *not* include: neither a penalty provision for hiring illegal immigrants nor permanent legislation to permit temporary agricultural labor as a nonimmigrant category—if U.S. workers could not be found. Both provisions had been integral parts of Senate Report 1515, on which the act was largely based.[8] The failure of the act to respond to the changing climate of opinion with regard to immigration led to a plethora of subsequent amendments as well as to the simultaneous liberalization of back-door opportunities. By the end of the decade, the substance of the 1952 legislation had changed beyond recognition. It was only a matter of time before President Kennedy's commitment to immigration reform and President Johnson's emphasis on the "Great Society" would give rise to the first major revision of U.S. immigration policy in nearly half a century.

The resultant 1965 Immigration and Nationality Act (P.L. 89-236) placed a ceiling on immigration of 300,000, which was split between the Western (130,000) and Eastern (170,000) hemispheres. This legislation has been hailed from virtually all quarters for having abolished national-origin and anti-Oriental discrimination and, in conjunction with the civil rights legislation of the 1960s, for tearing down the institutional racism of earlier U.S. immigration legislation. Yet it treated the two hemispheres differently. For the Western Hemisphere, visas were to be granted on a first-come, first-served basis. Relatives of U.S. citizens and residents had equal preference with workers, regardless of the order of relationship or skill level involved. In order to protect the labor market, a labor certification was required of all relatives not of the first order attesting that there was a shortage of "able, qualified, willing, and available" workers in a particular skill category and that the prospective immigrant would not affect "prevailing wages and working conditions" adversely.

Immigrants from the Eastern Hemisphere, however, were admitted in accordance with a system of seven preference categories, with each country awarded a certain proportion, but no more than 20,000, of the total number of visas.

• The first preference includes children of U.S. citizens who are unmarried and under twenty-one years of age, up to 20 percent of the total number of visas allocated.

• The second preference applies to the spouses and unmarried children of U.S. permanent residents, regardless of their ages, up to 20 percent of the total number of visas *plus* any percentages unused by the first preference.

• The third preference allows the entry of scientists, artists, and professionals of exceptional ability, for a total of 10 percent of the visas allocated.

• The fourth preference includes the married sons and daughters of U.S. citizens, regardless of their ages, up to 10 percent of the total number of visas *plus* any unused allocations from the first three categories.

• The fifth preference applies to brothers and sisters of U.S. citizens, up to 24 percent of total allocations *plus* any unused visas from the first four categories.

• The sixth preference allows a mixture of skilled and unskilled workers needed by the U.S. labor market, up to 10 percent of total allocations.

• The seventh preference applies to refugees and covers the remaining 6 percent of visas (see note 1).

• The remaining unused allocations fall into a final, nonpreference category.[9]

Additionally, the 1965 act not only prohibited immigrants from the Eastern Hemisphere entering under the third and sixth preferences from exhausting any unused visas from the other categories but also required them to obtain labor certification.

The preference system, although philosophically in basic accord with a neutrality concerning race, color, and language, is flawed by a series of pronounced intended and unintended inequalities. In practice, the system shows a preference for skilled workers over unskilled. There is a strong class bias in preference categories three and six in favor of those who can make immediate significant contributions to the American economy and society, but whose immigration represents a significant loss to the sending countries. The magnitude of this problem often escapes the attention of all but the specialists in immigration matters. For instance, this "brain drain" is responsible for the presence of a higher number of Filipino medical doctors in practice in the United States than the total number of black doctors and for licensing of more foreign medical doctors by the United States in certain years than the number graduating from American medical schools. The receiving society does not have to absorb the high costs of totally educating these welcome immigrants, but the sending societies cannot afford to subsidize the American professions or to replace the skills lost. The 1965 act thus may also dampen our own incentive to develop and train our own manpower. To meet the problem of the brain drain, compensatory schemes have been proposed for the countries of origin of the workers.

Furthermore, there are loopholes that have been exploited by immigration lawyers, such as having aliens travel to the United States for the birth of a child or bringing their retired parents, who can then bring along other children under preference two. Both these groups gain the right to immigrate without a labor certification, if the persons immigrating can afford the cost of coming. Indeed, almost a third of the total number of immigrants from the Western Hemisphere since 1965 have used the first loophole.[10]

Some other unintended consequences of the 1965 act reflect the naiveté of the architects of P.L. 89-236. The refugee category has proved to be grossly inadequate; the labor certification program has a Catch-22, in that applicants have to be offered jobs before they can be certified, in effect encouraging illegal immigration. As noted, there has been unequal treatment of the two hemispheres. The legislation failed to anticipate accurately the pressure for immigration from Mexico and the Carribean countries and consequently encouraged additional illegal immigration. The main gate has attempted to respond to some of the defects, however. In 1978, revision of the immigration laws under P.L. 95-412 extended to the Western Hemisphere the same preference system to which the Eastern Hemisphere had been subjected and eliminated the exemption from labor certification for preferences one and two as well as the separate numerical ceilings for the two hemispheres.

Parallel to these main-gate reforms, the 1965 act reaffirmed the continuation of a system of small-scale back-door waves of immigrants. Provision 101a (H) ii of the 1952 Immigration and Nationality Act, dubbed the "H-2 program," empowered the attorney general to authorize the entry of several categories of temporary workers as exemptions to the rule prohibiting the entry of nonimmigrant labor. Such an exemption may be granted when the Department of Labor certifies that "indigenous labor is unavailable and that recourse to temporary alien labor will not be detrimental to local wage scales or working conditions" and recommends to the Immigration and Naturalization Service (INS) that it issue temporary work permits.[11]

Although this program is intended to respond to genuine labor shortages, several problems hamper its operation. For instance, when is a shortage real and when contrived? What is the potential for confusion of the practice of having two separate agencies responsible for the program? How can one justify the fact that tying a worker to a single employer who has arbitrary powers over him during his tenure as an H-2 worker creates an extremely one-sided power relationship that can make of the worker something like an indentured servant? Finally, how can one justify the fact that issuance of permits may reflect the governmental contacts of a specific industry rather than demonstrable need?

Along with these back-door entrants, nearly 100,000 *border commuters* must be included; these, who reside in Mexico or Canada but hold permanent resident status under INS regulations (upheld by the Supreme Court in 1974), constitute up to 10 percent of the labor force in border counties. In addition, there are the visitor workers who enter the United States legally every day in search of work through a program that accords those who live permanently in Mexican border towns the privilege of entry into the United States within twenty-five miles of the border for a period of up to seventy-two hours. The INS does not know exactly how many such special cards have been issued—more than 2 million were issued in the 1960s alone—and how many such cards are being abused. Obviously, the number and impact of legal entrants in these categories into the United States are significant, although no studies of them have been made. Both cases, however, constitute de facto worker programs.[12]

With immigration policy thus responding on an ad hoc basis and with the numbers of foreign workers and their impact increasing dramatically, it is necessary to undertake a thorough assessment of the most significant components which a comprehensive immigration policy must address.

Assessing the Effects of Immigration on the United States: Four Components

The Economic (Labor Market) Component. The effect of international migration on the economies of the receivers is probably the most complex aspect of the immigration phenomenon. Foreigners are held responsible both for dampening and for fueling inflation by reducing and increasing aggregate demand; for depressing wages or at least moderating wage increases; for improving the economic condition of some of the indigenous work force but also for contributing to the deterioration of working conditions and of the economic condition of the receivers' disadvantaged native strata; for being crucial to the economic health of advanced industrial societies but also for creating a persistent economic dependence on continuous flows of migrants; for displacing indigenous workers and for filling a real shortage of labor; and, finally, for dampening industry's enthusiasm for capital investment, mechanization, and rationalization of the labor force and for redefining jobs or for having no discernible impact in these areas.

Evaluating both the logical consistency and the empirical foundations of the principal hypotheses must be given priority by the academic and research communities. A starting point for this assessment must be the fundamentally neutral observation that the growth of the economies of both Europe and the United States since the end of World War II has been premised, to varying degrees, on a ready supply of foreign labor. Policy analysis should distinguish between short-term and long-term effects; describe the way micro-level decisions of both individual immigrants and specific employers have helped shape the flow; assess the economic interests of the intended protagonists (workers and employers) and the unintended protagonists (the consumers of public and private goods) of the immigration process; distinguish between the manifest and latent consequences of the process; and, finally, outline the present and probable future economic impact of legal and illegal immigration.

In order to clarify some of the structural problems that contribute to the immigration dilemma and are endemic to our economic system, I will use the dual labor market model developed by some American labor economists and sociologists. Dualists identify two employment sectors. The first sector is made up of monopoly firms that control "a significant portion of their respective markets, rely on capital-intensive technology to enhance productivity, and are able to pass on increases in their wage bill to consumers through their control of the markets."[13] In the secondary market, the conditions, to some observers, approach those of earlier industrial capitalistic competition: the economic environment is uncertain; markets tend to be local or at best regional; labor-intensive processes of production are used; and, since the secondary market is not monopolistic or oligopolistic, it cannot pass on increases in its wage bill to consumers.[14]

The social relationships of production that prevail in each market are obviously shaped by their respective internal structures. Accordingly, the monopolistic-oligopolistic market emphasizes stability and tenure in the job and, by generating internal markets that divide work into "finely graded job ladders," provides for institutionalized promotion and advancement. The secondary labor market, on the other hand, is unstable, enforces "discipline" directly, arbitrarily, and harshly, does not generate an internal market, and offers no incentive for either employer or worker to stabilize employment. Mobility between the two labor markets is negligible because of institutional restraints, notably discrimination.

A necessary corollary to the dualist model is that as segmentation along the "competitive/monopoly axis interacts with existing historical divisions by race, sex, and age, the secondary labor market becomes, by and large, a minority market."[15] It is in this market that students of migration perceive a relative scarcity of labor as the economically and politically disadvantaged indigenous groups, and the second-generation immigrants as well, begin to reject jobs in the secondary market for themselves. Thus there must be constant replenishment of the streams of migration if an adequate secondary labor force is to be maintained. In the past, this force was largely filled by black migrants coming from the rural South. The internal rural labor reserves have been exhausted, however, and the secondary jobs are being filled by legal and, more often, illegal immigrants with far less access to political organization and information. This model, therefore, indicates that in the present segmented labor market the interruption of the illegal inflow might actually cause severe shortages of labor in such economic activities as restaurants and hotels, the garment industry, maintenance, and various agricultural jobs.

Recommendations for reorganization of the labor market abound. They range from the stringent enforcement of antidiscrimination legislation, retraining of redundant workers, and enforcement of minimum-wage legislation, to an increase in public-service employment specifically for workers from the secondary labor market, the aggressive defense of the rights of workers, and the improvement of working conditions.

The Social Component. The second aspect of the immigration phenomenon that requires serious reappraisal is the social one. As Martin points out, it is in the "social arena that benefits and costs are most important for policy prescription, yet even qualitative assessments are not unambiguous."[16] Evidence of the social impact of immigration on the United States, particularly on the use of social services by the illegal immigrants, is often impressionistic, methodologically suspect, and based on small or unrepresentative samples. The conclusions drawn are therefore inherently suspect. It appears, however, that the overwhelming majority of illegal immigrants neither use the various social services in the United States nor collect the social benefits that are the right of every other worker in the United States.[17] Since at least some disadvantaged indigenous workers are displaced from the secondary labor market and use welfare and unemployment insurance, however, the net effect of illegal immigration is an increase in the costs of such benefits to localities in which there is a high concentration of illegal immigrants.

Obviously receiving societies do benefit somewhat from the contributions of migrants to the various social insurance schemes. As Greenwood has pointed out, the cost of the use of public services by immigrants depends on whether these services are produced under conditions of falling or rising cost.[18] Since the local tax base of immigrants is usually low because of low rates of ownership of real property, they contribute less than their share of the cost of the local services that they use. This leads to higher-than-average contributions on the part of the natives. Furthermore, the cost of the service infrastructure will also rise when, through overuse, the quality deteriorates or when resources are spread too thin. These increasing costs must be juxtaposed, however, against the declining average cost of producing other public goods in areas such as health, retirement, unemployment, national defense, agricultural assistance, in which the taxes and withholding contributions of immigrants make a difference. Furthermore, immigrants afford opportunities for some workers in the primary labor market to advance, even as they may push some secondary workers downward.

Social marginality, however, constantly reinforced by the often institutionalized discrimination against immigrants and the widely discretionary and often capricious administrative practices on the part of immigration bureaucracies, encourages the development of a second-generation problem. The children of immigrants find themselves caught on a treadmill that portends severe sociopolitical consequences. At the heart of this problem is the political ambivalence of the receiving societies toward immigrants and their unwillingness to accept the challenge of new cultural, linguistic, and ethnic entities. In this evolving environment, receiving societies may come under increasing domestic and international pressure to grant their de facto citizens the rights and privileges that correspond to their economic contributions.

The Population Component. As the United States is coming to realize, importation of labor and illegal flows of migrants that are allowed to develop in the midst of policy voids become de facto immigration and population policies. Accordingly, the debate over the effects of immigration on population growth should not be defined exclusively by demographic concerns. It must also include the more critical discussion of the appropriate size for the population of the United States.

Again it is necessary for policy planners to take a long view. With the present rate of fertility falling to about 1.7 live births per woman—less than the 2.11 births that is the absolute population replacement level, and down from 2.9 births in the 1960s and 3.7 births in the 1950s—a stationary population can be expected within the next thirty years.[19] It is obvious, then, that with reduced immigration the population will soon begin to decline. Depending on the various estimates of permanent illegal settlement, the total U.S. population in the year 2000 will be between 234 million with no net immigration and 286 million with the present net number of legal immigrants plus 1 million net illegal immigrants per year.[20] The actual number will probably be much closer to the lower figure than to the higher.

The annual net flow of legal immigration to the United States is around 270,000, from a gross inflow of about 400,000, and the annual net flow of illegal immigration may be only about 100,000, from a gross illegal inflow as high as three quarters of a million.[21] Arguments advanced by groups such as the advocates of zero population growth that seek to restrict total immigration severely therefore make little sense, because they are premised on faulty data. Policy makers cannot afford such faulty premises, nor can they afford to act without a population goal in mind.

The Political Component. Although it has received only scant attention from researchers, the political component of immigration constantly intrudes upon all other components. In fact, it is in response to both domestic and international political pressures that the United States is now reconsidering its immigration policies. At stake is its ability to exercise one of the most jealously guarded expressions of sovereignty: the control of its borders and the formulation and implementation of policies that reflect its national interests. At present it is entirely plausible to argue that the United States is in effect reacting to conditions imposed upon it by the region and by the *fait accompli* of an illegal alien population in its midst, the size of which is roughly comparable to the total economically active foreign population in Europe—about 5 million.[22]

In view of the centrality of the immigration issue for advanced industrial societies, it is remarkable that the topic has not come to occupy a more central place in the international political agenda. In the United States, a debate is heating up over the issues of "over-foreignization" on one hand and the violation of the basic human rights of the illegal immigrants on the other.[23] The controversy seems to test the will and ingenuity of political elite groups that are uncertain exactly where immigration fits into the U.S. ideological spectrum. They instinctively seek consensus by appointing commissions, task forces, and study groups. As Cornelius vividly illustrates, illegal immigrants are often regarded by various segments of the public in negative terms, such as "racial and cultural contaminants," "free-loaders," "welfare cheats," and "*mañana* minded."[24] Fears of the creation of a Spanish-speaking Quebec in the Southwest are being fueled by such talk. Such public perceptions, however erroneous, are politically significant, because they reduce the degrees of policy space within which the United States and other governments, particularly that of Mexico, can maneuver and thus reduce the prospects for "gradualist, cooperative solutions . . . [while pressuring for] narrow punitive responses by the U.S. government."[25]

Uncertainty on the part of the elite has resulted in odd couples and strange bedfellows. The following list, adapted partly from David S. North, identifies some of these alliances.[26] The restrictionist camp includes racists, advocates of population control, environmentalists and conservationists, those eager to promote law and order, organized labor, and (often) the black leaders; antirestrictionists include employers of illegal immigrants in agribusiness and the secondary labor market, the State Department, the Mexican government, church groups, the Hispanic leaders, the civil libertarians, the left, and the immigration bar.

Among all these groups, organized labor has the greatest potential to be a veto group on immigration policy, yet it has failed to have a significant effect in this area and has usually been outmaneuvered by business interests, at least with regard to back-door policies. Underlying this lack of effect on policy is a basic ambivalence about the place of both legal and illegal immigrants in the union movement. Are the two groups in antithetical positions in relation to capital? Are immigrants a threat to the security, advancement, and organization of natives? Is exploitation of immigrants by employers in the secondary labor market detrimental to the union movement? It is only recently that some organized labor groups have begun to perceive illegal immigration in a different light.

Although illegal aliens may harm the well-being of some union members, it is in the interests of organized labor to organize immigrants and to demand and obtain equal economic and social treatment for all workers, regardless of nationality. Some embryonic attempts in that direction have already been made in the New York garment industry and, intermittently, in some agricultural areas of the Southwest. In so doing, the unions are taking a more active part in the formulation and implementation of new immigration initiatives in recognition of their crucial interests in this matter.

Concluding Remarks

Because the causes of illegal immigration are structural and are primarily related to the labor market, immigration pressure can only be relieved by reforming the labor market. Furthermore, an immigration policy may be ancillary to more fundamental questions such as population policy and social policies. In addition, an immigration policy must be sensitive to important internal and international political forces. Only when our priorities have become clear can immigration reform become the right tool in the attainment of our long-term national goals. A necessary first step in this direction is to study the effects of legal immigration on our society, a topic that has often taken a back seat to the study of illegal immigration. Only after we understand how legal immigrants behave can we begin to make intelligent choices about an overall immigration policy. But whether we have the time and the emotional distance to reach this level of understanding remains to be seen.

The various foreign labor programs under consideration, regardless of specific logical and philosophical problems, suffer from some basic deficiencies in that they address either the symptoms or the consequences, rather than the causes, of the problem. Often such programs are narrowly focused on certain problems, such as the problem of illegal aliens, to the exclusion of other equally critical issues.

There can be little disagreement that illegal immigration has been a source of troubled bilateral relations, has diminished the international prestige of the United States, has led to a divisive domestic debate over public policy with regard to such matters as the displacement of indigenous workers and the effect of illegal aliens on working conditions and wages in low-skill categories, and has "invited" the wholesale violation of immigration law.[27] At the same time, foreign workers often lack basic rights and services and are generally exploited by employers in the secondary labor market. Amid the competing claims with regard to the effects of illegal immigration, policy makers have apparently come to the conclusion that the status quo is unacceptable. The creation of the Select Commission on Immigration and Refugee Policy in 1979 seemed initially to reflect a high-level executive and legislative commitment to address the problem in all its facets and arrive at a consensus about the direction of our immigration policy.

Such expectations, however, were quickly dashed as the commission itself became the center of controversy with a series of professional staff problems and strained relations between the staff and several of the commissioners.[28] Political events further compounded these problems; President Carter, who had appointed the commission, was defeated, and the Democrats lost control of the Senate. These events both led to a substantial change in the membership of the commission and dissolved the remaining hopes that its final report would carry substantial political clout.[29]

In fact, that report became obsolete almost as soon as it was made public through the immediate empaneling by the Reagan administration of a task force to study the report. The recommendations of the task force to the cabinet, the cabinet's subsequent recommendations to the president, and, finally, the recently released program of the president followed in rapid succession. Mr. Reagan's program consisted principally of the following provisions: (1) A pilot guest-worker program with Mexico, involving 50,000 Mexicans for each of the next two years (rejecting the select commission's arguments against such a program). (2) A program of sanctions against employers who "knowingly" hire illegal immigrants (a recommendation in accord with that of the commission). The commission had been divided (eight in favor, seven against, one passing) on the question of developing a more secure identification system—something demanded by fairness and administrative reality. Mr. Reagan also skirted this fundamental issue by simply requiring employers to examine any two of the following documents: a birth certificate, a driver's license, a social security card, or a draft registration certificate. (3) The improvement of law enforcement in the border areas by expansion of the size of our border patrol in areas where the rate of illegal crossing is high. (4) The interdiction and return by the Coast Guard of boats of Haitians on the high seas. (5) A phased-in granting of legal status to qualified illegal residents who meet a series of requirements considerably more stringent than those recommended by the select commission. (6) And, finally, a doubling of the quotas of legal immigration from Canada and Mexico, allowing either to use those visas that are unclaimed by the other.[30]

The administration's proposals found considerable favor with the Congress, and several of their key provisions became integral parts of the bill introduced in Congress in the late summer of 1982. The bill (H.R. 6514), known formally as the Immigration Reform and Control Act of 1982 and informally as the Simpson-Mazzoli Immigration Bill, passed the Senate but never came to a vote in the post-election lame-duck House. H.R. 6514 got its informal name from Senator Alan Simpson and Representative Ron Mazzoli, the chairmen of the relevant subcommittees. It is expected that the bill will be reintroduced by its chief sponsors early in the Ninety-eighth Congress. This time, however, it is expected to receive considerably more opposition from those who object to certain of its key components—especially amnesty and sanctions against employers.

The Simpson-Mazzoli bill concurs with the administration's wishes in the border enforcement areas and the question of offering Mexico and Canada preferential treatment; it is more liberal than the administration's proposals on the conditions and timetable of its amnesty program; it is considerably more stringent than the administration wishes in its provisions for sanctions against employers in that it directs the president to develop a secure national worker identification system within three years on which the sanctions system would be anchored; and it seems to part company with the administration in the area of a temporary-worker program. The bill abandons that component but then seems to equivocate and reopen the back door to temporary migration by easing off the requirements and streamlining the procedure for H-2 entry to the point where that program could conceivably increase to several times its recent annual average of about 30,000 entries.

In the current climate in favor of more stopgap measures, I will take the minority viewpoint, namely, that even if there is a demonstrable need for more workers in the secondary labor market, we must first address the question why certain jobs are abandoned by native workers. Importing more workers solves nothing; it only postpones, reinforces, and eventually exacerbates structural problems of the labor market. If indeed we need large numbers of workers, let us address the issue first through mechanization and rationalization of the existing labor force and through improvement of both the wages and the working conditions in such jobs. Then, if we still have a shortage of workers, let us adopt an immigration policy with flexible quotas that can respond to our social, political, and human rights commitments. Changing the intolerable status quo with ill-conceived and optimistic plans for foreign-worker programs not only fails to remove the threat but, in our case, simply institutionalizes what Briggs calls a subclass of "rightless" and "deprived" persons.[31]

In reforming immigration policy, then, we should err, if err we must, on the side of caution. With regard to our labor market, we should focus on reform through a constellation of programs involving both direct intervention by the government—in job creation, retraining, minimum wage legislation, *strict enforcement of legislation about working conditions*—and incentives, such as tax credits, for business to reduce its dependence on illegal aliens through more aggressive efforts at rationalization and the redesign of the wage and skill structures of jobs that natives will not occupy. Concomitantly, we must begin to move in areas of immigration reform, which, without reduc-

113

ing our commitment to such noble goals as reunification of families and antidiscrimination, will allow us to tighten the labor-certification process, help communities that are burdened with significant legal and illegal immigration flows through special federal grants to defray immigrant-related costs, severely punish repeat offenders who employ illegal immigrants, and reorganize, modernize, and enlarge the Immigration and Naturalization Service.

Many of these proposals stem from the acknowledgment that although in a free society illegal immigration cannot be eradicated, it must be controlled. The *juste milieu* between a perceived need for controls and our (at times undeserved) international image as a nation that welcomes immigrants has been extremely elusive. The administration's proposals show only a halfhearted commitment to solving the immigration problem and seem to be opening the way—through the guest-worker option—for the resumption of back-door policies. Once again, palliatives appear to have won the day over long-term, politically difficult solutions.

Notes

1. A related but distinct problem concerns the multiple waves of "refugees" who have been entering the United States in increasingly large numbers during the last few years. Although refugee status has already been redefined in the Refugee Act of 1980 (Public Law 96-212, approved March 17, 1980), it is undeniable, as is poignantly attested to by the case of the Haitians, that a significant and increasing proportion among them are little more than economic refugees who have openly come to the United States to escape broad political repression accompanied by abject poverty. This category, if unchecked, can play havoc with the ability of the government to arrive at a comprehensive immigration policy. Significantly, the Refugee Act of 1980 removed the seventh preference of the 1965 Immigration and Nationality Act and added the 6 percent of total visas previously allocated to refugees to the second preference. The discussion of the refugee issue, however, is not within the scope of this essay.

2. Alejandro Portes and John Walton, *Labor, Class, and the International System* (New York: Academic Press, 1981), p. 4.

3. Helga Hveem, "The Global Dominance System: Notes on a Theory of Global Political Economy," *Journal of Peace Research*, vol. 10 (1973), p. 319.

4. Aristide R. Zolberg, "The Main Gate and the Back Door: The Politics of American Immigration Policy, 1950–76" (Paper presented at a workshop of the Council on Foreign Relations, Washington, D.C., April 12, 1978).

5. Ibid., p. 10.

6. Ibid., p. 11.

7. See David S. North and Allen Lebel, *Manpower and Immigration Policies in the United States* (Washington, D.C.: National Commission for Manpower Policy, 1978).

8. Zolberg, "The Main Gate," pp. 12–24.

9. See, for example, E. Abrams and F. S. Abrams, "Immigration Policy—Who Gets In and Why?" *The Public Interest*, no. 38 (1975), pp. 3–29; Interagency Task Force on Immigration Policy, *Staff Report* (Washington, D.C.: U.S. Departments of Justice, Labor, and State, March 1979); Zolberg, "The Main Gate," pp. 27–49; Charles B. Keely, *U.S. Immigration: A Policy Analysis* (New York: The Population Council, 1979); and Mark J. Miller and David J. Yeres, *A Massive Temporary Worker Programme for the U.S.: Solution or Mirage?* Migration for Employment Project, World Employment Programme Research Working Paper, WEP 2-26-/WP 44 (Geneva: International Labor Organization, 1979).

10. Abrams and Abrams, "Immigration Policy," pp. 13–15. The 1976 amendment to the Immigration and Nationality Act closed one of these loopholes by stipulating that a child may not use his citizenship to bring his parents into the United States until he or she is twenty-one years of age. See P.L. 94–571.

11. Miller and Yeres, *Massive Temporary Worker Programme*, p. 8.

12. Vernon M. Briggs, Jr., "Foreign Labor Programs as an Alternative to Illegal Immigration into the United States: A Dissenting View" (Paper presented at the Center for Philosophy and Public Policy, University of Maryland, College Park, February 2, 1980).

13. Alejandro Portes and Robert L. Bach, "Dual Labor Markets and Immigration: A Test of Competing Theories of Income Inequality," Comparative Studies of Immigration and Ethnicity, Occasional Paper Series (Durham, N.C.: Center for International Studies, Duke University, 1979), p. 7.

14. Ibid.; and Peter B. Doeringer and Michael J. Piore, "Unemployment and the 'Dual Labor Market,'" *The Public Interest*, no. 38 (1975), pp. 67–79. For a full exposition of the dualist thesis and immigration see Michael J. Piore, *Birds of Passage* (Cambridge: Cambridge University Press, 1979).

15. Portes and Bach, "Dual Labor Markets," p. 9.

16. Philip L. Martin, *Guestworker Programs: Lessons from Europe*, Report prepared for the Joint Economic Committee of the U.S. Congress, June 1979, p. 42.

17. See David S. North and Marion F. Houstoun, *The Characteristics and Role of Illegal Aliens in the U.S. Labor Market: An Exploratory Study* (Washington, D.C.: Linton and Co., 1976); see also Maurice D. Van Arsdol, Jr., et al., *Non-Apprehended and Apprehended Undocumented Residents in the Los Angeles Labor Market: An Exploratory Study*, Report prepared for the Employment and Training Administration, U.S. Department of Labor, May 1979.

18. Michael J. Greenwood, "The Economic Consequences of Immigration for the U.S.: A Survey of the Findings," *Staff Report Companion Papers*, Interagency Task Force on Immigration Policy, August 1979, pp. 1–108.

19. Ibid.

20. Keely, *U.S. Immigration*; Greenwood, "Economic Consequences of Immigration"; David M. Heer, "What Is the Annual Net Flow of Undocumented Mexican Immigrants to the U.S.?" *Demography*, 1979, pp. 417–23.

21. Wayne A. Cornelius, "Building the Cactus Curtain? Mexican Immigration and the U.S. Responses" (Paper delivered at the Latin American Program of the Woodrow Wilson International Center for Scholars, September 28–29, 1979), p. 11; Heer, "Annual Net Flow of Undocumented Mexican Immigrants."

22. See *U.S. Immigration Policy and the National Interest*, Final Report and Recommendations of the Select Commission on Immigration and Refugee Policy to the Congress and the President of the United States, Washington, D.C., March 1, 1981.

23. See *The Tarnished Golden Door: Civil Rights Issues in Immigration*, Report of the United States Commission on Civil Rights, September 1980.

24. Cornelius, "Building the Cactus Curtain?" p. 11.

25. Ibid., p. 22.

26. David S. North, "Comments on Vernon Briggs' Paper" (Commentary given at the Conference on Border Relations, La Paz, Mexico, February 9, 1980), p. 17.

27. Miller and Yeres, *Massive Temporary Worker Programme*, p. 35.

28. See Michael S. Teitelbaum, "Right versus Right: Immigration and Refugee Policy in the United States," *Foreign Affairs*, vol. 59, no. 1 (1980), pp. 21–59; see also the supplementary statements to the final report of the commission by several of the commissioners, *U.S. Immigration Policy and the National Interest*, pp. 331–421.

29. The commission was composed of four public members, the secretaries of health and human services, labor, and state, the attorney general, four U.S. senators, and four U.S. representatives, one of whom, Representative Elizabeth Holtzman, failed to win reelection.

30. See *U.S. Immigration Policy and the National Interest*, Final Report; *U.S. Immigration Policy and the National Interest*, Staff Report of the Select Commission on Immigration and Refugee Policy, April 30, 1981; Memorandum of the Attorney General to the Secretaries of State, Defense, Education, Labor, Health and Human Services, Transportation, and Treasury and to the Director of the Office of Management and Budget, May 19, 1981; Robert Pear, "White House Asks a Law to Bar Jobs for Illegal Aliens," *New York Times*, July 31, 1981; and John M. Crewdson, "Plan on Immigration," *New York Times*, July 31, 1981.

31. See Briggs, "Foreign Labor Programs"; Cornelius, "Building the Cactus Curtain?"; Wayne A. Cornelius, *Illegal Migration to the United*

States: Recent Research Findings, Policy Implications and Research Priorities (Cambridge, Mass.: Center for International Studies, MIT, 1977); and Edwin Reubens, *Temporary Admissions of Foreign Workers: Dimensions and Policies,* Special Report No. 34 of the National Commission for Manpower Policy (Washington, D.C., 1979).

6

Foreign Direct Investment in the United States: The Balance of Foreign and Domestic Policy

Don C. Piper

In the decade of the 1970s, the American public and government officials became increasingly, and in some cases dramatically, aware of growing foreign direct investment (FDI) in the United States. Newspaper headlines that proclaimed, among other things, "British Ready to Join Invasion of Investors,"[1] "Foreign Investing in U.S. Rises As Stocks Lag, Dollar Slips,"[2] "Wave of Foreign Investment Washing across U.S.,"[3] "Foreign Farmland Purchases Higher Than Earlier Thought,"[4] and "Oklahoma Strives to Undo Foreign Hold of Real Estate"[5] focused attention on the general condition of the American economy and aroused suspicion, even fear, that foreign nationals might be securing control of the economy to the detriment of the interests of American citizens.

The possibility that oil-producing states have already invested or will in the future invest their surplus revenues to purchase American land or industries is one of several reasons for the recent concern about FDI. Others are the substantial increase in FDI within the past decade, the emergence of new countries as investors, and the acquisition of American firms, rather than the establishment of new economic enterprises, by foreign investors. With regard to the last point, foreign acquisition of existing American-owned businesses generates a concern that American citizens may be forced out of certain economic sectors, which will then be dominated by foreign interests. There is also a growing concern about foreign ownership of American natural resources, such as agricultural land, coal, and timber. In a period of increasing shortage of certain natural resources, foreign ownership of natural resources generates a suspicion that the resources will not be used to accommodate American requirements but will be exported to meet the needs of other countries.[6]

In view of these general concerns and dramatic headlines, it is not surprising that there seems to exist among the American public a negative attitude regarding FDI in the United States. Such an attitude is reflected in a Roper poll of June 1979, in which respondents were asked, "We'd like to know whether you are in favor of or opposed to foreign companies investing in the United States—or don't you have any feelings one way or the other about it?" Responses were the following:[7]

Opposed	44 percent
In favor	34 percent
No feelings one way or the other	17 percent
Don't know	5 percent

With regard to specific types of foreign direct investment, a November 1978 Roper poll obtained the following responses:[8]

	More harm	More good	No difference	Not sure
			(percent)	
Acquiring American natural resources such as forests and coal mines	80	10	7	3
Buying out small companies	77	8	11	4
Investing in farm land	65	16	15	4
Buying shares of American companies	62	16	16	6
Investing in properties such as office buildings and shopping malls	56	21	19	4
Establishing multinational operations here in the United States	54	20	17	9

In this context it is worth noting that a June 1979 poll reported the American public to be evenly divided on the issue of American direct investment abroad. The Roper poll that month asked, "Generally, are you in favor of or opposed to American companies investing in foreign countries, or don't you have any feelings one way or the other about it?" The responses were as follows:[9]

Opposed	38 percent
In favor	38 percent
No feelings one way or the other	18 percent
Don't know	6 percent

It is instructive to realize that some of the expressions of concern about FDI in the United States reflect the same concerns that are set forth by officials in third world countries who fear that the local economy is controlled by industrial interests from Western, capitalist states. Although the problem of foreign penetration of the local economy is less acute in the United States than in the developing countries, the knowledge that there is some degree of alien control is unsettling and likely to precipitate some type of public policy response. As one economist has noted:

> However much the multinational enterprise may contribute to the objectives of economic growth and stability in the host country, the fact that the parent has the ability to alter the activities of the affiliates increases the uncertainty facing the host government. The further fact that the decision center is outside the jurisdiction of the host government increases the uncertainty. The normal means of control, such as persuasion and inducements—short of administrative regulation—are not as effective across national boundaries.[10]

The general uncertainty of the host government and its citizens about FDI centers on whether the foreign owner will pursue policies that will be economically beneficial to the host state. There is a suspicion that foreign investors may depart from rational economic policies and instead adopt policies that are intended to advance the political and economic interests of foreign governments at the expense of the local interests. A related concern is that foreign economic interests will use their economic holdings to intrude into the formulation of local domestic and foreign policy and thereby subvert local policy to support foreign interests and goals.

In general, a host government is likely to welcome FDI as long as the benefits of such investment will appear to outweigh any possible liabilities. Specifically, FDI is likely to be welcome if it contributes to the economic growth of the host state by bringing in capital for investment or new technology or if it opens up new markets or generates additional jobs among the local population. In addition, FDI is likely to be welcome when it enables existing local economic enterprises to remain in operation.

In an important study, C. Fred Bergsten and his colleagues identify some of the goals that host governments seek to achieve or to protect in permitting FDI that would appear to be appropriate goals for inflows of FDI into the United States.[11] One is the promotion of domestic economic growth, and as part of that general effort the expansion or retention of jobs appears to be the most important domestic economic goal of host governments. External economic advantages, including primarily improvements in the balance of payments as a consequence of inflows of foreign capital associated with the FDI and the expansion of exports, are a second goal of host governments.

The third goal of host governments is to be able to ensure that FDI is consistent with local governmental policy through mechanisms that will ensure local managerial control over the foreign-owned industry.

Besides being expected to make a positive contribution to local economic growth, FDI will be welcome only so long as it does not appear to bring economic, social, or political liabilities. FDI will probably be unwelcome if the result is:

1. ownership or control by aliens of economic activities considered to be sensitive for reasons of national security

2. depletion by aliens of local natural resources for foreign benefit and to the detriment of the local population

3. the ability of aliens to use their local economic activities to influence local policy to the benefit of foreign interests and to the detriment of local interests

4. the transfer of resources to the home states in such magnitude that there is a drain on the economy of the host country

5. restriction or prevention of economic opportunity of local nationals

6. preferential treatment of aliens, especially in matters such as taxes, that is generally not available to the local population

7. complete control by aliens of a specific economic sector and the consequent ability to dominate an important market

8. failure of alien owners to act as "good citizens" with regard to such matters as labor policy, pollution, and illegal activities

In situations in which FDI is perceived as bringing liabilities, the host government may prohibit the entry of FDI or require the divestiture of existing alien ownership through expropriation or forced sale of assets. A less extreme and perhaps more likely policy response is for the host government to establish regulations over the FDI in order to minimize the liabilities to the local economy.

FDI in the United States

Although it is recognized that additional detailed data are needed in order to obtain a more complete picture of FDI in the United States, the available data are sufficient to reveal the substantial growth of FDI during the past decade and the sources of such investment. The Commerce Department defines foreign direct investment, as the term is used in these data, as the "direct or indirect ownership of ten per cent or more of the voting securities of an incorporated business enterprise."[12] FDI does not equal the value of the assets in the economic sector that are foreign owned but the value of the funds brought into the United States by the foreign investors. Consequently the FDI position does not reflect the funds that foreign investors borrow in the United States or the increase in the equity of the investment. Because the data reflect the primary sources of investment, they do not disclose any difference between the country of origin of the investment and the country of ownership of the investment.

According to the 1974 bench-mark survey of FDI in the United States, the foreign direct investment position was $26,512 million, with a value of $174,272 million in total assets.[13] The marked discrepancy between the FDI and total assets is explained in part by the fact that a substantial number of foreign investors borrow in U.S. capital markets in order to finance their investments. Table 1 indicates the 1974 values of FDI and total assets for selected countries.

By 1981, FDI had increased to $89,759 million, an increase of 239 percent from the 1974 position. Extrapolating from the 1974 value of total assets, one can calculate that in 1981 the total assets of foreign investors could amount to more than $400,000 million.[14] As table 2 indicates, the greater portion of FDI still comes from OECD countries and with the exception of the Netherlands Antilles reflects rather a traditional investment pattern, although in 1981 there was apparently a sharp increase in FDI from Kuwait.[15]

In reporting earlier data, Fouch and Lupo set forth several reasons that investment opportunities in the United States were attractive to foreign investors during the period under study. These include a "strong rise in U.S. output since the 1974–75 recession, the

TABLE 1

VALUES RELATING TO FOREIGN DIRECT INVESTMENT IN THE
UNITED STATES, 1974
(millions of dollars)

Country of Origin	FDI Position	Total Assets	Gross Product	Net Capital Inflows
Canada	5,177	23,856	4,491	604
France	1,145	8,692	1,114	239
Germany	1,562	8,201	1,008	579
Japan	131	39,069	1,408	93
Netherlands	4,704	17,323	5,597	476
Netherlands Antilles	1,408	3,428	—	44
Switzerland	2,002	9,541	1,417	543
United Kingdom	5,714	32,226	5,965	229
All others	4,669	31,936	3,690	972
Total	26,512	174,272	24,690	3,779

SOURCE: U.S. Department of Commerce, *Foreign Direct Investment in the United States*, vol. 2 (April 1976), p. 10.

TABLE 2

SOURCES OF FOREIGN DIRECT INVESTMENT IN THE UNITED STATES, 1981

Country of Origin	FDI Position (millions)	Percent of Total FDI
Canada	12,212	13.6
France	5,844	6.5
Germany	7,067	7.9
Japan	6,887	7.7
Netherlands	20,177	22.5
Netherlands Antilles	5,993	6.7
Switzerland	4,368	4.9
United Kingdom	15,527	17.3
All others	11,684	13.0
Total	89,759	100.0

NOTE: Percentages do not add to 100 because of rounding.
SOURCE: Ned G. Howenstine and Gregory G. Fouch, "Direct Foreign Investment in the United States in 1981," *Survey of Current Business*, vol. 62 (August 1982), pp. 31 n2, 37.

depreciation of the U.S. dollar against a number of leading foreign currencies since 1971, the decline of U.S. costs of production relative to foreign costs, and the political stability of the United States, compared with several other major areas."[16]

The pattern of growth of FDI is also evident in the number of announcements of FDI in American manufacturing industries reported by the Conference Board during the decade.[17] As these figures reveal, there were more than 2,000 announcements during the decade, the number increasing as the decade progressed.

Year	Announcements	Cumulative Total
1970	70	70
1971	72	142
1972	93	235
1973	166	401
1974	252	653
1975	159	812
1976	250	1,062
1977	274	1,336
1978	358	1,694
1979	437	2,131

The contribution of FDI to the American economy can be measured in part by the value of the gross product that can be attributed to the American affiliates of foreign parent firms. In 1974, the value of gross product for American affiliates of foreign parent firms was $24,690 million. This constituted about 2 percent of the gross product of all U.S. business for that year. Although this is a relatively small percentage, gross product for affiliates of foreign parents that year was greater in the petroleum, chemical, food, tobacco, and mining sectors.[18]

In the attempt to understand FDI, it is also instructive to examine the distribution of FDI among the various economic sectors. Table 3 provides appropriate data and reveals that FDI is greatest in the petroleum and trade sectors. As noted earlier, it should be remembered that the FDI reflects the value of the funds brought into the United States by foreign investors and not the value of the funds that foreign investors borrow in the United States or the asset value of the investment. This is especially important in considering the FDI position in real estate. In this instance, the FDI reflects only a small portion of the asset value because real estate is highly leveraged —that is, the purchaser borrows a substantial portion of the funds

TABLE 3

FOREIGN DIRECT INVESTMENT IN THE UNITED STATES,
BY ECONOMIC SECTOR, 1981

Sector		Value (millions of dollars)	Percent of FDI
Petroleum		17,813	19.8
Manufacturing		29,533	32.9
Food	4,791		5.3
Chemicals	8,488		9.5
Metals	4,325		4.8
Machinery	4,626		5.2
Other	7,303		8.1
Trade		17,734	19.8
Finance		7,448	8.3
Insurance		5,896	6.6
Real estate		4,564	5.1
Other		6,771	7.5
Total		89,759	100.0

SOURCE: Howenstine and Fouch, "Foreign Direct Investment," p. 37.

for the purchase of the assets, usually from sources that are not affiliates of the foreign owners. Consequently, it should not be concluded that the value of foreign real estate holdings is only $4,564 million.[19]

It is also important in considering FDI to understand that the outward movement of investment from the United States to other countries substantially exceeds the inward flow of FDI. Table 4 provides comparable values for 1981 and shows inward FDI as a percentage of outward FDI. It is obvious from this table that in the aggregate, inward FDI is equal to less than 40 percent of outward FDI. For a few countries the inward flow of FDI exceeds the outward flow. I shall suggest later that this preponderance of outward FDI has important consequences for public policy with respect to inward FDI.

These data indicate that the inward flow of FDI to the United States has been increasing during the last decade, but they also indicate that the United States is not dependent upon FDI as a source of capital for economic growth and development. FDI in the United

TABLE 4

U.S. Position in Foreign Direct Investment Inward and Outward, 1981

(millions of dollars)

Country of Origin or Destination	Inward	Outward	Inward as Percentage of Outward
Canada	12,212	46,957	26.0
France	5,844	9,102	64.2
Germany	7,067	16,077	44.0
Japan	6,887	6,807	101.2
Netherlands	20,177	8,775	229.9
Sweden	1,402	1,403	99.9
Switzerland	4,368	12,437	35.1
United Kingdom	15,527	30,086	51.6
All others	16,275	95,698	17.0
Total	89,759	227,342	39.5

Source: Howenstine and Fouch, "Direct Foreign Investment," p. 37; Obie G. Whichard, "U.S. Direct Investment Abroad in 1981," *Survey of Current Business*, vol. 62 (August 1982), p. 22.

States appears to be a function of the fact that foreign investors find attractive investment opportunities here and that it is relatively easy to undertake investment in the United States. Some of the characteristics of the American economy and markets that make the United States an attractive opportunity for FDI are:[20]

1. the large size of the American market, which serves as an attractive magnet for foreign producers
2. political stability of the United States
3. greater freedom in the United States from economic controls and governmental intervention than in many other countries
4. the traditional American policy of welcoming FDI
5. American leadership in marketing and managerial skills
6. the existence of an efficient and highly skilled labor force
7. well-developed capital markets for investment financing, usually with interest rates lower than in other countries
8. technological leadership as well as substantial research and development capabilities
9. the traditional receptivity of American consumers to new products
10. the existence of large supplies of important natural resources

In addition to these characteristics that make the United States an attractive prospect for FDI, developments in Western Europe and Japan have enhanced the capabilities of foreign investors to participate directly in the American market. During the past decade, foreign corporations have increased in size and improved their managerial skills. There has also been a trend toward corporate mergers and consolidations that has given foreign industry greater assets and stronger capabilities for entering the American market. At the same time, foreign governments have also relaxed their restrictions on investment abroad, thereby giving private investors greater freedom to seek investment opportunities in the United States.[21]

Public Policy and FDI

Although in the nineteenth and early twentieth centuries the United States had been a major recipient rather than a supplier of FDI, public policy discussion and consideration of FDI for at least two decades following World War II focused primarily on American direct investment abroad. This was, of course, a period during which the United States became a principal supplier of capital and substantially expanded American investment abroad. The advocates of American FDI asserted the benefits and the efficiency for both the United States and the world economic system of a liberal policy of American investment abroad, and it was generally assumed that the same arguments of benefit and efficiency would apply to FDI in the United States. Public discussion of inward FDI was unnecessary because until recently there was little new FDI entering the United States. Consequently, the general American policy of welcoming FDI with minimal interference or intervention by the federal government seems simply to have evolved from the policy of supporting American FDI abroad and has not been the consequence of a deliberate public discussion or policy decision.

The issue of FDI and the formulation of appropriate policy appears to be unusual among those issues that combine elements of both domestic policy and foreign policy. This is not only because the formulation of appropriate policy involves the reconciliation and coordination of federal domestic and foreign policies, but also because the various state governments have an active share, especially in the formulation of land policy and the regulation of banking. Consequently, there are many domestic policies that may not be uniform or consistent and that may lead to conflict with foreign policies.

Notwithstanding the neutral policy of the federal government, it is important to note that some states and local governments as a matter of policy have deliberately sought to attract FDI into their communities in order to promote local economic growth and development. In fact the incentives offered by local communities to attract FDI are often considerable; the state of Pennsylvania offered to Volkswagen an incentive package that included loans, tax abatement, and a bond issue for site development. Recently two federal departments, Commerce and Housing and Urban Development, have been exploring opportunities to attract FDI as part of their programs to aid economically depressed areas in the United States.[22] In instances of this nature, the FDI usually entails the establishment of new economic enterprises rather than the acquisition of existing American firms. Consequently, there is a positive perception of economic growth, and there are no unsettling feelings that Americans are being squeezed out of the local economy or that the local economic interests are being taken over by foreign interests.

The basic policy of the federal government regarding FDI in general was articulated in 1977 by the Economic Policy Group, which declared, among other things:

> The fundamental policy of the U.S. Government toward international investment is to neither promote nor discourage inward or outward flows or activities.
> The Government, therefore, should normally avoid measures which would give special incentives or disincentives to investment flows or activities and should not normally intervene in the activities of individual companies regarding international investment.[23]

Although many will question whether such a neutral statement is an accurate reflection of government policy regarding FDI abroad, the statement does appear to be a correct statement of federal policy toward inward flows of FDI. To say that the policy of the federal government is neutral toward entering FDI is not to say that the policy is one of indifference to FDI. The federal government welcomes FDI, but it has not established government incentives to attract FDI; it prefers that foreign investors enter the United States because the economy is generally attractive to and supportive of private investment.

In accordance with this neutral policy, the federal government does not have the statutory authority to review in advance private FDI entering the United States. The authority to undertake such a review case by case has been deliberately rejected by the federal government because it would bode ill in the minds of the investors for the long term outlook for the investment climate in this country. If we are prepared to restrict entry of foreign companies today, tomorrow we might even be prepared to restrict the operations of foreign companies who have already come in.[24]

Since it is not obvious why possible review of initial entry of FDI should lead investors to fear future restrictions on existing FDI, it is possible to speculate that the purpose of such a policy as set forth above is not related solely to FDI in the United States. Indeed, the policy of the federal government in not seeking authority to review private FDI appears to be important in articulating for the benefit of other countries the openness of the United States to FDI, with the expectation that such openness should apply to American investment abroad.

Consequently, with the exception of existing restrictions on FDI in certain economic sectors, alien investors may enter the United States freely without securing government approval in advance. Although the federal government does not review entering FDI in advance, the Committee on Foreign Investment in the United States (CFIUS)—an interagency committee with representatives from the departments of State, Treasury, Defense, and Commerce and from the assistant to the president for economic affairs and the executive director of the Council on International Economic Policy, established by executive order in 1975—is charged with the task of examining "investment in the United States which, in the judgment of the Committee, might have major implications for United States national interests."[25] The committee's function is to advise other governmental agencies, and it is to focus on trends and developments rather than upon specific investments, although the committee may, if requested, review a specific investment proposal. It appears that most of the committee's efforts have been directed toward the matter of foreign governmental investment, although the committee does have the authority to review private FDI if it meets the description set forth above. In situations in which the committee considers that the private FDI does have adverse implications for national interests, it may ask the parties involved to enter into consultations. The committee and other federal agencies apparently have the power of persuasion in such situations rather than the statutory power to prohibit entry.[26]

The authority of CFIUS to conduct monitoring or consulting activities or to recommend appropriate policy regarding FDI does not appear to pose a threat to existing FDI or to constitute a departure from the general welcome extended to FDI by the federal government.

It should also be mentioned that the federal government does have certain emergency powers that are applicable to FDI. Under the provisions of the International Emergency Economic Powers Act of 1977, the president has the power, among other things, to regulate, nullify, or prohibit the acquisition or use of any property in which any foreign country or national has an interest. This is a broad grant of authority, but it can be employed by the president only when he declares that there is a national emergency because of an "unusual and extraordinary threat, which has its source in whole or substantial part outside of the United States, to the national security, foreign policy, or economy of the United States."[27] The statutory authority is consequently intended to have only limited use, if any, and does not grant to the federal government powers that would be considered threatening to foreign investors.[28]

International Standards regarding FDI

United States domestic policy regarding FDI at both the federal and the state levels must also be compatible with the existing international legal regime regarding protection of alien investment. This international legal regime serves both to protect American investment abroad and to define the rights and responsibilities of foreign investors in the United States and the responsibilities of the federal government to alien investors as well. Under the customary rules of international law regarding a country's responsibility for the treatment of aliens, a country has the right to restrict or prohibit the entry of FDI unless it has concluded a treaty with other countries guaranteeing such entry. Consequently, the United States has the right under international law to prohibit or restrict in advance FDI in some or all sectors of the American economy. As we shall see, the United States does in fact restrict or prohibit FDI in the national interest in certain sectors of the American economy.

Since, as a matter of public policy, FDI may generally enter the United States, the federal and state governments extend to existing investment the national treatment standard required by international law. National treatment, under international law, is the treatment that must be accorded to acquired property rights and does not require that a state extend to alien investors equal opportunity to acquire property. National treatment may be defined as "treatment under their laws, regulations, and administrative practices consistent with international law and no less favorable than that accorded in like situations to domestic enterprises."[29] National treatment requires

130

essentially that a government extend to existing alien investment the same standard of treatment regarding government policy that it extends to local nationals in similar situations. Discriminatory action against existing alien investment that is related to alienage is therefore contrary to the standards required by international law.

The rules of international law also permit a country to take alien-owned property so long as the taking is for public purposes, is not discriminatory, and is accompanied by the payment of compensation. In this regard, the United States has consistently insisted that the taking of American property abroad must be accompanied by the payment of "prompt, adequate, and effective compensation," the compensation to reflect the fair market value of the property in accordance with the rules of international law.[30] Such standards would clearly be applicable to any taking of alien property by American governmental authorities. In addition, alien investors in the United States also enjoy the constitutional protections regarding the taking of property by the government and accordingly receive compensation in accordance with both U.S. law and international law.

In addition to these customary rules of international law, the United States is also a party to a number of bilateral treaties of friendship, commerce, and navigation (FCN) that contain provisions concerning alien investment in the United States and American investment abroad.[31] The recent FCN treaties contain language that generally grants to foreign-owned businesses the same rights as are granted to alien individuals. These treaties explicitly extend to alien enterprises national treatment and most-favored-nation treatment within the territory of the other party to the treaty. These rights include the right of an alien enterprise to establish a local subsidiary or to purchase a local enterprise. Treaties allow the host government to limit the extent to which alien investors may participate in certain economic sectors, such as communications, air and water transport, and exploitation of land and other natural resources. The FCN treaties also contain provisions that permit the host government to deny benefits under the treaty to corporations that, though registered in the other country signatory to the treaty, are in fact directly or indirectly owned by nationals of a third country. Consequently, alien investors from third countries may not obtain a free ride on bilateral FCN treaties.

The United States is also party to several multilateral understandings concluded under the Organization of Economic Cooperation and Development (OECD) that deal with FDI and the international movement of capital. One of the basic OECD agreements is the Code of Liberalization of Capital Movements, in which the member states agree to abolish between themselves restrictions on capital movements to the extent that such movements are necessary for effective economic cooperation. The code also establishes a general equality of treatment standard for all alien-owned assets, but it does not require that states grant national treatment to alien owners with regard to the right of entry. Members are allowed to restrict capital movements either inward or outward if necessary for maintenance of public order, protection of essential security interests, or fulfillment of international obligations relating to international peace and security—decisions of the United Nations Security Council, for example, that require the imposition of mandatory economic sanctions.[32]

The OECD Declaration on International Investment and Multinational Enterprises (1976) is also a significant part of the international legal environment for FDI in the United States and other OECD countries. The declaration requires that members extend national treatment to alien-owned enterprises "consistent with their needs to maintain public order, to protect their essential security interests, and to fulfill commitments relating to international peace and security." Discriminatory practices against aliens that are contrary to national treatment must be reported to the OECD. The declaration also calls upon member states to "give due weight" to the interests of the other member states regarding laws and regulations "providing official incentives and disincentives to international direct investment."[33] In the 1979 Review Conference the members agreed that consultations would take place at the request of a member country "which considers that its interests may be adversely affected by the impact on its flow of international direct investments of measures taken by another member country specifically designated to provide incentives or disincentives for international direct investment."[34]

Although these international understandings are very important in creating a favorable international environment for FDI, they should not be interpreted to mean that the federal or state governments have no flexibility to regulate FDI in the United States. The international environment does not interfere with the capacity of American governmental authorities to control or perhaps prohibit FDI in certain economic sectors so long as the regulations relate to matters of entry and do not appear to violate the basic provision of national treatment or adversely affect the flow of international direct investment.

Restrictions on FDI

Any public discussion of FDI must take into account the various restrictions that are set forth in federal statutes and that have in the past been justified on grounds of protection of national interests. These statutory restrictions generally do not prohibit all foreign investment or participation in certain economic sectors, but they do limit the degree of foreign ownership of voting stock and establish requirements regarding alien participation as company officers or directors.[35]

These existing restrictions constitute conditions related to the entry of FDI into the United States and are thus not in conflict with provisions concerning national treatment in FCN treaties or customary rules of international law. They have to do with economic activities in domestic air transport and aircraft registration; coastal and freshwater shipping; dredging, salvage, and towing; licensing of radio and television stations; telephone and telegraph operations; natural resources related to energy, such as atomic energy, the outer continental shelf, and the use or lease of federal land for mining and fishing; and classified defense contracts.

The statutory limitations on the degree of foreign ownership of stock or participation in management are not identical for all the above-mentioned economic sectors. For example, aliens may own up to 25 percent of the voting interests in an American airline, but they may not own more than 5 percent of a firm seeking a classified defense contract unless the firm is organized so as to minimize foreign influence or control. In the latter case, foreign ownership of defense industries is not prohibited, but a firm more than 5 percent of which is owned by aliens runs the risk of losing its security clearance and thus would be ineligible for future classified government contracts.

A radio or television license may not be granted to an alien, to a corporation organized under foreign law, or to a corporation more than 25 percent of which is owned by aliens. In addition, an alien may not participate in management as either an officer or a director.

Aliens may not acquire or lease federal land for energy-related purposes unless they are domestically incorporated and are also nationals of a country that grants reciprocity to American nationals. As a consequence of the latter requirement, leasing of federal land is not a right that is available equally to all aliens.

A total prohibition of alien ownership or control exists with regard to licenses for operation of atomic reactors and reprocessing plants. In contrast, existing law does not limit FDI in production of petroleum or natural gas or in extraction of coal or uranium.

As has been suggested earlier, the pattern of prohibitions or limitations on foreign ownership or participation in management is mixed and varies from one economic sector to another. Notwithstanding this mixed pattern of regulations, the present statutory

133

provisions appear to be working and are effectively administered. According to the conclusions reached in a recent GAO study: "None of our findings suggests the need for revising U.S. foreign investment policy and we propose no fundamental change in the independent administration of foreign investment restrictions by the Federal Agencies presently authorized to do so. We believe that existing procedures, if strengthened, will be adequate."[36]

It should also be noted that existing antitrust laws are applicable to acquisition by aliens of enterprises in the United States. Consequently, acquisition of an American firm by an alien firm that would tend to lessen competition in that economic sector and consequently lead to a monopoly situation may be challenged under the Clayton Act. In this respect, alien-owned firms receive national treatment.

Alien Ownership of Agricultural Land

Because the existing prohibitions or limitations on FDI are justified as serving or protecting the national interest and because they have been in place for a number of years, it is unlikely that they will be relaxed in the future. It is more likely that the future public discussion will be focused on the desirability or need to extend the prohibitions or limitations to other economic sectors. In addition, there has already been public policy discussion of the need to obtain more complete information about FDI in the United States and about the firms, governments, or persons who are the beneficial owners of the investment.

Two economic sectors can be identified in which increasing attention is being given to FDI because of the alleged threat to American interests that it represents. These are the purchase of agricultural land and of American banking institutions by aliens. The problem of direct investment by foreign governments, rather than private firms, can also be identified as a recent development. Both these problems include some emotional components that cannot be ignored and will keep the issue before the public eye as a matter of public policy.

Foreign ownership of land, especially landholdings that are large and publicly visible, is potentially disturbing to a local population, especially if local purchasers and funds are available and have been ignored or rejected. Because land is a finite resource, alien control of land diminishes the opportunities for local purchase and control. Control of land by local nationals is fundamental to the notion of statehood and sovereignty. National ownership of land is also essential to the idea of national identity and the belief that this is "our" land and country. Foreign ownership of land shakes these funda-

134

mental ideas and can lead to fears that one has lost control of one's state and consequently of one's identity and destiny.

Although the issue of alien ownership of agricultural land is an important matter at present, it is useful to understand that the purchase of American agricultural land by alien investors is not new in American history. Throughout the nineteenth century, alien investors made extensive purchases of American land. In fact, foreign landholdings had become so extensive by the beginning of this century that thirteen states enacted legislation to restrict purchases of land by aliens. In this century, alien landholdings have generally declined, but the issue has once again become a matter of public discussion at both the federal and state levels, and there have been several congressional hearings on the matter. The fundamental question of alien investment in agricultural land is whether the alien investors use the land for a productive purpose or whether they purchase land as a speculative venture or as a relatively secure investment.[37]

Related to this is the question of who is making such purchases, especially whether the purchasers are from the oil-producing countries. Other issues are whether the alien purchasers, as absentee owners, are contributing to the decline of the American family farm and also whether the foreign investors are driving up the price of land to the extent that local purchasers are unable to compete for agricultural land.

In response to the question of ownership, Congress enacted the Agricultural Foreign Investment Disclosure Act of 1978, which requires all alien owners of American agricultural land to report their holdings to the secretary of agriculture.[38] In its initial report under the act, the Department of Agriculture disclosed that aliens own 5.2 million acres of agricultural land, which constitutes less than 0.5 percent of all privately held agricultural land and 0.25 percent of all land in the United States. Seventy-six percent of the agricultural land that is identified as foreign-owned is held by corporations registered in the United States with foreign owners. Corporations with interests from the United Kingdom, the Federal Republic of Germany, and Luxembourg own 52 percent of all the alien-owned land in the United States.[39]

The alien landholdings are not evenly distributed throughout the United States; the largest concentrations are in Tennessee, Georgia, and South Carolina. In its initial report the Department of Agriculture summarized the general situation by concluding:

> Effects of foreign ownership cannot be determined with certainty, based on the initial data. Additional studies are being conducted that compare foreign owners with other

135

owners. The quantity of foreign-owned agricultural land is so small that it is unlikely that any aggregate impact on agriculture, positive or negative, could be detected. In areas of heaviest concentration, however, some communities could be locally affected.[40]

Because alien ownership in the aggregate does not appear to pose a threat to American agriculture or to American national interests in general, the matter of alien ownership is not likely to be a major issue for the federal government, although that government will continue to monitor acquisitions of land by aliens. Because alien ownership is concentrated and therefore highly visible in some areas, however, and because there may be a detrimental effect on local communities, the demand for restrictions or limitations on alien ownership will probably occur at the state level and become a matter of state policy rather than federal policy. At present, approximately twenty-five states have some statutory limitations on foreign purchases of agricultural land. One of these states, Iowa, recently enacted a total prohibition of acquisition of agricultural land by aliens, except when the land is to be used for commercial or industrial development. In such instances ownership by alien investors is limited to 320 acres.[41] A more extreme position appears to prevail in Oklahoma, where the attorney general has apparently ruled that both alien individuals and alien-owned corporations are prohibited from owning property, including agricultural land, in the state.[42] It must be recognized that statutory provisions which limit or prohibit acquisition of land by aliens also serve to restrict the right of American owners to dispose of their property to the highest bidder without government intervention.

With regard to the question of whether oil-producing states were responsible for purchases of American agricultural land, in a study by the General Accounting Office (GAO) in which the ownership of American agricultural land was surveyed, no evidence was found to show that Arab interests were a factor in the acquisition of American land. According to the GAO report, most investors purchased American land for general investment purposes. "[U.S. land] is generally considered a low maintenance investment and, over the past years, has proven a sound choice in maintaining security and obtaining long-term profits through steady capital appreciation."[43] The GAO also found that most alien investors had improved and upgraded the land for agricultural production. The GAO also reported that alien investors "did not consistently pay more than U.S. buyers for similar land."[44]

Alien Ownership of Banks

In the United States banking institutions may be chartered under either federal or state law. Consequently, both governmental authorities may be involved in the establishment or operation of foreign banks in the United States. Statutory requirements and practices regarding banks that are controlled by aliens vary among the several states, and some states are more liberal than others on the matter. In addition, foreign banks tend to concentrate in important commercial or industrial centers. As a result, 96 percent of all foreign banking assets are located in New York, California, and Illinois.[45]

Foreign banks that seek a charter under federal law are controlled by the International Banking Act of 1978, which generally extends to foreign banks national treatment with regard to other federally chartered banking institutions and which also attempts to ensure competitive equality between foreign and domestic banks.[46] It is not clear that competitive equality has been attained, however. The GAO reports that, notwithstanding the International Banking Act, foreign banks still have an advantage over domestic banks for certain activities.[47]

Foreign banks enter the United States either by establishing branches, agencies, or subsidiaries or by the acquisition of existing domestic banking institutions. According to a GAO study, assets in the United States of foreign banks totaled $146.2 billion in May 1979. During the 1970s, foreign banks expanded their assets in the United States by more than 400 percent. The overwhelming portion of foreign banks operating in the United States come from Japan, Western Europe, and Canada. Banks from other countries have also expanded and control about 8.3 percent of the standard assets of foreign banks in the United States.[48]

Public attention to the establishment of foreign banks has tended to be focused more on the acquisition of domestic banks by foreign interests than on the establishment of new branches or subsidiaries. The GAO has identified seventy-one domestic banks that were acquired by foreign interests during the 1970s. At the time of acquisition, these banks had assets of $21,965.4 million. Foreign individuals or nonbank corporations control sixty-five of the seventy-one acquisitions, the total assets of which are $13.2 billion.[49]

One matter of concern is the rapid increase in the number of foreign acquisitions. In the three years 1977, 1978, and 1979, foreign investors acquired forty-eight domestic banks, twice the number of acquisitions made during the previous seven-year period. Although most of the banks acquired are medium-sized institutions, foreign investors have acquired control of some large American banks, including the Marine Midland Bank in Buffalo, Crocker National Bank in San Francisco, and Financial General Bankshares in Washington, D.C. The last acquisition, by private Arab interests, including the former head of the Saudi Arabian intelligence service, followed a long and bitter fight with its previous owners.[50]

The chairman of the Federal Reserve Board, Paul Volcker, has indicated his opposition to any moratorium on foreign entry into the American banking system and has declared that the anticipated problems with foreign banks "have not materialized." The Federal Reserve Board has, however, established a new system to monitor foreign-owned banks operating in the United States.[51]

Although the present situation with regard to foreign banks appears to be manageable and not to pose a threat to U.S. interests, continuing acquisition of American banking institutions by foreign interests could become a problem. It would be a problem especially if a domestic bank sought to resist the takeover or if the takeover was believed to reflect a new investment pattern in the United States. Takeovers by investors from oil-producing states appear to be sufficiently emotional that there might be demands for government intervention to prevent foreign acquisition.

Direct Investment by Foreign Governments

Although my primary concern has been private FDI in the United States, it is important to acknowledge that some of the FDI is from foreign governments rather than from private sources. Data on government FDI in the United States do not appear to be available; as a consequence, a specific dollar value cannot be given for investment by foreign governments. Nevertheless, it is probably reasonable to conclude that the amount of government FDI is small. The most frequently mentioned examples are the joint venture of the Romanian government with the Island Creek Coal Company and the proposed investment, never consummated, by the government of Iran in the Occidental Petroleum Company.[52]

Government FDI is different from private FDI at least to the extent that while a private investor generally seeks profit from the investment, a foreign government may be willing to forgo profit in the investment in order to secure other objectives. Government FDI may reflect a policy objective of the investing government that may or may not be compatible with the interests of the host government. There is consequently a greater possibility of a conflict of public policy interests between the two governments in the case of government FDI than in the case of private FDI. In addition, local public sensitivity to investment by foreign governments is likely to be greater because it may be seen as serving "foreign" interests to the detriment of local interests and placing the host government in an inferior position in relation to the investing government.

Notwithstanding these differences, it is still the policy of the federal government to welcome appropriate, nonthreatening government FDI. Such a welcome reflects a basic belief among officials in the federal government that FDI is beneficial to the American economy. Because of the particular nature of government FDI, the federal government may ask for advance consultations with foreign governments regarding any prospective sizable investment by a foreign government in the United States. The review and consultations will be requested if the government investment has significant implications for American national interests. The Committee on Foreign Investment in the United States is the agency charged with the responsibility to undertake such a review and consultation. If the government investment is considered to be undesirable because of its adverse implications for American national interests, diplomatic representation to that effect will be made to the foreign government.[53]

Balancing Foreign and Domestic Policy

FDI in the United States could decline if general economic conditions here or abroad deteriorated to such an extent that investment capital was no longer available or became so expensive that there was a moratorium on investment. In the absence of such a situation, it is reasonable to expect that FDI in the United States will continue to grow, unless specific policies are adopted by the government for the purpose of restricting certain types of FDI. Consequently, it is useful to offer some concluding assessment about future domestic and foreign policies concerning FDI.

Although public officials appear to be persuaded that FDI promotes the economic interests of the United States, the public opinion polls mentioned earlier indicate a generally negative attitude toward FDI among the American public. Although the negative attitude toward FDI may be based more upon emotion, dramatic headlines, and feelings of national pride than upon economic analysis, the existence of negative opinions will set the boundaries for public discussion of the issue and the parameters of public policy. The existence of a negative attitude suggests that public officials have an important educational task to undertake if the United States is to continue offering its general welcome to FDI. The negative attitude also suggests that when problems or negative publicity regarding FDI emerge, the public may favor the adoption of restrictive policies.

In addition to a negative public attitude toward FDI, there also appears to be a negative, critical congressional attitude toward existing federal policy and the activities of various executive departments dealing with matters concerning FDI. A recent report by the House Committee on Government Operations asserts: "Notwithstanding repeated assurances by administration officials, the U.S. Government does not have a sound, sensible, or rational policy on FDI in the United States. The present U.S. policy of 'neutrality with encouragement,' the reasons for it, and the U.S. Government's extreme reluctance to change it, place in jeopardy U.S. economic and political interests."[54] The committee is also specifically critical of the CFIUS, saying that it has "grossly neglected its responsibilities to the President, Congress, and the public."[55]

The report of the committee offers a number of valid recommendations, such as a requirement for a system of full registration for all FDI, that should be considered. Nevertheless, the extremely negative, critical tone of the report in reference to existing government policy and agency performance suggests that although Congress recognizes the benefits from appropriately regulated and monitored FDI, the public discussion is likely to be set forth in negative terms and in an environment of an adversary relation between the executive branch and the Congress that is not likely to be healthy for the formulation of a responsible public policy.

It is also important to understand that at the present time the largest share of FDI comes from other developed countries, primarily in Western Europe, and that these countries are also the principal recipients of American FDI abroad. Thus, there is a familiar and reciprocal pattern established among the countries involved. To the extent that this pattern continues to prevail, the issue of FDI is not likely to become an emotional or divisive public issue or to bring about extreme or dramatic changes in present public policy regarding FDI. Public sensitivity and reaction to FDI, however, are likely to increase in the future if FDI begins to come in substantial amounts from nontraditional sources—that is, from foreign governments or from the surplus revenues of oil-producing states. In such a situation, fears of the adverse consequences of FDI may be accentuated, with the result that there may be increasing demands for dramatic changes in public policy regarding the entry of FDI.

It is also clear that there must be consistency between American domestic and foreign policies regarding FDI. Any discriminatory or unwelcome restriction on FDI in the United States may invite reciprocal restrictions on American FDI abroad. So long as it is the policy of the federal government to permit American investment abroad and if necessary to employ diplomatic or legal means to protect that investment, the substantial volume and potential vulnerability of American investment abroad will be a restraining influence in the formulation of any restrictive domestic policy toward FDI in the United States. Concern with direct American investment abroad was one reason for the State Department's opposition to a congressional proposal to impose a moratorium on foreign investment in U.S. mineral companies. Such action would create "a potential precedent and justification for retaliation by foreigners against U.S. investment abroad, particularly in the strategic minerals sectors which are vital to our national interest."[56] Clearly, any domestic policy toward FDI will need to be consistent with the standards that the United States requires other countries to meet in the protection of American investment abroad.

For the future, it is also likely that because of the greater volume of U.S. investment abroad and because the general policy discussion has so far been focused on U.S. investment abroad rather than on FDI in the United States, any inconsistencies between appropriate policies for incoming and outgoing FDI will be resolved in favor of the latter investment pattern. It can thus be seen that the present foreign policy for the support and protection of American FDI abroad is the dominant public policy on the matter. Policy issues concerning FDI in the United States are not inconsequential, but they are nevertheless likely to be subsumed by well-established policies and patterns concerning FDI abroad that will be difficult to change. With increasing public and congressional interest in FDI there will probably be new challenges to the present policy priority. An example of such a challenge is the recent charge by the House Committee on Government Operations that the existing policy bias is mistaken and unwarranted and holds domestic policy "hostage" to foreign policy interests.[57] The dispute over priorities presents a classic dilemma for policy makers. It will require astute and assertive policy makers to formulate policies that will maintain foreign and domestic policies in a compatible balance and not hold either policy "hostage" to the other.

With increasing FDI, there will probably be increasing interest in public disclosure of the beneficial owners. Although the data on FDI and the various reporting laws or monitoring systems make it possible to identify certain assets or investments as foreign-controlled, the data and procedures are not adequate in all instances to identify the ultimate beneficial ownership of the investment. Some foreign investment is held by foreign banks and law firms without any disclosure of the beneficial ownership. Indeed some foreign states, such as the Netherlands Antilles, have domestic laws that are clearly intended to make it possible to prevent disclosure of beneficial ownership. Investors may seek to prevent disclosure of ownership in order to avoid problems with American law or with the laws of their own countries. It is quite possible that some of the FDI in the United States is in fact owned by American nationals who use foreign corporations as convenient covers for their investments.

The interest in disclosure is not intended to invade the legitimate privacy of the investor. Knowledge of beneficial ownership, however, may be necessary information in the formulation of appropriate domestic and foreign policy. It is therefore a very important matter of American public policy if foreign investors seek to invoke foreign laws in order to hide from either the American public or government authorities beneficial ownership of investments located in the United States. The continuing refusal of the Treasury Department to disclose to congressional committees the extent of portfolio investment in the United States by Arab oil-producing countries indicates that the matter of disclosure is complex and that there are some investors, both foreign and domestic, who will oppose any efforts to improve the disclosure requirements.[58]

The reach of American law on this matter is limited, because foreign corporations may be protected by the law of the home country, which may permit hidden ownership. Such countries will resist any efforts by the United States to force disclosure of corporate ownership as an intrusion into their internal affairs and as contrary to their own public policy.

Public demands for disclosure of beneficial ownership will increase if the public becomes suspicious that beneficial ownership is deliberately being hidden from the American public with the intent to enable foreign investors to protect or increase their participation in the American economy. In such a situation, the general welcome extended to FDI by the United States may be restricted or limited to those countries or investors who are willing to make full disclosure of beneficial ownership.

Notes

1. *Washington Star,* November 17, 1979.
2. *Washington Star,* September 16, 1979.
3. *Washington Post,* July 24, 1979.
4. *Washington Star,* August 2, 1979.

5. *Washington Post,* June 10, 1979.

6. See U.S. Department of Commerce, *Foreign Direct Investment in the United States,* vol. 1 (April 1976), p. 1.

7. U.S. Department of State, "Public Is Wary of Foreign Investments in the United States," Briefing Memorandum, September 6, 1979 (mimeo.).

8. Ibid.

9. Ibid.

10. Jack N. Behrman, *National Interests and the Multinational Enterprise* (Englewood Cliffs, N.J.: Prentice-Hall, 1970), p. 82.

11. C. Fred Bergsten, Thomas Horst, and Theodore H. Moran, *American Multinationals and American Interests* (Washington, D.C.: Brookings Institution, 1978), pp. 342–48.

12. U.S. Department of Commerce, *Foreign Direct Investment in the United States* (December 1977), p. 2.

13. U.S. Department of Commerce, *Foreign Direct Investment in the United States,* vol. 2 (April 1976), p. 10.

14. A recent congressional report concludes that the total assets of foreign-owned firms operating in the United States are $350 billion. See U.S. House of Representatives, Committee on Government Operations, *The Adequacy of the Federal Response to Foreign Investment in the United States,* 96th Cong., 2d sess. (August 1, 1980), p. 7.

15. The Netherlands Antilles is a relatively new source of FDI and apparently is popular because it permits corporations to operate without revealing the beneficial ownership of the corporation. This is attractive to investors who do not wish to have their investments identified. The volume of investment coming from this source is not, however, sufficiently large to distort or change the existing, traditional investment pattern. For comments on Kuwait FDI, see source cited for table 2.

16. Gregory G. Fouch and L. A. Lupo, "Foreign Direct Investment in the United States in 1978," *Survey of Current Business,* vol. 59 (August 1979), p. 40.

17. The Conference Board, "Announcements of Foreign Investment in U.S. Manufacturing Industries," Fourth Quarter 1976 and Fourth Quarter 1979 (mimeo).

18. Ned G. Howenstine, "Gross Product of U.S. Affiliates of Foreign Companies," *Survey of Current Business,* vol. 59 (January 1979), p. 30.

19. Fouch and Lupo, "Foreign Direct Investment," p. 39.

20. U.S. Department of Commerce, *Foreign Direct Investment in the United States,* vol. 1 (April 1976), p. 98. In this study FDI in specific economic sectors and the principal sources of the FDI in the particular sector are examined.

21. Ibid., pp. 99–100.

22. *Washington Post,* May 31, 1980. For a discussion of some of the incentives employed by state and local governments and of their interest in securing greater assistance from American embassies in attracting FDI.

see U.S. General Accounting Office, *Foreign Direct Investment in the United States—The Federal Role. Report by the Comptroller General of the United States*, ID 80-24, June 3, 1980.

23. U.S. Department of the Treasury, *News*. Statement by C. Fred Bergsten, assistant secretary of the Treasury for international affairs, "U.S. Policy toward Foreign Direct Investment in the United States: The Role of the Committee on Foreign Investment in the United States," July 29, 1979, p. 2. See also State Department memorandum 185216, "U.S. Government Policy on Direct International Investment," August 1977 (mimeo).

24. Bergsten, "U.S. Policy toward Foreign Direct Investment," p. 20.

25. Executive Order 11858, May 7, 1975.

26. For a discussion of the role and activities of the CFIUS, see Bergsten, "U.S. Policy toward Foreign Direct Investment."

27. P.L. 95-223, *International Legal Materials*, vol. 17 (1978), p. 139.

28. The provisions of this act were invoked by President Carter in the imposition of economic sanctions against Iran; see Executive Orders 12170, November 14, 1979; 12205, April 7, 1980; and 12211, April 17, 1980.

29. OECD, "Declaration on International Investment and Multinational Enterprises," *International Legal Materials*, vol. 15 (1976), p. 967.

30. See U.S. Department of State, "Statement on Foreign Investment and Nationalization," December 30, 1976, *International Legal Materials*, vol. 15 (1976), p. 186.

31. For a discussion of these treaties, see Robert R. Wilson, *United States Commercial Treaties and International Law* (New Orleans, La.: Hauser Press, 1960); and Don C. Piper, "New Directions in the Protection of American-owned Property Abroad," *International Trade Law Journal*, vol. 4 (1979), pp. 315–48.

32. OECD, Code of Liberalization of Capital Movements (June 1978), article 3.

33. OECD, "Declaration on International Investment."

34. See the revised decision of the OECD Council on International Investment Incentives and Disincentives, July 20, 1979, *International Legal Materials*, vol. 18 (1979), p. 1175.

35. For a discussion of these restrictions, see U.S. General Accounting Office (GAO), *Controlling Foreign Investment in National Interest Sectors of the U.S. Economy, Report by the Comptroller General of the United States*, ID 77-18, October 7, 1977; U.S. Department of Commerce, *Foreign Direct Investment in the United States*, April 1976, Appendix K; and U.S. Senate, Committee on Agriculture, Nutrition, and Forestry, *Foreign Investment in U.S. Agricultural Land*, 95th Cong., 2d sess. (January 1979), pp. 191–201.

36. GAO, *Controlling Foreign Investment*, p. 38.

37. A useful source of information on this matter is Senate, Committee on Agriculture, Nutrition, and Forestry, *Foreign Investment in U.S. Agricultural Land*.

38. P.L. 95-460, *International Legal Materials*, vol. 18 (1979), p. 128.

39. U.S. Department of Agriculture (USDA), *Foreign Ownership of U.S. Agricultural Land*, Agricultural Economic Report no. 447, February 1980. A second report was issued in November 1980; see USDA, *Foreign Ownership of U.S. Agricultural Land, February 1, 1979, through February 1, 1980*, Agriculture Information Bulletin no. 440.

40. USDA, *Foreign Ownership of U.S. Agricultural Land* (February 1980), p. iv.

41. *Washington Post*, July 25, 1979.

42. *Wall Street Journal*, September 19, 1979.

43. U.S. General Accounting Office, *Foreign Investment in U.S. Agricultural Land—How It Shapes Up*, Report by the Comptroller General of the United States, CED 79-114 (July 29, 1979), p. vi.

44. Ibid., p. 67.

45. U.S. General Accounting Office, *Considerable Increase in Foreign Banking in the United States since 1972*, Report by the Comptroller General of the United States, GGD 79-75, August 1, 1979, p. 17.

46. Michael J. Fienman, "National Treatment of Foreign Banks Operating in the United States: The International Banking Act of 1978," *Law and Policy in International Business*, vol. 11 (1979), pp. 1109–47.

47. GAO, *Increase in Foreign Banking since 1972*, p. 4.

48. Ibid., pp. 10, 15–16.

49. Ibid., pp. 19–20.

50. *Washington Post*, August 12, 1982; *Wall Street Journal*, August 26, 1981.

51. *Washington Post*, July 9, 1980.

52. See responses by C. Fred Bergsten to letter from Congressman Benjamin Rosenthal, July 18, 1979, in U.S. Department of the Treasury, *News*, July 30, 1979 (mimeo.), pp. 14–18.

53. Ibid.

54. U.S. House of Representatives, Committee on Government Operations, *The Adequacy of the Federal Response to Foreign Investment in the United States*, 96th Cong., 2d sess. (August 1, 1980), p. 37.

55. Ibid., p. 22.

56. John T. McCarthy, "International Investment Issues," *Department of State Bulletin*, vol. 81 (July 1981), p. 32.

57. Ibid., pp. 22, 37.

58. Ibid., pp. 33–36.

7

American Politics and the Law of the Sea

GERARD J. MANGONE

For nine years representatives of more than 150 states of the world met in Caracas, Geneva, and New York in the largest and longest international conference in modern history to fashion a comprehensive convention on the law of the sea. Finally on April 30, 1982, the Third United Nations Conference on the Law of the Sea adopted a convention by 130 votes to 4 with 17 abstentions. On December 10, 1982, in Montego Bay, Jamaica, representatives of 117 states signed the UN Law of the Sea Convention, to be in force after ratification by 60 states.

The effort to develop international law by this means has a fascination for every scholar of world politics. Of equal interest, however, are the domestic forces within each state that propel or retract the diplomatic positions of its delegation. In such negotiations the marginal compromises and concessions of national interest groups ultimately blend into an international consensus and serve as the basis for a widely acceptable treaty. In the case of the UN Law of the Sea Convention, the United States participated fully in the bargaining process that elaborated the Draft Convention of 1981, always influenced by domestic considerations and bureaucratic politics. In the end, however, the United States rejected the document because of dissatisfaction with the provisions on deep-seabed mining.

Obviously the ideal policy objectives of any single state cannot be realized in multilateral bargaining among delegations that represent both coastal and landlocked nations, both maritime powers and negligible navies, both highly developed and poorly developed economies, and all the diverse cultures of the continents of the earth. Yet each state at the Third UN Law of the Sea Conference had set priorities among its own interests in the ocean, remaining intractable on some issues, yielding on others, as its domestic politics allowed. The conduct of the United States illustrates the adage that foreign policy is domestic policy.

From the opening of the conference in December 1973 through its twelfth session in March 1982 the central interests of the United States in the outcome of an international convention were (1) national security, (2) maritime transport, (3) exploitation of marine resources, (4) scientific investigation of the ocean, and (5) economic development and equity for the peoples of the world through international institutions. As the negotiations proceeded through both formal meetings and informal consultations for seven years, arriving at a Draft Convention (Informal Text) in 1980,[1] the domestic advocates of the five major American interests worked to influence official policy on the law of the sea. The traditional means of bureaucratic politics, congressional pressures, and appeals to public opinion had their effect. Some American interests were bound to gain and others to lose in the diplomatic considerations of compromise with the other states that bargained at the conference and produced a least common denominator of international acceptance.

The Territorial Sea and International Straits

Since 1793 the United States has observed a three-mile limit on its territorial sea. At the beginning of the twentieth century virtually all the great maritime powers maintained such a narrow territorial sea, leaving the freedom of navigation of the open ocean as wide as possible. But not all states accepted that limit. Indeed, the trend, even before World War II, was to widen coastal jurisdiction, especially to protect fisheries. But the advent of the submarine, whose power had been demonstrated against the Allied forces in two world wars, raised serious concerns about the difficulty of detection of such destructive vessels, which might be lurking illegally in the widened territorial sea of a neutral state.

As a great naval power with surface fleets and world maritime trade, the United States maintained a national security policy that dictated that the territorial sea of all states be kept as narrow as possible and that passage through the straits of the world's oceans, as well as flight over them, be unimpeded. Throughout the negotiations in the First and Second UN conferences on the law of the sea in 1958 and 1960, and from 1973 to 1981 in the Third UN Law of the Sea Conference, the interests of the Department of Defense were paramount. Every consideration of the American representatives in fashioning the Draft Convention was predicated on preserving the mobility of the United States Navy and Air Force over the seas.

By 1958 the Soviet Union had already achieved superiority over the United States in numbers of submarines. Arthur Dean, the head of the American delegation to the First UN Law of the Sea Conference reported the U.S. position at the conference:

> Clearly the advance in striking power and in underwater range of the new submarines raises extraordinary implications as to appropriate breadth for the territorial sea. The United States was, in the interests of the free world, constrained to keep the territorial sea within as narrow a limit as possible.[2]

The breadth of the territorial sea, however, was never defined either by the first conference in 1958 or by the second conference in 1960, largely because many of the coastal states of the world wanted to extend their jurisdiction over adjacent fisheries. The Department of Defense, especially the navy, had hoped to preserve the three-mile territorial sea, but international pressures compelled the United States to support a compromise that would have provided for a six-mile territorial sea and an additional six miles beyond the territorial sea in which the coastal state would have exclusive jurisdiction over fisheries. That compromise failed of adoption at the 1960 conference by one vote.

Frustrated in its effort to contain the extension of the territorial sea to six miles by international agreement, the United States again proclaimed a three-mile limit as the standard of customary law. Nevertheless, the trend by other coastal states to claim wider margins of the sea under their jurisdiction continued during the 1960s, some asserting control over fisheries only, others widening their sovereignty over their territorial seas from three to six to twelve miles and even beyond. By the time the Third UN Law of the Sea Conference opened in December 1973, some sixty-four states had declared a territorial sea of twelve miles. Thus, as the negotiations for a comprehensive convention began in Caracas in 1974, a preoccupation of the Department of Defense was the fact that if a twelve-mile limit were adopted as positive international law, a number of straits used for international navigation that narrowed to fewer than twenty-four miles would come completely within the territorial sea of one or more coastal states.

Under present international law such a change in regime would mean that all vessels transiting such straits would have to be in "innocent passage," not threatening the peace, good order, and security of the coastal states, in which case "innocent passage" might be suspended; all submarines would have to transit such straits on the surface; and there would be no right of overflight of the straits, with permission of the coastal state specifically required for air force planes and general agreement upon regularly scheduled commercial flights. For the United States, with its mighty, wide-ranging surface and submarine fleets as well as its interests in maritime trade, these potential restrictions by coastal states seemed intolerable.

In 1969 the Office of the Geographer of the Department of State had already discovered some 121 straits of the world that would no longer have a "high seas" channel if a twelve-mile territorial sea regime were applied, and it was alleged that about a dozen of these straits, such as Dover, Bab el Mandeb, Hormuz, Malacca, Sunda, Gibraltar, Ombai-Wetar, Osumi Kaiko, and Western Chosen, were of strategic importance to the United States.[3] Then, on July 30, 1971, the United States submitted to the UN Seabed Committee, which was preparing for the Third UN Law of the Sea Conference, two draft articles that included provisions that all ships and aircraft in straits used for international navigation not otherwise governed by an international convention "shall enjoy the same freedom of navigation and overflight for the purpose of transit through and over such straits as they have on the high seas." The head of the delegation of the United States to the UN Seabed Committee, John R. Stevenson, thereafter stated that the United States and others have made it clear that "their vital interests require that agreement on a twelve-mile territorial sea be coupled with agreement on free transit of straits used for international navigation, and these remain basic elements of our national policy which we will not sacrifice."[4]

Thus, from the beginning of the negotiations at the Law of the Sea Conference at Caracas, the American delegation, girded by the Defense Department, trumpeted its position that it would not accept a twelve-mile territorial sea article in any convention that did not also provide for unimpeded passage through and over straits used for international navigation. But with such a sine qua non on the negotiating table, it was incumbent upon the diplomats from other countries to calculate and bargain for the price the United States was willing to pay for these essential articles on straits; put another way, the coastal and landlocked states, having no shipping but wanting to exploit or share in the exploitation of marine resources, could make strong demands for their interests, confident the United States would sacrifice other marine interests for its policy on straits. In any case, the 1980 Draft Convention largely incorporated the views of the United States on the transit by ships and overflight by planes of straits used for international navigation.

Many observers of the American negotiations at the Law of the Sea Conference from 1974 to 1981 did not accept the idea that articles on the free transit of straits, agreed to by the delegates and embodied in a convention, were absolutely indispensable to American strategic interests. They argued that there was a physical limitation of some straits for submerged ships, that allies would probably border many straits in time of need, and that the increased ranges of submarine-launched ballistic missiles made transit through straits into closer approaches to the Soviet Union unnecessary. While the movement of general-purpose forces, including the overflight deployment of supplies for limited warfare in some parts of the globe, might be slowed by restrictions on the transit of certain straits, an international convention was not likely to overcome the intransigence of a few coastal states that might feel their national security threatened by such passage.[5] Considering the complexity of law of the sea negotiations, the involvement of many states with virtually no interest in international straits, and the price that would have to be paid to them for support of such articles, it might be far better American diplomacy to negotiate, in concert with other maritime powers, special regimes, such as those for the Dardanelles or the Panama Canal, with the few coastal states involved.

It may be argued, in fact, that the profound suspicion and fears of the U.S. Defense Department, always eager to have the most power in the most places, so dominated the bargaining for a convention on the law of the sea that the other interests of the United States, including fisheries, exploitation of mineral resources, scientific investigation of the oceans, the equitable economic development of poor countries through international institutions, and even maritime transport, were reduced, stifled, or denied. But that would be only partially true, for the United States has managed so far to gain control over an extraordinary share of marine resources while providing safeguards against arbitrary coastal acts against its shipping on most of the ocean.

Exploitation of Mineral Resources

In transmitting his annual report of the Department of the Interior to President Harry S. Truman for fiscal year 1945, the forceful Secretary Harold L. Ickes recounted a somber tale of the costs of World War II to the natural resources of America. Four years of battle around the world, with millions of tons of supplies sent to all the Allies, had depleted the known usable reserves of twenty-two essential minerals in the United States to a supply that would last thirty-five years or less. It was estimated that the assured domestic deposits of petroleum would last only fourteen to twenty years. Nevertheless, Secretary Ickes held out some hope in 1945 that the prospects of new oil supplies were "fairly good."[6]

Truman Proclamation of 1945. What the Interior Department had in mind was the continental shelf of the United States. In 1937 the first successful offshore well out of the sight of land had been drilled in the Gulf of Mexico off the coast of Louisiana, and it was suspected that billions of barrels of oil might lie within the submerged lands adjacent to American shores. Upon Ickes's recommendation, therefore, after a study by an interagency committee and the approval of the Department of State, Truman issued a proclamation on September 28, 1945, in which the United States "regarded the natural resources of the subsoil and seabed of the continental shelf beneath the high seas but contiguous to the coasts of the United States as appertaining to the United States, subject to its jurisdiction and control."[7]

By this proclamation the United States, acting from purely domestic interests, appropriated for itself mineral resources in an area of 700,000 square miles of submerged lands to which it had no previous title. Moreover, it precipitated revolutionary changes in the maritime boundaries of all coastal states in the world and modified the customary international law of the seas that had prevailed for more than a century. In brief, after 1945 coastal states, following the lead of the United States, asserted ever-increasing and widely divergent claims over both the continental shelf and the seas adjacent to their shores. By 1981 the legal issues had still not been positively resolved by the Third UN Law of the Sea Conference.

The rationale for this unilateral American claim over the resources of the continental shelf was that (1) technology had made the submarine minerals exploitable, (2) conservation and prudent use of them were required, and (3) it was "reasonable and just" that the contiguous nation should exercise jurisdiction over the continental shelf, which could be regarded as an extension of the land mass of that state. Finally, the Truman Proclamation said, "self-protection compels the coastal nation" to keep a close watch over activities that might be required for use of these resources.[8] Thus have tenuous arguments from natural law provided the foundation for innovative positive law throughout history.

The claims of Washington to the resources of the appropriated seabed not only revamped international law, but impelled the federal government to assert jurisdiction over the submerged lands right up to the low-water mark of the coastal states of the United States. California and other coastal states had long assumed that dominion over the coastal seabed, like dominion over the beds of navigable rivers, was inherent in the states. But only four months before the Truman Proclamation the federal government attempted to enjoin the extraction of oil by a company that had obtained offshore leases from California.[9] In 1950 the U.S. Supreme Court supported the federal position that the United States had paramount rights over the seabed, since the marginal sea was a national concern.[10] But the Congress balked at this utter arrogation of federal power and passed the Submerged Lands Act of 1953, which recognized the property rights of the coastal states of the United States to the natural resources of the waters and the submerged lands to a distance of three geographic miles from their coastlines in the Atlantic and Pacific oceans.[11] The act also provided that in the Gulf of Mexico or in the Great Lakes, if either its historical boundary or its boundary when admitted to the Union had been greater than three miles, a state was entitled to the water and mineral resources up to nine geographical miles from its shore. Thus Florida and Texas obtained dominion over marine resources nine miles from their shores in the Gulf of Mexico.

The Continental Shelf Convention of 1958. The United Nations International Law Commission in 1949 had begun its work by selecting the regime of the high seas as suitable for codification. It soon faced a completely new legal question, however, as one state after another followed the American example of 1945 and claimed the resources of the continental shelf for itself: what should be the width of the continental shelf over which a state might exercise jurisdiction? Some coastal states in Latin America, moreover, with narrow continental shelves, had gone far beyond the U.S. initiative, claiming not only the resources of the continental shelf but also the resources of the water column above as far out as 200 miles from their shores. Such claims not only threatened the free catch of American tuna and shrimp fishermen in distant waters, but also implied controls over navigation on the high seas, which would be intolerable to the U.S. Navy and merchant marine.

In the Geneva Convention on the Continental Shelf of 1958, after preparation of the articles by the International Law Commission and their general adoption by the First UN Law of the Sea Conference, the width of the continental shelf was left indefinite. The International Law Commission had considered both a test of exploitability—that is, a width dependent upon the coastal state's ability to control its drilling for offshore oil and gas on the shelf—and 200 meters as the depth of water to which the coastal state's control over the seabed would be limited. Since the Inter-American Specialized Conference at Ciudad Trujillo had adopted the depth test, the final text of the Geneva convention adopted both criteria—namely, to a depth of 200 meters *or* beyond that limit where the superjacent waters admit exploitation.

From the point of view of the United States, keeping in mind that in 1958 no one had yet recovered petroleum resources from lands submerged under more than 200 feet of water, let alone 200 meters, both the depth and the exploitability tests were compatible with the potential developments of the American oil industry, both at home and abroad. The real issue was to ensure that jurisdiction over the resources of the continental shelf did not mean sovereignty over the seabed itself or the water column above it. In the intervening years between 1958 and 1973, when the Third UN Law of the Sea Conference met, the uses of the world ocean changed remarkably. The submarine-launched ballistic missile and the nuclear-powered ship had altered the course of strategic warfare; the average size of the tanker at sea had more than doubled, with supertankers carrying 200,000 to 400,000 tons of oil; the world catch of fish had soared from about 33 million metric tons to 70 million metric tons,[12] a large portion taken by great fleets of Japanese (more than 9 million tons), Russian (more than 7 million tons), and other vessels that operated close to American and Canadian shores; and a movement to protect the environment, especially the marine environment, from pollution had captured public attention and called for both national and international regulation. Not the least change was the march of drilling rigs into ever deeper water, farther from shore, for the exploitation of petroleum. Even more dramatic was worldwide realization after 1959 that it might be possible to extract manganese, cobalt, nickel, and copper from nodules lying on the seabed of the deep ocean, an idea that attracted adventurous miners and covetous governments.

Trusteeship of the Continental Shelf. Before the Third UN Law of the Sea Conference began, following a recommendation of the Commission on Marine Sciences, Engineering, and Technology, the United States had constructed an ingenious scheme to satisfy three major interest groups with respect to the continental shelf. An interagency group, with the approval of Elliot Richardson, under secretary of state in 1969, prepared for President Richard Nixon an important ocean policy statement, which the White House issued on May 23, 1970.[13] The United States proposed that the continental shelf area beyond the water depth of two hundred meters should be designated as trusts to be governed by adjacent coastal states, but in this area a substantial portion of the income from the exploitation of resources should be used for "international community purposes," especially to assist developing countries. The United States also proposed that a treaty should provide international machinery for the resources beyond the continental margin, so that the resources of the seabed could be exploited as a common heritage of mankind.

From the point of view of American security, such a regime still involved control over resources only of the continental shelf, maintaining the legal status of the superjacent waters as high seas for the navigation of vessels. From the point of view of the American petroleum industry, control over the entire continental shelf adjacent to the United States would still be in Washington's hands, and no limit was placed on the depth of exploitation in either American or foreign waters. It hardly mattered to the oil companies that the United States Treasury might share some of its income with an international agency; from the point of view of the vociferous, internationally minded groups of nongovernmental organizations, such as the Commission to the Study of the Organization of Peace and Save Our Seas, the trusteeship provision and the possibility of substantial income for an international development fund from petroleum resources on the shelf beyond the water depth of 200 meters, while not ideal, was nevertheless satisfactory. And it would be a revolutionary breakthrough in the financing of international organizations by direct sharing of revenue with national governments.

Perhaps Congress would never have approved this remarkably generous proposal of the federal officials to the Third UN Law of the Sea Conference, which began its substantive work in 1974, but it hardly mattered. The American draft document died quickly and quietly, with little or no support from either developed or developing countries, which retained a suspicion of trustees as a colonial heritage and which were also eager to claim complete jurisdiction over the wealth of adjacent continental shelves for themselves. After six years of negotiations at Caracas, Geneva, and New York, moreover, the appetite of the coastal states in the Law of the Sea Conference to devour a wider and wider area of the continental shelf had been whetted by the startling rise of world oil prices.

The Continental Shelf in 1982. By 1979 the diplomats at the Third UN Law of the Sea Conference had arrived at a revised Informal Composite Negotiating Text (ICNT) to extend national jurisdiction of the coastal states to the outer edge of the continental margin—that is, where the underlying basaltic rock is no longer covered by sedimentary rock. And even where the covering of sedimentary rock might be thin or ill distributed, a coastal state could fix base points for its continental shelf up to sixty miles beyond the foot of the continental slope. Indeed, a coastal state could claim a continental shelf up to 350 miles seaward of its coastal base lines used to measure the territorial sea or up to 100 miles seaward from the 2,500-meter isobath. The provisions of the ICNT passed almost intact into the 1981 Draft Convention, except that on submarine ridges, the outer limit of the continental shelf could not exceed 350 miles from the base lines. Even those states that had narrow or negligible geographic shelves, moreover, could claim jurisdiction over the resources of the adjacent seabed up to a distance of 200 miles from shore.

Again, American petroleum interests had no objections to jurisdiction over the shelf that had enormously expanded from water depth of 200 meters to the deep ocean; again the U.S. Department of Defense had kept the superjacent water free for navigation. Plainly, however, the hopes of the internationally minded groups had been sacrificed. Only a token of the potential revenues from exploitation of resources on the continental shelf was left for international development in the ICNT of 1979, for only in the area of the shelf beyond 200 miles would a portion of the value be diverted to an international agency. Indeed, no payments would come from a site until after five years of production at that site, and only 1 percent of the value or volume of production would be paid in the sixth year, rising annually to a payment of 7 percent in the twelfth year of production, with no increase thereafter.

As the Third UN Law of the Sea Conference resumed its negotiations in 1982, the consensus on the continental shelf was clear, with the broadest possible claims for jurisdiction of the coastal states over their continental shelves and little or nothing for the international fund for development. This agreement was consolidated in the final text of the UN Convention on the Law of the Sea. The national interest of the United States in maintaining the superjacent waters of the shelf free for navigation and obtaining unlimited control over adjacent resources in the seabed had been protected.

The Nodules of the Deep Seabed. By far the most contentious issue of the Third UN Law of the Sea Conference was the legal regime for the exploitation of the ferromanganese nodules, discovered by the *Challenger* expedition of 1873, that are strewn upon the ocean floor under several thousand feet of water. Previously these resources of manganese, copper, nickel, cobalt, and other metals had seemed technically and economically beyond reach, so no question had arisen about customary international law under which the deep seabed was regarded as belonging to no one. So long as the use of the seas for fishing, navigation, the laying of cables, scientific research, and so forth was unimpeded, the deep seabed was of little importance. This attitude was radically changed after 1959 by the supposition that immense wealth in minerals could be recovered from the seabed by dredging, sweeping, or sucking manganese nodules to surface vessels for transshipment to processing plants on shore. Who then had lawful title to the manganese nodules beyond the territorial sea and beyond the continental shelf of any state?

In 1967, on the initiative of a dramatic speech and proposal by Arvid Pardo, who had been a member of the UN Secretariat and a representative of the UN Development Program and had become the representative of Malta to the United Nations, the General Assembly began considering a declaration and treaty to reserve the seabed and the subsoil beyond the limits of national jurisdiction for peaceful purposes only and the use of their resources "in the interests of mankind." Two years later a coalition of developing countries pushed through the General Assembly a resolution that all states and persons were bound to refrain from all activities of exploitation of the area of the seabed and subsoil beyond national jurisdiction and that no claim to any part of that area or its resources would be recognized.[14] But this was too much for the United States and other countries, which felt that the boundary line of national jurisdiction had not yet been fixed, that mining technology in which the United States was a leader might be inhibited, and that the legal regime for the exploitation of the "international area" was still unsettled. Although the resolution was approved by sixty-two states, twenty-eight, including the United States, voted against it, and another twenty-eight abstained from the vote.

In 1970, however, the United States joined the unanimous vote of the General Assembly, with only fourteen abstentions, in a resolution that the seabed and ocean floor, and the subsoil thereof, as well as the resources of the area, were "the common heritage of mankind," that no person or state could appropriate them by any means, and that no state could claim or exercise sovereignty over any part of the area. Exploitation of the area, moreover, was to be carried out for the benefit of mankind under some "international machinery" to be established by treaty to ensure equitable benefits for all states, especially developing states.[15] At the same time the assembly approved the convening of the Third UN Law of the Sea Conference in 1973, and in 1974 the delegates began to negotiate a regime for the deep seabed following the lines of the General Assembly resolution.

The American politics of the deep-seabed-mining issue before the Law of the Sea Conference, as fought in the executive agencies of the administration and the committees of Congress, have involved questions of national defense and economic development, international equity, and the trade-offs in the conference negotiations that would lead to adoption of a comprehensive convention. On an ideological plane, there were also sharp cleavages between Americans who would accept a large, complex international organization with complete control over a vast area of the seabed and the right to collect and distribute revenues from its exploitation and other Americans who believed that such an international organization would not exercise its powers efficiently and equitably, to the detriment of American interests.

Although there was no disagreement in the United Nations that the area should be exploited for "the benefit of mankind" and there was no objection to some "international machinery" for the orderly management of claims, with some revenues to be distributed to economically disadvantaged nations, the negotiations from 1974 to 1981 in the Law of the Sea Conference clearly exposed the differences in interpretation of these ideas, among both developed and developing countries and among partisans in the United States itself.

In the beginning the developed states had hoped for a simple system of registration of claims to a mining site by a public or private entrepreneur, with an international agency as a clearing or authenticating device, and for a formula for revenue contributions to be made to an international fund for development of the disadvantaged states. But from the first negotiating session at Caracas in 1974 to the ninth in New York in 1980, the developing states advocated ever-widening powers for an International Seabed Authority over the resources of the ocean floor and an International Seabed Enterprise that might itself exploit the "international area." By 1976 U.S. Secretary of State Henry A. Kissinger had not only conceded broad powers for the Authority, including supervision of the sharing of revenues from mining activities and the establishment of an Enterprise by the convention, but he was also willing (1) to require a miner to offer the Enterprise a choice of half of any proposed mining site or sites that the miner nominated for a claim; (2) to assist developing countries to enhance their skills and their access to deep-seabed-mining technology; (3) to limit to some degree the production of minerals from the nodules where their effect on the world market might cause economic hardship to mineral-producing states; and (4) to help provide economic assistance to such states that suffered adverse effects domestically or upon their export earnings from deep-seabed mining. But Kissinger warned that "if agreement is not reached this year, it will be increasingly difficult to resist pressure to proceed unilaterally."[16]

In fact, no agreement was reached in 1976, 1977, 1978, 1979, or 1980 despite extensive public negotiating sessions and countless private diplomatic negotiations. By 1979 the revised Informal Composite Negotiating Text contained provisions about interest-free loans and borrowing guarantees for the Enterprise; controls over production from nodules that would limit the production of nickel for an interim period of twenty-five years to 60 percent of the anticipated annual increase in demand for nickel; a review conference after twenty years and the possibility of suspending all new production five years later; a provision that applicants make their technology available to the Enterprise; and other highly debatable provisions, not to mention the lack of accord on the structure of the vital decision-making Council of the Authority itself. In 1981 the new administration of Ronald Reagan adopted a different stance about the text of the 1980 Draft Convention.

At the instance of the mining industry, which was eager to gain investment support for the development of its technology and pilot projects for recovering hard minerals lying on the deep seabed, in 1974 and again in 1976 the Interior and Insular Affairs Committee of the U.S. Senate had reported bills to establish interim federal regulation of such mining. But the bills never reached the floor of the Senate. In 1976, the Senate Commerce Committee believed that the pending bill might spur negotiations at the prolonged Law of the Sea meetings, but it opposed provisions of the legislation that would give investment guarantees and insurance to American miners for their operations. Although the Senate Armed Services Committee was not averse to the bill, it felt that legislation should wait until either the conclusion of the Law of the Sea Conference or 1977. The Senate Foreign Relations Committee was opposed to the bill, however, not only because it was against investment guarantees, but also because it was doubtful that the lead of American technology would be impaired by a few more years of waiting or that the United States would be denied manganese, cobalt, nickel, or copper by world events in the near future. Most of all this internationally minded committee believed that the negotiations at the Law of the Sea Conference would be hurt by any unilateral action of the United States on seabed mining at that time.

In retrospect, the Department of Defense was not convinced of any threat to national security in the immediate future for lack of the metals to be found in the seabed, and it was satisfied that the negotiating text posed no difficulty for the free navigation and over-flight of the proposed international area. The balance-of-payments argument was hardly convincing, since the metals constituted such a small part of the total value of imports to the United States. The American public, moreover, was entranced in the late 1970s with the soaring costs of imported oil, not manganese, cobalt, copper, or nickel. With its national security arguments and no painfully evident economic consequences from lack of seabed mining, the State Department and its conference officials could press their point for waiting, for not disturbing the "delicate" negotiations as they sought to arrive, after six years, at a "successful" international convention. In this political stance the State Department had the support of internationally minded groups that stigmatized the thrust of a U.S. deep-sea-mining bill as nationalistic and serving only the interests of the mining industry.[17]

Nevertheless, by 1977 the arguments of the mining industry that the sluggish progress of the Law of the Sea Conference and the informal negotiating text clearly biased access to seabed mining by the developed states and was hindering American ability to exploit the nodules attracted wider congressional support. And it was difficult for the U.S. government to deny, after years of negotiation, largely over the regime for the deep seabed, a sense of frustration at the demands of developing states that they be allowed to control and reap virtually all the alleged wealth of the enormous ocean floor.

In 1978, therefore, the Ninety-fifth Congress had six different bills before it on the mineral resources of the deep seabed. Of these, one made its way successfully through the House, failing passage in the Senate only for lack of unanimous consent by one senator to limit debate on the measure. In the House, American politics worked overtime in winning the approval of a bill that would have affected U.S. foreign relations significantly. The Merchant Marine and Fisheries Committee, the Interior and Insular Affairs Committee, the Foreign Affairs Committee, and the Ways and Means Committee were all involved in fashioning this legislation, each with its own interests. To approve licenses for the American miners in the deep seabed, for example, the Merchant Marine and Fisheries Committee wanted the Commerce Department, which it oversees, as the decisive agency. But the Interior Committee, of course, wanted the Department of the Interior in control. Among the several other conflicts of political value were the idea of investment guarantees (dropped), requirements for transporting the manganese nodules on American-documented ships (partly dropped), environmental controls (strength-ened), and the means of sharing revenues with a future international agency (trust fund established to hold a percentage of the value of nodules in escrow). All parties, moreover, agreed on the idea of an "interim" arrangement, pending the establishment of a new international regime, but the language ensuring that the U.S. diplomats at the Law of the Sea Conference obtain an agreement that protected established claims by American miners was modified and revamped several times without complete satisfaction.

For want of passage by the Senate for reasons that were somewhat technical, the 1978 bill never reached the president. But on February 27, 1979, no fewer than sixteen public-interest and conservation groups appealed to the White House that a deep-seabed-mining bill could disrupt the Law of the Sea Conference. Congress had heard it all before. On December 14, 1979, therefore, the Senate passed the Deep Seabed Mineral Resources Act (S. 493) by a unanimous consent measure, within twenty minutes and with only five senators present. The bill had already run the gamut of the Energy, Commerce, Foreign Relations, Finance, and Environment and Public Works committees, with one final concession to the importunities of the State Department—namely, that the House be requested not to pass a companion measure until the end of the March 3–April 11, 1980, session of the Law of the Sea Conference.[18] In June 1980 the House did pass a companion measure (H.R. 2759), which became the act finally approved by the Senate and signed by the president.[19]

Congress intended the Deep Seabed Mineral Resources Act to be an interim measure, pending the establishment of a convention governing the international area, and, if no convention was adopted, to ensure the progressive development of seabed mining for American nationals. The act provided, among other things, for a tax of 3.75 percent of the imputed value (20 percent of fair market value) of any nodules mined, which would be held in escrow for the international fund planned under the Draft Convention on the Law of the Sea. But the key elements of the act, which agreed with doubts of the Reagan administration in 1981 about the Draft Convention and demands for changes in the text, were the provisions that the United States should adopt no convention that did not recognize the assured and nondiscriminatory access of American nationals to deep-seabed mining, that did not maintain substantially the same rights to seabed mining that had been acquired earlier by American nationals under the act, or that might impair the value of investments already made by American nationals in deep-seabed mining.

At the final session of the UN Law of the Sea Conference in New York at the end of April 1982, the Draft Convention text was revised to meet U.S. concerns about access to deep-seabed mining. Four sites in the deep seabed would initially be reserved for "pioneer investors" of Western Europe and North America, and four sites would also be reserved for the Soviet Union, France, Japan, and India. In exchange the "pioneer investors" would have to make commitments to interest-free loans and loan guarantees to two initial mining operations of the Enterprise, and would have to explore for the Enterprise, transfer technology to it, and train its personnel, all on a cost-plus basis or at fair market value. Another revision of the text made it necessary to obtain a voting majority of three-fourths rather than two-thirds to amend the convention.

These concessions to the United States were not enough. Washington still believed that the operation of the convention would deter the development of deep-seabed resources, frustrate rational economic development, and deny the play of market forces: future access to the international area was not ensured, privileges granted to the Enterprise would discriminate against national miners, and production limitations upon mining the seabed were contrary to consumer interests. Finally, the United States felt that the decision-making process of the International Seabed Authority did not give sufficient weight to the states most affected by its decisions and that the government could never accept an international convention in which substantive amendments might come into force without its consent, clearly a treaty process incompatible with the Constitution.

Fisheries

With fisheries the political context was different. The opening strategy of the State Department in negotiating a multilateral convention for the law of the sea, in accordance with the views of the Defense Department, was to keep claims to marginal seas as narrow as possible. It was feared that the claims of coastal states to the resources of the water column beyond the territorial sea and above the continental shelf would lead to claims of jurisdiction over navigation and overflight. In fact, the State Department had for years opposed American extension of exclusive jurisdiction over fisheries from the three-mile territorial sea to an additional nine miles from U.S. shores. Only in 1966 did the department yield to congressional action to protect near-shore fisheries from the increasing catch of Russian, Japanese, and other foreign vessels when legislation provided exclusive U.S. jurisdiction over fisheries out to twelve miles from the coasts.

In August 1971 the United States introduced to the UN Seabed Committee draft articles for an international convention that would have allowed fisheries and other living resources of the high seas to be regulated by international or regional organizations without discrimination between states and with the allocation of the total permissible catch to both coastal and distant fishing states by the international organization. American coastal fishing interests raised howls of protest, arguing forcefully that they had not been adequately consulted by the State Department in determining U.S. policy. They received strong support from the House Merchant Marine and Fisheries Committee. In 1972, therefore, the United States switched its position 180 degrees. The U.S. delegate admitted that American views had changed since 1971 and that the delegation had been persuaded that "the coastal state should have the right to regulate the fish stocks inhabiting the coastal waters off its shores as well as its anadromous (e.g. salmon) resources."[20]

Indeed, the trend of the coastal states to claim exclusive fisheries zones, initiated by Peru, Chile, and Ecuador in 1952, had continued during the 1960s. By 1971, countries such as Canada and Brazil, with very long coastlines and adjacent waters fished by Americans, had also begun to regulate the catch out to 200 miles from their coasts. The political strength of the American fishermen, moreover, always greater than their actual share of the national economy, came to bear in 1971, not only upon Congress, but also upon the new National Marine Fisheries Service in the National Oceanic and Atmospheric Administration and upon the new coordinator of marine affairs in the Department of State. The fisheries interests obtained two seats on an advisory group to the Law of the Sea delegation. Here, coastal fishermen largely from New England and Alaska held views different from the California (tuna) and Gulf (shrimp) fishermen who made catches off the shores of Latin America. Distant-water fishermen naturally feared retaliation by other countries if the United States extended its jurisdiction two hundred miles from shore, but the politically powerful coastal fishermen, railing against Russian and Japanese depletion of American coastal stocks, won the votes. Against the specific opposition of the Department of State,[21] and some arguments from the Department of Defense in its perennial fear that navigation on the high seas might be affected, the Senate extended the contiguous fishing zone of the United States to two hundred miles in December 1974 by a vote of sixty-eight to twenty-seven. That bill lapsed in the Ninety-third Congress, but companion bills were introduced in both the House and the Senate in 1975.

Meanwhile, the United States delegation at the Law of the Sea Conference, which had first tried a "species" approach to regulation and had called for management of stocks by cooperative action rather than by geographical demarcation of coastal waters, relented. John

Stevenson, head of the U.S. delegation to the Law of the Sea Conference, said on July 11, 1974, that he perceived a large measure of agreement on a willingness to accept a territorial sea of twelve miles and an "economic zone" of 200 miles and that the United States would accept such an arrangement as part of "an acceptable comprehensive package including a satisfactory regime within and beyond the economic zone and provision for unimpeded transit of straits used in international navigation."[22]

Thus the central difference between the majority congressional political viewpoint and the State Department's conduct of foreign policy lay not in the acceptance of a 200-mile exclusive economic zone for the coastal state but in the means of effecting it. Plainly Congress had tired of repeated assurances from the U.S. delegates that the adoption of a convention was in sight and that unilateral legislation not only would be contrary to international law but also would harm U.S. bargaining for other objectives at the Law of the Sea Conference. Abetted by such senators as Edward Kennedy of Massachusetts, Edmund Muskie of Maine, and John Pastore of Rhode Island, Senator Warren Magnuson of Washington, chairman of the Commerce Committee, which examined the bill, turned back the arguments of Senator John Tunney of California, who represented a distant-water constituency, by saying, "I think the argument that somebody is going to retaliate on navigation or air space because we protect our own fisheries is ridiculous. . . . The military worries about this all the time." And in response to the opposition by one of the senators from Alaska, who asked why the United States should not also claim jurisdiction over seabed minerals, Magnuson replied, "the minerals are going to be there; the oil is going to be there, but the fish . . . are going down and down and down."[23]

Thus, the Fisheries Management and Conservation Act of 1976, made effective March 1977, passed. Under it the United States unilaterally took control over the allocation of the catch of fish within 200 miles of its shores; claimed management over anadromous species, principally salmon, spawned in the United States beyond that zone in the high seas; exempted migratory species, such as tuna, that should be regulated by an international organization; and theatened restrictions on the importation of the fish products of any country that did not consider the customary or conventional rights of foreign fishermen in the management of their conservation zones or did not adhere to an international arrangement for migratory species.

In truth, by 1976 about forty states of the world had already approved ordinances that regulated fisheries in a two-hundred-mile zone from shore. There was an indisputable consensus by the states at the Law of the Sea Conference that an "exclusive economic zone," not just for fisheries, but for all economic resources in the water column, on the seabed, and in the underlying soil, should be created in the area lying beyond a twelve-mile territorial sea and up to a boundary 200 miles from shore. Once the Defense Department was assured that the exclusive economic zone would not be a territorial sea, that navigation and overflight there would be unimpeded, with specific provisions in the negotiating text to that effect, the interests of the United States were not only protected but enhanced. It should not be forgotten that the extension of jurisdiction over all resources in the adjacent ocean and its seabed gave more area—1,676,600 square miles—to the United States than to any other country in the world; Australia was next, followed by New Zealand, Japan, the Soviet Union, and Indonesia.

Pollution from Ships

Another issue of importance to the United States and other coastal states was international agreement on the regulation of ships to prevent pollution from oil and other hazardous or despoiling wastes. Several international conventions from 1952 to 1973, largely under the auspices of the Intergovernmental Maritime Consultative Organization (IMCO), had begun to make progress on safety standards of navigation, marine casualties on the high seas that endangered the coastal state, and compensation for damages from pollution. But the Law of the Sea Conference was bent on clarifying the limit of a state's jurisdiction over its coastal waters, not only for the exploitation of resources but also for the protection of a coastal state's shores from marine pollution within that resource zone.

Although the United States began the Law of the Sea negotiations with a preference for a narrow territorial sea and international regulations through IMCO for navigation on the marginal waters and high seas, in 1974 it accepted the idea of a two-hundred-mile exclusive economic zone with the proviso that nothing in the chapter would affect the rights of freedom of navigation or overflight and other rights recognized by the general principles of international law. Washington, prompted by the Council on Environmental Quality and the Environmental Protection Agency, was not averse to a rule of law that allowed the coastal state to protect its waters and shores from pollution by foreign vessels, even as far out as two hundred miles at sea. But the main policy objective of the United States was to prevent interference by coastal states with American ships by arbitrary national regulations for the design, manning, and operating equipment of vessels and other special requirements. Such unilateral action by coastal states, under the guise of environmental protection, could lead to diverse requirements for navigation throughout the world ocean and cause delays, arrests, and intolerable costs for shipping. In this policy the State Department had, of course, the support of the Defense Department, as well as that of the Interior Department, with its interests in international movement of oil, the departments of Commerce and the Treasury so far as the costs of maritime transportation were involved, and the advice of the Coast Guard, which ultimately would be responsible for policing the vast marine coastal area.

In December 1976, however, the *Argo Merchant*, a Liberian-registered tanker, was twenty-four miles off course when it hit the shoals off Nantucket, Massachusetts, and lost 7.7 million gallons of oil into the sea. Within days the secretary of transportation of the outgoing Nixon administration, William Coleman, stated that in the absence of a treaty, the United States might have to impose shipping standards unilaterally, and the administrator of the Environmental Protection Agency, Russell Train, said that it was "time to set tight regulations" for foreign shipping in U.S. waters.[24] At the same time, Congress began to plan new legislation for the protection of the U.S. coast from marine pollution. On January 13, 1977, Admiral Owen Siler stated that the U.S. Coast Guard had planned to ban the *Argo Merchant* from U.S. waters, but was told that such action would weaken negotiations at the Law of the Sea Conference.[25] Thereafter the Council of Governors of the fifty states, meeting in March 1977, called for the imposition of U.S. navigational rules upon foreign vessels.[26]

Other oil spills in the territorial waters and marginal seas of the United States hardly helped the restraint of the American delegation at the Law of the Sea Conference on unilateral action by the United States to regulate the passage of foreign vessels along its shores or into its ports. It was no coincidence that President Carter on March 18, 1977, called for a $200 million oil spill fund that would compensate victims of pollution from marine oil spills. Under these domestic pressures, as well as the determination of many coastal states without substantial merchant marines of their own to protect their coasts from pollution by vessels, the United States gradually yielded at the Law of the Sea Conference more regulatory rights and enforcement powers to the coastal nation over navigation under foreign flags. The rupture of the *Amoco Cadiz* off the coast of France, spilling 85,000 tons of oil on the beaches of Brittany on March 18, 1978, was the final blow, and on April 21, 1978, Elliot Richardson, head of the

165

American delegation at the Law of the Sea Conference, stated that the lessons of the recent tragic accident show the need to "bolster the rights of coastal states to prevent pollution by ships off their shores."[27]

By 1979, therefore, the revised Informal Composite Negotiating Text (ICNT) of the Third UN Law of the Sea Conference contained three sections, worked out in prolonged negotiations and compromises through the years, on international rules and national legislation to prevent, reduce, or control pollution of the marine environment. So complete and delicate was the consensus that the articles passed virtually intact into the 1980 Draft Convention and finally into the 1982 UN Convention on the Law of the Sea. With respect to land-based sources of pollution, the convention merely calls upon states to establish *national* laws and "to endeavor to establish" global and regional rules. With respect to pollution from seabed activities under their jurisdiction and pollution caused by ocean dumping, states were called upon to establish *national* laws to prevent pollution and to work through international organizations to establish global and regional rules. But pollution from vessels was another matter.

The first article in the convention dealing specifically with pollution by vessels (article 211) calls upon states, acting through international organizations or a general diplomatic conference, to establish *international* rules for the prevention, reduction, and control of pollution of the marine environment by ships. Some concessions, however, were made to the national authority of coastal states. First, power was given to the coastal state to fix its own requirements to prevent, reduce, or control pollution as a condition for the entry of foreign vessels to its own ports and inland waters or calling at its offshore structures. Second, the coastal state was given authority to set its own conditions to avoid pollution by the passage of a foreign vessel through its territorial sea so long as such conditions did not apply to the design, construction, manning, or equipment of the foreign vessel, except to give effect to international rules or standards. Third, beyond the territorial sea and within the exclusive economic zone, a coastal state—or a port state—can investigate evidence of oil spills (1) in violation of international standards or (2) in violation of national laws giving effect to international regulations, and, when it is clearly warranted, a coastal state can initiate proceedings against the ship, including detention, in accordance with its laws.

Having yielded these three powers to coastal states, the defense, shipping, and energy interests of the United States, in concert with other maritime nations, insisted on "safeguards," which were point-edly enumerated as section 7 of part 12 of the Draft Convention. To begin with, the legal proceedings against a vessel and its detention by the coastal state for an alleged violation of pollution regulations have been carefully circumscribed. At any time within six months the flag state may remove proceedings to impose penalties to its own jurisdiction, provided that the flag state itself has not flagrantly disregarded enforcement of international regulations by its own vessels. Moreover, no discrimination between foreign vessels and coastal state vessels is permitted, no unreasonable delay of the passage of foreign ships is allowed, and nothing but monetary penalties may be assessed for proven violations. Most important, nothing in the convention regarding marine pollution applies to any vessels owned and operated by a state and used in noncommercial government service.

Such safeguards were essentially satisfactory to the United States, culminating a diligent effort to balance its own maritime and environmental interests in dense paragraphs of carefully wrought legal verbiage. Indeed, the very complexity of these articles—and of the rest of the Draft Convention—in their effort to balance diverse domestic and international interests, placed a heavy burden on the intricate dispute settlement provisions of the convention. Largely the province of jurists and not as dramatic as the constitutive articles on the use of the seas, procedures for the settlement of disputes were always a constant concern of the whole American delegation as the keys to resolving future conflicts over the interpretation and application of the convention. Objective commissions, arbitration, and adjudication appeal to the United States as consonant with its own domestic rule of law, although the record of Washington in submitting disputes to international judgment has hardly been exemplary.

Scientific Research

Although of great importance to the small community of oceanographers in the world, scientific research, as a political issue, was given scant attention in the negotiations at the Third UN Law of the Sea Conference. American interests in this subject have been frustrated, if not poorly served.

In that narrow territorial sea observed by most maritime nations before 1950, coastal states had the same jurisdiction as on their land, save only over the easement of innocent passage by vessels through the territorial sea. For a foreign vessel to engage in scientific research in the territorial seas clearly required the permission of the coastal state. The new claims to jurisdiction over the resources of the continental shelf beyond the territorial sea, however, initiated by the United States, posed an important question about the legality of

167

scientific research by foreign vessels in that "limited jurisdiction" zone. The 1958 Continental Shelf Convention, which several states never ratified, admonished the coastal state that its exploration and exploitation of the resources of the shelf must not result "in any interference with fundamental oceanic research or other scientific research carried out with the intention of open publication." But the convention went on to say that the consent of the coastal state would have to be obtained in respect of any research concerning the continental shelf, though the coastal state would not normally withhold its consent *if* the request were submitted by a qualified organization for purely scientific investigation of the physical and biological characteristics of the shelf, *if* the coastal state had the right to participate in the research, and *if* the results of the research were to be published.[28]

The ambivalence of the Continental Shelf Convention, requiring the consent of a coastal state for scientific research yet dictating that such consent was not normally to be withheld for open research, pervaded the negotiations at Caracas, Geneva, and New York from 1974 to 1980 in the effort to reach a satisfactory text for the proposed comprehensive convention on the law of the sea. Compromise was further complicated by the expansion of "limited jurisdiction" zones to include a two-hundred-mile exclusive economic zone and, for some coastal nations, a much wider continental shelf. The totally new legal concept of an "international area" under the jurisdiction of an international authority for the exploitation of mineral resources, moreover, raised another issue about the freedom of scientific research in the ocean.

Although the UN Seabed Committee began its work in 1968 and the idea of a Third UN Law of the Sea Conference was adopted in 1970, the U.S. ocean science community hardly entered the policy process until 1972. The International Marine Science Affairs Policy Committee of the Ocean Affairs Board submitted its recommendations to the president of the National Academy of Sciences in March 1972. Five months later the American representative to Subcommittee 3 of the UN Seabed Committee made the first U.S. policy statement on scientific research, indicating that the language of the Continental Shelf Convention remained satisfactory, "if implemented in the spirit intended," but that for any other areas of limited jurisdiction or special competence there should be "minimal restrictions upon the conduct of research."[29] Not until July 1973, however, did the United States submit its first draft articles on the subject. Among other things, one of those articles quixotically tried to mitigate the ominous trend toward a wider territorial sea by requiring states "to cooperate in facilitating the conduct of scientific research in their territorial sea."[30] That suggestion proved an absolutely dead letter in the succeeding negotiating texts of the Law of the Sea Conference.

Important oceanographic research has been carried on by only a handful of developed states in the twentieth century—the United States, Canada, Great Britain, France, Germany, the Soviet Union, Japan, Australia—and even among those nations the program of the United States has loomed large, for modern oceanographic research is very expensive. Arguments that basic oceanographic research was beneficial to mankind or that the developing countries should welcome, participate in, and support basic oceanographic research were greeted with skepticism, if not derision, by nearly all the Asian, African, and Latin American countries. Entranced by the vision of exploiting for themselves all the resources of the water column, the seabed, and the soil beneath out to a distance of 200 miles or more from their shores, the representatives of developing states suspected that basic research, which could only be conducted and comprehended by developed states, might provide valuable security or economic data that could not be fully shared, used, or controlled by the coastal state. The plea of the scientists that it would be "open" research carried little weight with many governments that ruled closed societies.[31]

Oceanographic research, moreover, hardly pressed the policy makers in Washington as a political interest in the same way as military, mineral, or fishery concerns. By definition military intelligence could never rely upon open research for its needs. Under any legal regime for the seas the Department of Defense would resort to a variety of means to secure the knowledge essential to its security mission. While easier access to zones of limited jurisdiction might be desirable, it was not essential. For the mineral industry, any research associated with its operations in a zone of limited jurisdiction had to be concerned with mineral resources and would need the consent of the coastal state to warrant the risk of investment, so that the issue of open research for the industry was virtually moot. And the domestic fishing interests were more intent on eliminating foreign competition in coastal waters than in seeking research opportunities in the exclusive economic zone. In any case, there was a long history of fisheries research through international or regional commissions that could be relied upon, if needed, as a source of the specific data and behavioral patterns of stock for fishing interests.

Testimony before the Subcommittee on Oceanography of the House of Representatives Committee on Marine and Fisheries in 1978 clearly indicated the collapse of the American position on scientific research in Law of the Sea negotiations. Ambassador Elliot Richardson stated that the provisions in the ICNT on scientific research were not satisfactory to the United States, that he was trying to get them changed, and that this had been "one of my major preoccupations for the last year." But he went on to add that "even if we do not succeed in getting additional improvements . . . this is not an issue that in my judgment should affect the ultimate acceptability of the treaty from the standpoint of ratification or non-ratification by the United States."[32] John Norton Moore, who had been deputy representative of the United States to the Law of the Sea Conference, pointed out to the subcommittee that after granting no normative rights for marine science research in the exclusive economic zone, the coastal states were still so worried that they turned around and did away with any kind of compulsory settlement dispute for the few remaining obligations in the chapter on marine scientific research.[33] It must also be noted that the Subcommittee on Oceanography in these briefings on the Law of the Sea Conference from February through August 1978 devoted very little time to oceanographic research, spending most of the time questioning the witnesses on issues of deep-seabed mining.

The articles in the 1980 Draft Convention, which became the 1982 UN Convention on the Law of the Sea, taken almost verbatim from the ICNT, contained rhetorical flourishes about the right of states and international organizations to conduct marine scientific research, but always "subject to the rights and duties of other states" as provided in the convention. Thus, not only would the coastal states have the "exclusive right to regulate, authorize, and conduct marine scientific research in their territorial sea," but they also would have a right "in the exercise of their jurisdiction" to regulate, authorize, and conduct marine scientific research in their exclusive economic zones and on their continental shelves. In these areas of limited jurisdiction coastal states "in normal circumstances" would grant their consent when the research was exclusively for peaceful purposes, when it would increase scientific knowledge of the marine environment for the benefit of mankind, and when the proposal conformed to a set of rules requiring that details of the research be given to the coastal state. The coastal states could, however, "in their discretion" withhold their consent if they believed that the research (1) was of direct significance to the exploration and exploitation of resources; (2) involved drilling or the use of explosives or might introduce harmful substances into the environment; (3) contained inaccurate data about the objectives or methods of the research project; or (4) unjustifiably interfered with activities undertaken by the coastal state in the exercise of its sovereign rights and jurisdiction. Any international dispute that might arise from the exercise of the "discretion" of the coastal state in these circumstances, moreover, would be specifically exempted from the procedures for settling disputes elaborated in the Draft Convention.

Through all the meticulous verbiage, one point emerged: The coastal state might have any number of reasons to delay or deny marine scientific research by foreign vessels in its economic zone or on its continental shelf. Although some minor amendments were kept under discussion by the Law of the Sea delegates, at least to allow untrammeled research on the continental shelf more than 200 miles from shore and to require compulsory conciliation for international disputes over the discretion of the coastal state, the ultimate legal subjection of marine scientific research to the jurisdiction of coastal nations in the zones of limited jurisdiction had little hope of amendment. Complaints of the ocean science community and negotiations by the American representatives in redrafting the ICNT into the Draft Convention in 1980 obtained no relief from the restraining provisions, except an agreement that "normal circumstances" might exist in spite of a lack of diplomatic relations between the coastal state and the researching state.

Finally, with respect to the International Seabed Area, at one time the developing countries wanted marine scientific research to be carried out exclusively by the International Seabed Authority, but the ICNT in 1979 and the subsequent 1980 Draft Convention had been amended to permit states to carry out marine scientific research in the international area so long as they (1) promoted international scientific cooperation by participation in international programs, (2) encouraged cooperation with the personnel of other countries and the authority, (3) ensured that such programs were developed through international organizations or the Authority for the benefit of developing countries, and (4) disseminated the result of such research through the authority or other appropriate international channels.

1981 and Beyond

The election of Ronald Reagan to the presidency in November 1980, with his conservative ideology in fiscal policy, government regulation, and foreign policy, cast a new light upon the negotiations of the Law of the Sea Conference. Many of the hard-won compromises that had been molded into the draft articles during a period of six years and were largely acceptable, if not rather favorable, to U.S. political interests could not be assailed by the new administration. The widened territorial sea, the 200-mile exclusive economic zone, the extensive continental shelf, coastal state control over marine pollution from vessels, and the regime of free transit through straits fit nicely, if not perfectly, into American objectives. But the mining interests, as well as those in Congress and elsewhere who were skeptical about the performance and the costs to the American treasury of international agencies, found new support for their views in the Reagan administration.

At its tenth session, in April 1981, at which it had been expected that the Draft Convention would be adopted, the Law of the Sea Conference accomplished practically nothing. Among other things, the rules for delimiting the overlapping maritime boundaries for the exclusive economic zone or the continental shelf and the participation in the convention by such entities as nonindependent territories and liberation movements had not been resolved. But these were trifling compared with the American objections to the conditions for mining the deep seabed beyond national jurisdiction and the role of the International Seabed Authority and the International Seabed Enterprise in the Draft Convention. The United States bluntly informed the conference that it was reviewing the entire Draft Convention and that its review would not be completed until early 1982.

In testimony before the Subcommittee on Oceanography of the House Committee on Merchant Marine and Fisheries, the new assistant secretary of state for the Bureau of Oceans and International Environmental and Scientific Affairs in the Reagan administration, James L. Malone, reported on the work of the April 1981 session of the Law of the Sea Conference and outlined the features of the Draft Convention that needed review to satisfy the interests of the United States. He stated that the Draft Convention placed burdens of international regulation upon the development of all the resources on the seabed and in the subsoil beyond the limits of national jurisdiction, which is an area of about two-thirds of the earth's submerged lands. He pointed out that the convention would establish an International Seabed Enterprise that would have significant discriminatory advantages in mining this area over the companies of industrial countries and would perhaps monopolize production in time. He noted that the initial capitalization of the Enterprise would require contributions from the United States.

The assistant secretary observed, moreover, that the Draft Convention would compel the sale of proprietary information and technology now largely in the hands of the United States, with certain restrictions, to the Enterprise and to developing countries planning to go into seabed mining. The annual production of manganese nodules as well as the amount any one company might mine could be limited by the International Seabed Authority under the Draft Convention for the first twenty years of production.

Not the least of the worries of the U.S. government, under both President Carter and President Reagan, were, first, the provisions of the Draft Convention that created a one-nation, one-vote Assembly as the supreme organ of the International Seabed Authority, to which the other principal organs would be accountable and which could establish general policies in conformity with the convention; second, and more important, the creation of a thirty-six member Council as the executive organ of the Authority in which, through a complex formula, the developing countries and the Soviet bloc would have greater voting leverage than the United States and Western Europe.

In the summer of 1980, with Elliot Richardson still heading the U.S. delegation under the Carter administration, intensive negotiations in the Law of the Sea Conference had led to an extraordinarily complex voting procedure for the Council. Procedural questions would be settled by a simple majority of those present and voting; questions of substance, however, under certain articles would be decided by a two-thirds vote of those present and voting, provided that the vote included a majority of the Council; other questions under other articles, largely the powers and functions of the Council, including its borrowing power, would be decided by a three-fourths majority vote, provided again the vote included a majority of the Council. Finally, there were four types of decisions that required "consensus" for adoption: (1) questions about the protection of developing countries from adverse effects upon their economies and export earnings as a result of price reductions or volume of production as a result of mining the International Seabed Area; (2) recommendations to the Assembly on the sharing of economic benefits from the activities in the International Area or from exploitation of nonliving resources beyond the two-hundred-mile exclusive economic zone; (3) the provisional rules, regulations, and procedures of the Authority that would apply to the Area pending their approval by the Assembly; and (4) the adoption of amendments to all the articles applying to the International Area.

Nevertheless, as the Reagan administration took charge of the negotiations of the UN Law of the Sea Conference, there was no doubt that the United States was not satisfied with the Draft Convention, especially the articles on the International Seabed Authority that applied to the decision-making process, the limitation on the production of manganese nodules, the access and tenure of private companies to the resources, and the heavy financial burdens that might be placed upon both the private companies and the U.S. government.

In August 1981, at the eleventh session of the conference, the delegates plunged ahead in approving Jamaica as the headquarters for the International Seabed Authority and Hamburg as the home of the future International Tribunal for the Law of the Sea. But little else was done to change the substantive articles of the Draft Convention. Thus at the final session of the conference in April 1982, the United States called for a vote on the convention, revised by the provisions for "pioneer investors" and the requirement of a three-fourths vote for the approval of amendments. The convention was adopted by 130 votes to 4 with 17 abstentions.[34] In Montego Bay on December 10, 1982, the United States, joined by such states as the United Kingdom, the Federal Republic of Germany, Italy, and Belgium, refused to sign the convention, although 117 other states did.

Conclusion

Despite the serious doubts of the Reagan administration about the 1982 UN Convention on the Law of the Sea and its provisions on deep-seabed mining, doubts that were probably shared by more than a third of the United States Senate, there was a tremendous momentum both at home and abroad to adopt this comprehensive convention. From a political point of view the United States had achieved a great deal in the document: the interests of the Defense Department were largely secured by a definitive twelve-mile territorial sea and free transit through straits used for international navigation; the exclusive economic zone of 200 miles seaward from the baselines would put the resources of about 1.7 million square miles of ocean and seabed under the exclusive jurisdiction of the United States, most generous for American fishing and mining interests; and marine pollution control, sought by the United States, was certainly assisted by the provisions for investigation and arrest by the coastal state of polluting vessels within the exclusive economic zone. Scientific investigation, important to Americans, did not fare so well in the convention, but if no convention had been adopted, scientific investigation off foreign coasts might depend upon national regulations, varying in content and application, a worse alternative than the articles of the convention.

A large part of the convention was a codification of customary international law and the law of the sea to be found in previous conventions. Codification in a single comprehensive convention fitted American policy well, and, in retrospect, the negotiations of the several American delegations from 1974 to 1980 seem to have served the political interests of Washington rather well, considering the complexity of dealing with 150 states and their multiple interests. Only the issue of seabed mining, which contemplated the creation of an utterly new kind of international organization that would take jurisdiction over the resources of vast areas of the ocean floor and receive independent revenues and that would have a large bureaucracy, a separate international tribunal, and many other rights and privileges, gave pause to the American government.

In 1983 the UN Convention on the Law of the Sea was still far from being in force, especially lacking ratifications by the large industrialized states that might actively participate in deep-seabed mining. Political attitudes in the United States were divided, reflecting support for an orderly regime for world ocean management partly under the aegis of an international agency and the contrary view that the orderly regime was not worth the price of uncertain and discriminatory access to the deep seabed under an international agency with virtually sovereign powers. With defense and fisheries interests satisfied and scientific research interests minimized, the refusal of the government to sign the convention in 1982 signaled its adherence to conservative and traditional domestic interests of the United States rather than more liberal, innovative, but uncertain approaches to international law.

Notes

1. UN Document A/CONF, 62/WP10/Rev 3, August 27, 1980.

2. Arthur Dean, "The Geneva Conference on the Law of the Sea: What Was Accomplished," *American Journal of International Law*, vol. 52 (1958), p. 611.

3. U.S. Department of State, Office of the Geographer, "Sovereignty of the Sea," *Geographic Bulletin*, no. 3, rev. (1969).

4. Statement of John R. Stevenson before UN Committee on Peaceful Uses of the Sea and Ocean Floor beyond National Jurisdiction, July 17–August 18, 1972, Session, *Department of State Bulletin*, vol. 67 (July–December 1972), p. 383.

5. See, for example, Robert Osgood, "U.S. Security Interests in Ocean Law," *Ocean Development and International Law*, vol. 2, no. 1 (Spring 1974), pp. 1–36; and Richard G. Darman, "The Law of the Sea: Rethinking U.S. Interests," *Foreign Affairs*, January 1978, pp. 372–95.

6. U.S. Department of the Interior, Annual Report, Fiscal Year Ended June 1945, p. v.

7. *Public Papers of the Presidents of the United States: Harry S. Truman* (Washington, D.C.: National Archives and Records Service, 1963), p. 211.

8. Ibid.

9. United States v. California, 322 U.S. 19 (1947).

10. United States v. Louisiana, 339 U.S. 699 (1950); and United States v. Texas, 339 U.S. 707 (1950).

11. Public Law 31, May 22, 1953, *U.S. Statutes at Large,* vol. 67 (1963), p. 29.

12. UN Food and Agriculture Organization, *Yearbook of Fisheries Statistics,* vol. 32 (1973), Rome.

13. *Public Papers of the Presidents of the United States: Richard M. Nixon* (Washington, D.C., 1971), p. 454.

14. General Assembly Resolution 2574D (General Assembly session no. 24), December 15, 1969.

15. General Assembly Resolution 2749 (General Assembly session no. 25), December 17, 1970.

16. Speech of Secretary of State Henry A. Kissinger before the Foreign Policy Association, U.S. Council of the International Chamber of Commerce, and UN Association of the U.S.A., April 8, 1976.

17. For a complete study of the arguments, see U.S. Congressional Research Service, Library of Congress, *Deep Seabed Minerals: Resources, Diplomacy, and Strategic Interest,* prepared for House of Representatives, Committee on International Relations, Washington, D.C., 1978.

18. *Congressional Quarterly Almanac, 1979,* 96th Cong., 1st sess., 1979, vol. 35, p. 685.

19. *U.S. Code: Congressional and Administrative News,* 96th Cong., 2d sess., 1980, vol. 3, p. 1600.

20. Statement of Donald L. McKernan before Subcommittee 2, UN Seabed Committee, Geneva, August 4, 1972.

21. See the speech of Henry A. Kissinger, U.S. secretary of state, before the annual convention of the American Bar Association, Montreal, August 11, 1975.

22. Statement of Ambassador John R. Stevenson, special representative of the president to the Third UN Law of the Sea Conference, Caracas, Venezuela, July 14, 1974.

23. Congressional Research Service, Library of Congress, *Legislative History of the Fishery Conservation and Management Act of 1976,* pp. 376–77.

24. *New York Times,* January 12, 1977.

25. *New York Times,* January 13, 1977.

26. *New York Times,* March 2, 1977.

27. *New York Times,* April 21, 1978.

28. Geneva Convention on the Continental Shelf, 1958, article 5.

29. Statement of U.S. Representative Donald L. McKernan before the UN Seabed Subcommittee 3, August 11, 1972.

30. See Draft Articles for a Chapter on Marine Scientific Research, UN Doc. A/AC. 138/SC. III/L.44 (1973), Art. 6.

31. Excellent background and analytical studies of marine scientific research at the Law of the Sea Conference are John A. Knauss, "Development of the Freedom of Scientific Research Issue of the Third UN Law of the Sea Conference," *Ocean Development and International Law,* vol. 1, no. 1 (Spring 1973), pp. 93–120; Russ Winner, "Science Sovereignty, and the Third Law of the Sea Conference," *Ocean Development and International Law,* vol. 4, no. 3 (1977), p. 297; and *Ocean Development and International Law,* Daniel S. Cheever, ed., vol. 9, nos. 3 and 4 (1981), Jon L. Jacobson, special editor.

32. June 1, 1978, Hearings before the Subcommittee on Oceanography and the Committee on Merchant Marine and Fisheries, serial no. 95-44, (Washington, D.C., 1978), p. 64.

33. Ibid., p. 199.

34. The complete text of the UN Convention on the Law of the Sea is in UN Document A/CONF, 62/122, October 7, 1982.

8

Human Rights in United States Foreign Policy: The Rhetoric and the Practice

LARMAN C. WILSON

In applying the concepts of continuity and change, ends and means to U.S. foreign policy, the case can be made that the commitment to idealism in foreign policy by U.S. administrations has for the most part been rhetorical. There has been some continuity in the rhetorical commitment to human rights, which were defined initially as inherent in democracy and representative government, with great importance assigned to elections. There has been a large gap, however, between the commitment and efforts to translate it into policy; the commitment to human rights, whether as the end or as the means of foreign policy, like the commitment to other ideals, has usually been transcended by other policy considerations—namely, those having to do with national security. An early example of the difference between commitment and practice on ideals was the decision to create a national democratic society in the United States but to eschew giving aid to other threatened democratic governments or societies. A more recent example has been the use of the commitment to democracy as a rationalization to justify supporting nondemocratic regimes that are being threatened by communist subversion.

 Several U.S. administrations, however, including those of Presidents Wilson, Roosevelt, Kennedy, and Carter, have made a particularly strong rhetorical commitment to representative government and human rights and have attempted to convert these ideals into principles of foreign policy. As a result of the efforts of these presidents to implement as policy what they advocated concerning human rights, they were faced with the dilemma of "the politico-moral balancing" of "what *ought* to be done with what *can* be done."[1] In the process of trying to resolve the dilemma, to balance the commitment to human rights with other policy considerations, their original rhetorical commitments to human rights had to be greatly modified and reduced in the crucible of foreign policy decision making. In fact, the commitment of every president to human rights appeared to assume a decreasing priority.

President Carter's pronounced commitment to the place of human rights in his administration's approach, contrary to that of the Reagan administration, provides the most recent case. President Carter's public statements about human rights—that it would be the "soul" of his foreign policy, for example—appeared to have broken the so-called conspiracy of silence on the subject generally attributed to the Nixon and Ford administrations. And his ready acceptance of and zealous efforts to implement the human rights program mandated by the Congress in the early 1970s signified to some that "humanitarian concerns have moved from the wings to center stage in the foreign policy decision-making process."[2] President Carter's statements and efforts on behalf of human rights provoked great controversy; his policy, in fact, renewed the debate about the national interest between idealists and realists.

There were three interesting aspects of President Carter's human rights approach involving both foreign and domestic policy. First, his high-intensity commitment to human rights and his earnest early efforts to translate the former into action were in response to a human rights program mandated by the Congress before he assumed office. Although he was happy to comply with the program of Congress, what was unique was that this was the first time that the Congress had legislated human rights policy. Second, the active pursuit of human rights as a goal of foreign policy—its institutionalization in the executive branch—indicated a departure in policy, one that could not be sustained. The third aspect was President Carter's unique rationale for human rights in foreign policy. Unlike his predecessors, he maintained that all members of the United Nations were bound under the 1945 Charter and the Universal Declaration of Human Rights of 1948 to respect human rights, which justified certain U.S. actions against countries that violated the human rights of their citizens. Related to this stance is the question whether human rights are now—or are becoming—a matter of public policy. That is, does there exist an international law of human rights, based upon both treaties and custom, that imposes legal duties upon all states in the treatment of their citizens and that justifies states in taking action against violators of human rights? This is a widely debated question.

The major purpose of this essay is to examine the place of human rights in U.S. foreign policy, with special emphasis on the relation between rhetoric and practice in the policy mandated by the Congress and pursued by recent administrations.[3] This will include an answer to the following question: Will humanitarian concerns in U.S. foreign policy move from center stage, as some believed in the late 1970s, back to the wings?

The Human Rights Initiative of Congress

Beginning in the late 1960s and continuing in the early 1970s, there was a mounting congressional challenge to limit the executive's prerogatives in matters concerning Vietnam. One manifestation of this challenge by the Congress was a growing concern about the place of human rights in U.S. foreign policy. This concern was initiated mainly by liberals but was soon supported by a conservative-liberal coalition in which the former were opposed to leftist governments and the latter opposed to rightist governments.

The first legislative initiative occurred in 1973, when the House Foreign Affairs Subcommittee on International Organizations and Movements, of which Representative Donald M. Fraser (Democrat, Minnesota) was chairman, conducted a series of hearings on the international protection of human rights. From this beginning there flowed an extensive body of legislative restrictions, introduced by a group of Democratic congressmen—namely, Representatives Fraser and Tom Harkin (Iowa) and Senators James Abourezk (South Dakota), Alan Cranston (California), Hubert H. Humphrey (Minnesota), and Edward M. Kennedy (Massachusetts)—upon U.S. bilateral aid to states that were guilty of violating human rights. There was also a partially successful effort to apply these restrictions to the actions of the U.S. members of certain multilateral lending agencies—the World Bank and the International Monetary Fund—and the regional development banks.

It was during Congressman Fraser's subcommittee hearings that one witness presented a widely accepted—and often quoted—characterization of human rights as "the stepchildren of United States foreign policy."[4] The subcommittee's report reflected this viewpoint in its conclusions:

> The human rights factor is not accorded the high priority it deserves in our country's foreign policy. . . . The State De-

partment . . . has taken the position that human rights is a domestic matter. . . . Unfortunately, the prevailing attitude has led the United States into embracing governments which practice torture and unabashedly violate almost every human rights guarantee pronounced by the world community. . . . A higher priority for human rights in foreign policy is both morally imperative and practically necessary.[5]

The subcommittee's high priority for human rights contrasted sharply with the views expressed by Henry Kissinger at the 1973 hearings for his confirmation as secretary of state. He stated:

I believe it is dangerous for us to make the domestic policy of countries around the world a direct objective of American foreign policy. . . . The protection of basic human rights is a very sensitive aspect of the domestic jurisdiction of . . . governments.[6]

Congress was more responsive to Congressman Fraser than to the new secretary of state, however, and initiated its "new directions in development aid" in the Foreign Assistance Act of 1973. This act, stressing basic human needs and the needs of the poor majorities in developing countries, sought to deny to some countries economic and military aid and funds for police training on the grounds that they had violated human rights and called upon the president to take action for the protection of human rights in Chile. A year later, the Congress added a new section—502B—to the Foreign Assistance Act. That section declared that "a principal goal of the foreign policy of the United States shall be to promote the increased observance of internationally recognized human rights by all countries" and set forth the following human rights formula for U.S. action: "The President shall substantially reduce or terminate security assistance to any government which engages in a *consistent pattern of gross violations of internationally recognized human rights.*"[7]

In late 1975, the Department of State indicated its reservations and preference for "quiet but forceful diplomacy" as the best means for promoting human rights. The department's report stated, among other things, the following:

Experience demonstrated that the political, social, and cultural problems which cause seemingly intractable human rights abuses to occur need to be resolved *before* real improvements in human rights conditions can apparently take place—with or without bilateral or international pressure. . . .

In view of the widespread nature of human rights violations in the world, we have found no adequately objective way to make distinctions of degree between nations. This fact leads us, therefore, to the conclusion that neither the U.S. security interest nor the human rights cause would be properly served by the public obloquy and impaired relations . . . that would follow the making of inherently subjective . . . determinations that "gross violations" do or do not exist or that a "consistent" pattern of such . . . does or does not exist in such countries.[8]

This report prompted a strong reaction by the Congress and the enactment of additional legislation, including the addition of section 116, the Harkin amendment, to the Foreign Assistance Act by means of the International Development and Food Assistance Act of 1974. No longer setting forth the "sense of Congress," Congress in this section legally *prohibited* development assistance to a country that had "a consistent pattern of gross violations . . . *unless* such assistance will directly benefit the needy people in such country" (emphasis added). The president was required to submit an annual report to the Congress regarding compliance.

In 1976 the Congress extended the restrictions that applied to bilateral aid to two regional development banks. In Public Law 94-302 the U.S. executive directors of the African Development Fund and the Inter-American Development Bank were directed "to vote against any loan, any extension of financial assistance, or any technical assistance" to a country violating the human rights of its citizens. (This directive was relaxed the following year.)

In the same year Congress included extensive human rights directives in the International Security Assistance and Arms Export Control Act. This act included the creation of the position of coordinator for human rights and humanitarian affairs in the Department of State, to be appointed by the president and approved by the Senate,[9] and the requirement of annual reports to the Congress by the secretary of state on human rights practices in each country receiving security assistance.

When the Arms Export Control Act was first passed, it permitted the Congress by a concurrent resolution to end military assistance to a country because of violations of human rights. This led to President Ford's veto of the measure because he believed that such congressional authority intruded upon his prerogatives in the foreign policy field. At the same time he expressed the opinion that such restrictions

would most likely be counter-productive as a means for eliminating discriminatory practices and promoting human rights. The likely result would be a selective disassociation of the United States from governments unpopular with the Congress, thereby diminishing our ability to advance the cause of human rights through diplomatic channels.[10]

He did accept the measure, however, when the Congress changed it to provide that a joint resolution was necessary in order to terminate aid.[11]

Notwithstanding Secretary of State Kissinger's earlier statements about human rights in foreign policy and the low priority he assigned to them, he responded to the pressure from Congress. This was indicated by the change in his attitude and policy toward Africa and by his criticisms of the Pinochet government in Chile. At the 1976 meeting of the General Assembly of the Organization of American States (OAS), held in Chile, he gave an entire speech on the subject, entitled "Human Rights and the Western Hemisphere." He declared: "One of the most compelling issues of our time, and one which calls for the concerted action of all responsible peoples and nations, is the necessity to protect and extend the fundamental rights of humanity."[12]

The Carter Administration and Human Rights

While he was campaigning for the presidency, former Governor Carter introduced the issue of human rights in foreign policy, and his effort seemed to evoke a favorable public response. He criticized the incumbent administration for its preoccupation with national security and lack of interest in human rights. Insisting that the pursuit of human rights was in the national interest, he promised that, if elected, he would place great stress upon human rights. Once he became president, he made it clear that human rights would be central to the foreign policy of his administration. This commitment was indicated in his inaugural address when he declared:

> Because we are free we can never be indifferent to the fate of freedom elsewhere. Our moral sense dictates a clearcut preference for those societies which share with us an abiding respect for individual human rights. . . . Our commitment to human rights must be absolute.[13]

Following this pledge and his statement four months later at the University of Notre Dame reaffirming "America's commitment to human rights as a fundamental tenet of our foreign policy,"[14] President Carter reiterated his commitment to human rights in a series of public addresses and press releases, and he stressed five points.[15]

First, he rejected the domestic jurisdiction argument advanced by his predecessors and critics that the pursuit of human rights in

U.S. foreign policy would violate the domestic jurisdiction and sovereignty of a foreign state, thus constituting intervention in its internal affairs. President Carter rejected this view as an invalid rationalization, maintaining that the United States, along with other members of the United Nations, had a responsibility and a "legal right" under the Charter and Universal Declaration of Human Rights to criticize violations of human rights. In his March 1977 speech at the United Nations, he declared:

> All the signatories of the UN Charter have pledged themselves to observe and to respect human rights. Thus, no member of the United Nations can claim that mistreatment of its citizens is solely its own business. Equally, no member can avoid its responsibilities to review and to speak when torture or unwarranted deprivation occurs in any part of the world. . . .
>
> . . . The solemn commitments of the UN Charter, of the UN's Universal Declaration for Human Rights . . . and of many other international instruments must be taken just as seriously as commercial or security agreements.[16]

There is considerable debate among experts in international law concerning the binding nature of the human rights articles of the United Nations Charter and of the Universal Declaration.[17] Two leading scholars have recently made a legal case rejecting the traditional domestic jurisdiction sovereignty obstacle to international protection of human rights and justifying humanitarian intervention in support of human rights.[18] There is no debate, however, about a state's being legally bound if it has become a party to one of the human rights treaties drafted by the United Nations.[19] One reality involving these treaties, an embarrassing one to President Carter, is that the United States at the time of his United Nations speech had not even signed all of them and had not ratified the principal ones, such as the two United Nations covenants. This is why he also promised in his speech to sign the unsigned ones and to seek the approval of the Senate.[20] President Carter subsequently fulfilled his pledge to sign the unsigned treaties. Ironically, the reservations he proposed in his message transmitting the four human rights treaties to the Senate seriously undercut the significance of the signing by the United States. In fact, some states will surely object to the nature of the U.S. reservations.[21]

Second, President Carter denied the "linkage" concept of former Secretary of State Kissinger. In rejecting the view that the human rights goal would jeopardize more important goals, such as national security and world order, Carter emphasized that his administration would pursue objectives in human rights at the same time that it sought economic, military, and political goals.

Third, President Carter declared that the United States would honor its pledge to human rights even if it strained bilateral relations.

Fourth, he rejected the claim that the efforts of the United States to draw world attention to human rights would cause an increase in the number of violations of human rights. He believed, instead, that such an approach by the United States would promote human rights and reduce violations in the long run.

And fifth, President Carter maintained that concern with human rights was in and would serve the national interest. He also referred to this idea in his University of Notre Dame speech: "I believe that we can have a foreign policy that is democratic, that is based on fundamental values, and that uses power and influence which we have for humane purposes." And he further observed that there was a "trend" in behalf of the individual in the world and that "to lead it will be to regain the moral stature that we once had."[22]

Implementation. President Carter moved rapidly to translate into action his own commitment to human rights and to carry out the congressional program. He signed the two United Nations covenants on human rights and the American Convention on Human Rights and sent them to the Senate, along with the Convention on the Elimination of All Forms of Racial Discrimination, requesting that they be approved. The work of the Human Rights Commission of the Organization of American States was strongly supported, and at the 1977 meeting of the General Assembly Secretary of State Cyrus Vance made an important address on human rights and announced that the United States was increasing its financial contribution to the Human Rights Commission of the OAS. One of the most forceful actions taken was the announced cutoff by the administration of military aid to Argentina, Ethiopia, and Uruguay, a cutoff that was subsequently applied to other countries. This provoked a strong reaction, and the countries charged the United States with intervention in their internal affairs. The Carter administration also successfully lobbied for repeal of the 1972 Byrd amendment, which permitted U.S. imports of chrome from Rhodesia (now Zimbabwe) in violation of a resolution of the United Nations Security Council. These actions and others evoked criticism of the policy, and the president also had some difficulties with the Congress. Before turning to a discussion of the controversy and his problems, it may be helpful to examine the institutionalization of the human rights machinery in the executive branch.

An important aspect of President Carter's implementation of human rights was his prompt expansion and development of a human rights bureaucracy. He was interested in upgrading and broadening the functions of the Human Rights Office, created in 1975 as the Office of the Coordinator for Human Rights and Humanitarian Affairs. In order to pressure the Ford administration into paying greater attention to human rights, the Congress in 1976 elevated the position to that of an assistant secretary of state. To head this three-division bureau—Office of Human Rights, Office of Refugee and Migration Affairs, and section on Prisoners of War and Missing in Action, each headed by a deputy assistant secretary—President Carter appointed Patricia Derian, a former activist in the civil rights movement in Mississippi, as the first assistant secretary of state for human rights and humanitarian affairs.[23]

Another body was created by the National Security Council in early 1977 for the purpose of coordinating decisions concerning human rights—the Interagency Committee on Human Rights and Foreign Assistance, commonly called the Christopher Committee because its chairman was Warren Christopher, the deputy secretary of state. The Christopher Committee was composed of representatives at the deputy assistant secretary level from the departments of Defense and the Treasury, the Agency for International Development (AID), and the National Security Council, plus representatives from all the functional and regional agencies, such as the departments of Agriculture and Commerce and the Export-Import Bank (EXIM) and the Overseas Private Investment Corporation (OPIC).

Despite the alacrity with which the Carter administration carried out the human rights program mandated by the Congress and institutionalized and developed its own initiatives, some conflicts with the Congress arose. One serious difference between the two branches that developed in 1977, and also involved differences between the House and Senate, concerned the role of the U.S. member in each of the multilateral lending agencies regarding questions of human rights. The approach of the House, reflected by the amendment of Congressman Herman Badillo (Democrat, New York), *required* the U.S. members in these international lending institutions to oppose loans to countries that violated human rights *unless* such loans directly served the basic needs of the citizens of the recipient countries.[24] The Senate, however, preferring a more moderate approach, wanted the U.S. members in these institutions to exert their influence in directing aid away from countries with poor records in human rights. The Foreign Relations Committee was opposed to mandating that the U.S. members vote against loans to countries that violated human rights. President Carter favored the approach of the Senate and obtained a compromise between the two houses, which instructed, but did not require, the U.S. members in the multilateral lending institutions to oppose loans *unless* the aid would serve basic human needs.[25]

During the 1977 debate, the president of the World Bank, Robert S. McNamara, expressed his negative reaction to the U.S. approach. He stated:

> The Bank . . . is helping large numbers of . . . people to move out of absolute poverty towards a more decent life. What we are not capable of is action directly related to civil rights. Such action is prohibited by our Charter, it would require information and competence which we lack, and there is no agreement among our member governments on acceptable standards of civil rights.[26]

Mr. McNamara warned further that the bank "could not accept funds from the U.S. if they were not to be 'pooled' but 'tied' to prohibitions on loans to certain countries."[27]

Subsequently, the Congress placed additional restrictions on the executive concerning the multilateral lending institutions. In 1978, legislation on the Supplementary Financing Facility of the International Monetary Fund (IMF) required the secretary of the treasury, in consultation with the secretary of state, to submit an annual report to the Congress on the observance of human rights by countries taking advantage of the IMF facility. In addition, the Foreign Assistance and Related Programs Appropriations Act of 1979 required the president to direct the U.S. executive directors in the multilateral agencies to attempt to amend the Articles of Agreement of these agencies and to establish human rights criteria to be applied to loan decisions.[28]

Although during President Carter's first year in office Congress amended the Export-Import Act of 1945 to include provisions concerning human rights, the next year it limited the provisions applying to U.S. trade. This action reflected the belief that EXIM dealt with trade, not aid, and that its purpose was to promote U.S. exports, which positively contributed to the U.S. balance of payments and employment. Also in 1978, the Congress amended and added provisions concerning human rights to the statute of OPIC, which included exceptions upon the basis of national securty and basic human needs.

Reaction to Carter's Human Rights Policy. The commitment and style of the Carter administration in carrying out the human rights program developed and mandated by the Congress provoked great controversy and renewed the idealist-realist debate of the 1950s about U.S. foreign policy. Much of the criticism was focused upon style and rhetoric rather than upon substance; some concentrated upon the problems of implementation. Related to the last point were the problems of the Carter administration and the inherent difficulties for any government to "differentiate among the categories of the impossible, the desirable and the possible."[29] The bulk of the criticism directed at President Carter included both style and substance and revolved around charges of two specific sorts. The first was that the human rights policy was inconsistent and represented a double standard; the second was that it was counterproductive and ineffective.[30]

The problems of the relation between commitment to human rights and implementation of a policy concerning human rights confronting the Carter administration were indicated by the titles of a critical article, "The Hell of Good Intentions,"[31] and a recent critical book, *American Dream, Global Nightmare: The Dilemma of U.S. Human Rights Policy.*[32] Another scholarly critic, one actually in favor of human rights in U.S. foreign policy, criticized President Carter's approach and style, in these words:

> [The Carter administration] announced it with trumpets. It gave it a general and abstract statement in advance of particular issues and apart from specific controversies. It hung strong and unqualified words around its neck, and when, as was inevitable, it has had to soften or bend these words, it has been vulnerable to charges that it is irresolute. . . . The Carter Administration's initial pronouncements gave its policy the quality of a categorical imperative.[33]

This is a valid opinion, even though President Carter had rejected "rigid moral maxims" and had admitted the "limits of moral suasion" in his University of Notre Dame speech.[34] Only after the first eighteen months in office did the administration move away from the general approach and start to deal with problems of implementation case by case.

The presidential rhetoric that raised false and unreal expectations lent credence to charges of inconsistency and a double standard in American policy, especially when human rights seemed to clash with the goal of national security. An example often cited is the administration's action to cut off military assistance to Argentina, Chile, El Salvador, Ethiopia, and Uruguay because of violations of human rights while continuing such assistance to Iran, the Philippines, and the Republic of Korea despite their violations of human rights. It was also argued that the human rights policy was being applied to small states, particularly in Latin America, in which the United States had no strategic interests.

Related to the charges of inconsistency and a double standard was the assertion that the human rights policy was both counterproductive and ineffective. Countries to whom aid was terminated did not appear to change their policies, but they refused any further U.S. assistance and, in some instances, expelled the U.S. military training missions and turned elsewhere for their purchases and aid. This had the effect of greatly reducing the influence of the United States in relation to that of other suppliers—from Asia, Europe, or the Soviet bloc—and causing a loss of business for American businessmen.

The efficacy of the human rights policy was challenged by a number of critics. One of the strongest charges of the ineffectiveness of the policy was presented by Ernst Haas, who believed that a human rights policy could not possibly succeed, given the heterogeneity and pluralism of the world and the nature of the international political system.

A consistent and energetic policy in the human rights field makes impossible the attainment of other, often more important, objectives of American policy. Once this was realized, something had to give. The human rights policy was the first victim of the realization that politics is the art of the possible, the practice of carefully considering the trade-offs between competing but equally legitimate objectives. . . .
. . . What was understood by previous administrations also became clear to Carter: international politics is not like the politics of the American civil rights movement.[35]

These criticisms and views were persuasive and relevant. With regard to the conflict between individual and collective rights, the Carter administration's approach to human rights certainly reflected a minority position in the world. The emphasis upon individual, civil, and political rights was juxtaposed with the emphasis upon collective, economic, and social rights on the part of a majority of countries—the third world, the Communist countries, and even some of the Western democracies. The perspective on individual rights was indicated by the Carter administration's official definition of human rights. Secretary of State Cyrus Vance set forth, in his April 1977 speech at the University of Georgia, three categories of rights:

(1) "the right to be free from governmental violations of the integrity of the person," (2) "the right to the fulfillment of such vital needs as food, shelter, health care, and education," and (3) "the right to enjoy civil and political liberties."[36] Most of the emphasis was on the first and third categories; Secretary Vance stated in Georgia that the first category was assigned that priority because it was the first to be dealt with by U.S. diplomats.

The Carter administration discovered how easy it was to make public commitments to human rights in foreign policy and how difficult it was to carry them out. The gap between the two, commitment and implementation, steadily widened as the reality of balancing was accepted, although reluctantly. The following dilemma has been acknowledged by policy makers:

> The question is not human rights versus no human rights; instead it is human rights versus national security versus friendly relations with existing regimes versus economic benefits to the U.S. economy and U.S. investors versus humanitarian aid to impoverished people.[37]

The chief executive's personal relations with the generals heading three Latin American countries—Videla of Argentina, Pinochet of Chile, and Somoza of Nicaragua—also undercut his stress upon human rights.[38] At the time of the fall 1977 ceremonial signing of the Panama Canal treaties in Washington, President Carter met individually with each attending head of state, including those from Argentina and Chile (Somoza did not attend). This conveyed the impression that the treaties were more important than human rights as an issue of hemispheric solidarity.[39] In the summer of 1978, President Carter sent a letter to General Somoza, praising him for his improvements in human rights. This case of great praise for cosmetic improvements in one of Latin America's most unpopular dictatorial dynasties indicated the primacy given by the administration to maintaining political stability in this strategic area. During the 1978–1979 insurrection in Nicaragua, the principal concern of the United States was the possibility that the toppling of Somoza by the Sandinistas would bring into being "a second Cuba," and the United States pursued a variety of efforts, both in the OAS and outside it, to mediate and reconcile the differences between the two sides. The United States was slow to join the growing Latin American consensus that Somoza had to leave and that a Sandinista government would be an improvement from the standpoint of human rights. Finally, Secretary Vance introduced a resolution at an OAS meeting in June 1979, the month before the defeat of Somoza, calling upon General Somoza to step down and leave his country; the revised resolution passed with a two-thirds majority.[40]

These actions, even though limited to this hemisphere, communicated the general message, in the words of one observer,

> that human rights would have a significant place in nearly all decisions regarding U.S. foreign policy, but that the *amount* of significance would depend upon (1) the nature of other variables involved (2) the type of human rights violations, and, therefore, (3) the countries involved.[41]

After the initiatives of 1977, the Carter administration used international organizations to advance the cause of human rights, but only to a limited extent. President Carter preferred to rely on a bilateral approach rather than upon either the United Nations or the OAS. Following his policy statement delivered before the General Assembly in March 1977, as noted above, he decided to present inter-American issues to the regional forum, the OAS, where the United States could exercise considerable influence. The low priority assigned to the United Nations and its Human Rights Commission as useful forums was indicated in the Carter administration's policy of appointing to the commission part-time representatives selected upon the basis of patronage rather than expertise.[42] In the first year, President Carter also considered the OAS to be important and used it significantly. Following Secretary Vance's address on human rights at the 1977 General Assembly of the OAS, however, and his announcement that the United States would increase its contribution to the budget of the OAS Human Rights Commission, the administration used the OAS only irregularly—for the signing of the Panama Canal treaties, efforts to resolve the Nicaraguan crisis, and so on. One exception was the continued strong U.S. support of the Human Rights Commission, which, although more effective than that of the United Nations, has quite limited powers.

Once the Carter administration had institutionalized and expanded the human rights machinery in the executive branch, particularly in the State Department, and had begun actively trying to implement a human rights policy, two aspects of the process emerged —the internal and the external. The former involved the bureaucratic struggle for influence among competing interests within the executive branch and between it and the legislative branch. The latter involved a human rights constituency outside the government that came to the fore in support of President Carter's commitments to human rights.

The first year of the Carter administration's efforts in behalf of human rights was characterized by factionalism and bitter debates. Many people in various agencies resented what they considered to be a single-minded approach on the part of those in the Human Rights Office. This brought about the formation of various coalitions. In the State Department, for example, there was usually a joining of forces by the Human Rights Office, the Office of Congressional Relations, and the Legal Adviser's Office in opposition to the Defense Department, certain regional bureaus of the Department of State, and such functional bureaus as Political-Military Affairs and Economic and Business Affairs. One serious estrangement developed between the Human Rights Bureau and the Bureau of East Asian Affairs over the Philippines and the Republic of Korea. There also was great tension between the Human Rights Bureau and the Bureau for Inter-American Affairs. The desk officers and regional officers in particular argued that the exponents of human rights were damaging relations with those countries with which the desk officers were concerned as well as with U.S. interests in general. Although many of the early debates and much of the tension were later moderated and dissipated, the Christopher Committee both brought out the strong disagreements and helped smooth them over. In the words of one report, however, "the costs in terms not only of confusion and disillusionment, but of sheer time and energy expended have been high."[43]

The efforts of the Congress first, and then of the Carter administration, were strongly supported by an emerging human rights constituency. Growing out of the civil rights movement and catalyzed by Vietnam and Watergate, this constituency consisted primarily of a coalition of liberals and minority groups. More specifically, the constituency included a vast array of religious, minority, women's, educational, service, and research organizations. A number of the organizations formed the Human Rights Working Group of the Coalition for a New Foreign and Military Policy. The coalition, along with other associations working independently or cooperating informally, applied pressure and made its position known in support of human rights by lobbying, testifying before congressional committees, publishing newsletters, using the mass media, and raising funds.[44]

Human Rights as Public Policy

In considering the human rights policy of the United States under international law, it is necessary to expand the discussion of President Carter's argument that the United States had both a legal duty and a legal right with respect to human rights because it was a party to the United Nations Charter.[45] I seriously doubt the validity of his argument. Instead, it is more reasonable to maintain upon the basis of the existing evidence, and particularly of the practice of the United States, that human rights have not yet achieved the status of internaional public policy. It is the case, however, that an international law of human rights is emerging. In legal parlance, such a body of law at present is *lex ferenda* (law that it is desired to establish), not *lex lata* (law that exists).

Richard Bilder, among others, has maintained that there exists a "law of human rights" in the form of "a body of international law, institutions, procedures and precedents."[46] He identifies two relevant sources of international law, treaties and custom, and cites the former as "the most important source of international human rights law for lawyers."[47] In considering treaties as a source of legal obligations of the United States, it should be remembered that the United States maintains an important distinction between self-executing and non-self-executing treaties and has placed the United Nations Charter in the latter category, which is a significant qualification of the provision in the U.S. Constitution (article VI, section 2) that treaties "shall be the supreme law of the land." In the classic *Fujii* case,[48] the court took the position that, since the United Nations Charter was a non-self-executing treaty and the human rights articles had not been implemented by special congressional legislation, the human rights provisions of the charter were not applicable as domestic law. This continues to be the U.S. approach, and President Carter, in recommending to the Senate reservations to the human rights treaties, maintained the non-self-executing distinction and consequently weakened the position of the United States on human rights.

Considerable debate surrounds custom as a source of legal obligation regarding human rights. A minority view of increasing popularity is that human rights and duties are now derived from principles of customary international law—that is, that the increasing number of legal documents dealing with human rights, both domestic and international, and with popular reaffirmations of human rights, have become a part of customary international law. The Universal Declaration of Human Rights is cited as an example of a source of customary international law and conceptually as legally binding on all states in the international community.[49] I find this argument to be unpersuasive, although at the same time this minority view does contribute to the incremental process that may lead to the future acceptance of duties toward human rights under custom. At present, however, the practice has not been broad enough or the consensus adequate to establish human rights obligations under customary international law. To cite one example, the two human rights covenants of the United Nations, derived from the Universal Declaration and completed in 1966, came into effect in 1976 and so far have some forty ratifications. This limited treaty participation in a United Nations with some 150 members is inadequate and cannot be employed as evidence of a custom that binds those nations, such as the United States, that have not ratified.

Interestingly, both the chief executive and the Congress have been inconsistent in their approaches to human rights under international law, whether from the perspective of treaties or customary rules. President Carter stressed customary rules, but at the same time undercut his approach to treaty approval by proposing damaging reservations to the UN covenants. The Congress, in legislating a human rights program, provided as one justification for its concern about human rights the international obligations of the United States as a member of the United Nations. The Senate, on the other hand, has consistently refused both before and since the enactment of the human rights program to approve the human rights treaties for fear that they would prompt the United Nations to intervene in the domestic affairs of the United States. Until the United States becomes a full party to these treaties, or until many more years have elapsed and legal duties regarding human rights have been established under customary international law, the case of national duties concerning human rights as international public policy cannot be effectively made.

The Reagan Administration and Human Rights

The 1980 presidential campaign raised once again the important question of balance in foreign policy—namely, the proper equilibrium between national security and human rights—and Governor Ronald Reagan indicated that he favored a shift in emphasis to the former. During the campaign he spoke in favor of human rights and did not challenge President Carter's call for improvements in human rights in foreign countries, but he did criticize the incumbent's inconsistent application of human rights in U.S. foreign policy. Governor Reagan attacked the Carter administration for neglecting U.S. national security, stressed that the Soviet Union was the principal threat to the United States—and human rights—and world peace, and made it clear that human rights in U.S. foreign policy would receive a lower priority as national security was given primary attention. It was indicated that "quiet diplomacy" would be the hallmark of the new administration in the field of human rights. These views were brought together and expressed by Governor Reagan during the late October presidential debate when he declared:

> Because someone didn't meet exactly our standards of human rights, even though they were an ally of ours, instead of trying patiently to persuade them to change their ways, we have, in a number of instances, aided a revolutionary overthrow which results in complete totalitarianism, instead, for these people. I think that this is a kind of a hypocritical policy when . . . we're maintaining a détente with the one nation in the world where there are no human rights at all—the Soviet Union.[50]

Although Governor Reagan spoke in favor of human rights in an address on the eve of the election and assured the nation of his commitment as president-elect, he replied to a question on human rights at his first press conference as president-elect in these words:

> Yes. I think that all of us in this country are dedicated to the belief in human rights. But I think it must be a consistent policy. I don't think that you can turn away from some country because here and there they do not totally agree with our concept of human rights, and then . . . maintain relations with other countries, or try to develop them where human rights are virtually nonexistent.[51]

The practice of the Reagan administration, in appointments, statements of officials, and changes in foreign policy, illustrates a new balance between national security and human rights. Three nominations to high office symbolized the stress upon national security and the Soviet Union. The first was that of Jeane Kirkpatrick, professor of government at Georgetown University, to be ambassador to the United Nations; the second was that of General Alexander Haig, former commander of the North Atlantic Treaty Organization, to be secretary of state; and the third was that of Ernest Lefever, a former senior fellow at the Brookings Institution and president of the Ethics and Public Policy Center, to be assistant secretary of state for human rights and humanitarian affairs.

Dr. Kirkpatrick's nomination as the only Democrat in the cabinet was not a controversial one, and the Senate Foreign Relations Committee supported it unanimously in mid-January. Certain of her views on human rights were expressed before her nomination and have been reiterated since, for they represent frequently expressed views of members of the Reagan administration, including the president himself. In 1979, she wrote an article, "Dictatorships and Double Standards," which was critical of the human rights policy of the

Carter administration. In this article, which attracted Governor Reagan's attention, she expressed certain views that have become important in U.S. foreign policy. She insisted:

> What makes the inconsistencies of the Carter administration noteworthy are, first, the administration's moralism—which renders it especially vulnerable to charges of hypocrisy; and, second . . . [its] predilection for policies that violate the strategic and economic interests of the United States. . . .[52]
>
> The foreign policy of the Carter administration fails not for lack of good intentions but for lack of realism about the nature of traditional versus revolutionary autocracies and the relation of each to the American national interest. Only intellectual fashion and the tyranny of Right/Left thinking prevent intelligent men of good will from perceiving the *facts* that traditional authoritarian governments are less repressive than revolutionary autocracies, that they are more susceptible of liberalization, and that they are more compatible with the U.S. interests.[53]

Before her nomination had been approved, she said that she hoped that the foreign policy adopted by the Reagan administration would embody "a mixture of morality and power" and criticized the human rights policy of the Carter administration: "Ideals never exist in the abstract. If you try to apply it in that context, the result will be havoc." She also stated that if she had to choose between a "traditional autocrat" such as Nicaragua's Somoza or a "Cuban-backed dictatorship," she would select the former, for "there are degrees of repression."[54]

General Haig's nomination caused a certain amount of controversy, partly because of his past association with President Richard M. Nixon and Watergate and his being a career military man, but primarily because of his preoccupation with the Soviet Union and national defense. At his first press conference as secretary of state he expressed the following opinion concerning human rights: "The assurance of basic human liberties will not be improved by replacing friendly governments which incompletely satisfy our standards of democracy with hostile ones which are even less benign." He saw no need, however, to change the provisions in the Foreign Assistance Act that linked U.S. aid to human rights, for he believed that the law was "not overly restrictive."[55] In answering a question dealing with human rights and terrorism, he indicated the priorities of the new administration. After affirming that "human rights is an essential and fundamental aspect of American foreign policy and domestic policy," he declared:

And as such when you move it from the mainstream of fundamental policy making and give it an extraordinary role in organizational terms, you frequently result in distortions that probably put in jeopardy the well-meaning objective you seek to achieve. So I would like to see some organizational change in the period ahead—no de-emphasis; a change in priorities.

Now the greatest problem to me in the human rights area today is the area of *rampant international terrorism* on both sides of the Iron Curtain.[56]

The nomination of Dr. Lefever, however, provoked a great controversy that culminated in the rejection of his nomination in early June by the Senate Foreign Relations Committee and his subsequent withdrawal from consideration. His nomination by the Reagan administration to head the Bureau of Human Rights was surprising, for he was the most outspoken critic of President Carter's human rights policy in general and toward Chile, the Republic of Korea, Rhodesia (under Ian Smith), and South Africa in particular. He had published a number of articles and had testified in favor of abolishing the human rights machinery. He appeared to be the antithesis of the previous incumbent, Patricia Derian, who was a forceful and outspoken advocate of human rights in U.S. foreign policy. He had the strong support of Senator Jesse Helms (Republican, North Carolina), chairman of the Subcommittee on Western Hemisphere Affairs of the Foreign Relations Committee, who supported him to the end.

In an article published in 1978, "The Trivialization of Human Rights," Dr. Lefever identified "Six Flaws in the Human Rights Policy" of the Carter administration, the second being "confusing totalitarianism with authoritarianism."[57] He believed that the national interest justified assisting authoritarian regimes (Chile, Iran, and the Republic of Korea) while totalitarian regimes (Cambodia, Cuba, North Korea, and the Soviet Union) were the real enemies of the United States. His distinction between totalitarianism and authoritarianism has become another hallmark of the new administration. In general he saw as limited what the United States should attempt to do in promoting human rights:

> In a formal and legal sense, the . . . [U.S.] Government has no responsibility—and certainly no authority—to promote human rights in other sovereign states. . . .
> Beyond serving as a good example and maintaining our security commitments, there is little the . . . [U.S.] Government can or should do to advance human rights, other than

using quiet diplomatic channels at appropriate times and places.[58]

Before his nomination, he recommended that Congress repeal the human rights legislation. He proposed that

> the United States should remove from the statute books all clauses that establish a human rights standard or condition that must be met by another sovereign government before our government transacts normal business with it, unless specifically waived by the President.
>
> It shouldn't be necessary for any friendly state to pass a human rights test before we extend normal trade relations, before we sell arms or before we provide economic or security assistance. This approach I believe should be adopted toward adversary states like the Sovet Union.[59]

Following the vote of the Foreign Relations Committee against his confirmation in early June, he withdrew his name from consideration by the Senate.[60] The apparent failure of the Reagan administration to initiate a prompt search for another candidate suggested to some observers that the administration might leave vacant the position of assistant secretary for human rights.[61]

In late October, however, almost five months after Dr. Lefever withdrew his name, President Reagan nominated Elliot Abrams, assistant secretary of state for international organization affairs, for the position. Mr. Abrams's support of the president, for whom he had campaigned in 1980 by speaking to Jewish groups throughout the United States about Reagan's foreign policy, had come about in a way similar to that of Ambassador Kirkpatrick. Abrams had been a liberal Democrat during his law school days at Harvard University and later worked for two Democratic senators. He became disillusioned with President Carter's foreign policy, however, and switched to the Republican party.[62] His appointment was not controversial and received little press coverage. He was approved unanimously by the Senate Foreign Relations Committee in November.

The administration's stress upon national security and the apparent unlinking of human rights and foreign policy is demonstrated by a number of recent policy changes, especially concerning relations with Latin America. In keeping with the distinction between authoritarian and totalitarian governments, U.S. assistance, both economic and military, to certain military governments has been resumed. In February, the administration announced that Chile would be eligible for EXIM financing, which had been denied it since 1976. The next month President Reagan asked Congress to repeal a 1977 amendment to P.L. 95-148 that prohibited military aid and the sale of arms to Argentina. While agreeing to the request, the House Foreign Affairs Committee and the Senate Foreign Relations Committee specified that such aid should be contingent upon the president's certifying that "significant progress" in human rights had been made in Argentina.[63] Although the administration opposed this requirement, the Congress approved it. (The two committees and the Congress took a similar approach in April and May in response to the administration's $26 million military aid package to El Salvador in requiring presidential certification of progress in human rights. Secretary of State Haig presented a formal objection to these qualifications.)[64]

Although military aid was to be resumed to Argentina, the outbreak of war in the spring of 1982 between England and Argentina over the control of the Falkland/Malvinas Islands and Argentina's strong reaction against the United States for siding with England postponed indefinitely the resumption of aid.[65] Military aid was resumed, however, to Honduras and Uruguay and was strongly favored for Guatemala.

The Reagan administration's preoccupation with national security in Latin America has been especially apparent in El Salvador. The fighting between the left and the right, that is, the efforts of the Farabundo Marti Front for National Liberation to overthrow the government, has been presented as a cold war struggle in which the Soviet Union, Cuba, and the Sandinista government of Nicaragua are arming and helping the left. To document this view, the U.S. government released in February 1981 a White Paper on El Salvador, accompanied by a summary entitled *Communist Interference in El Salvador*, which was widely criticized.[66] This approach resulted in (1) the removal of President Carter's ambassador to the country, Robert White, who had stressed reform and urged the United States to pressure the government of El Salvador instead of providing it arms, (2) the denial of economic aid to Nicaragua on the ground that it was helping the left in El Salvador, and (3) an increase in military aid, training, and U.S. advisers to the Salvadoran government. Despite great controversy about the government's human rights record—and that of its rightest allies—the Reagan administration has made the required certifications that the government is "making a concerted and significant effort" concerning human rights and is "making continued progress" in the field of economic and political reforms.[67] Three certifications have been made so far—in January 1982, in July 1982, and in January 1983—and each has been widely debated and challenged by spokesmen of the human rights constituency, including Pat Derian, Elliot Abrams's predecessor.[68]

Another indication of the changing of past policies is in the development of President Reagan's arms-transfer policy. When the administration announced seven guidelines for conventional arms transfers to foreign countries, human rights was not one of them. In a speech in May 1981, James L. Buckley, deputy secretary of state for security affairs, while explaining the new arms policy, criticized President Carter's human rights and nuclear proliferation criteria as ones that had "substituted theology for a healthy sense of preservation."[69]

In early July, another policy change was announced, which involved the U.S. representatives in the multilateral lending institutions. In a proposal to the chairman of the House Subcommittee on International Development Institutions and Finance (of the Committee on Banking and Finance), the assistant secretary of the treasury for legislative affairs proposed a change in P.L. 96-259. The change would free the U.S. representatives in the World Bank and in the Inter-American Development Bank from voting against or abstaining on loans to states on grounds that they were violators of human rights, namely, on loans currently being considered to Argentina, Chile, Paraguay, and Uruguay.[70] The change in policy was justified because "there have been significant improvements in the human rights situations" in the four countries.[71] The new policy was implemented in late July 1981, thus reversing a four-year practice, when the U.S. representative to the World Bank voted in favor of two loans to Chile.

A final example of change toward human rights in foreign policy is the Reagan administration's first annual report on human rights.[72] The report's introduction articulated an approach different from that in the four preceding annual reports of the Carter administration.[73] The report stressed civil and political rights and made no mention of economic and social rights. It stated that much more attention will be given to the human rights conduct of "opposition and terrorist groups" and that "Soviet bloc human rights violations" would be regularly exposed. It also made clear that among the "instruments" for pursuing human rights, "traditional diplomacy" will be stressed along with the "criterion of effectiveness." The introduction did refer to the problem of balance and consistency, in these words:

> Since the United States will continue to seek the redress of human rights abuses even in friendly countries, human rights policy will sometimes be very troubling. We will sometimes be forced to make hard choices between the need to answer human rights violations and other foreign policy interests, such as trade or security. In some cases we will

have to accept the fact that bilateral relations with a friendly country may be damaged because of our human rights concern. This is the unavoidable price of a consistent policy.[74]

In addition to the 1981 annual report, the Reagan administration's expenditures and requests for funds for economic and military assistance also suggest a change in orientation. In relative terms, the amounts requested or expended for military aid have increased markedly, and requests and expenditures for economic development assistance and Food-for-Peace have declined.[75] Although the resignation of Secretary of State Haig in June 1981 and his replacement the next month by George P. Shultz, who was approved unanimously by the Senate Foreign Relations Committee, have resulted in a decline of cold war rhetoric, it is too early to note any shifts or to be able to characterize Secretary Shultz's approach. It does appear, however, that human rights concerns are being "factored in" more than previously. It has been reported that Secretary Shultz did visit the Human Rights Office shortly after his appointment and indicated his personal commitment to human rights; he has also increased Mr. Abrams's staff.[76]

Conclusion

In answering the question posed in the introduction, whether human rights would move from the center of the stage back to the wings, certain qualifications are necessary. First, the experience of the Carter administration revealed that human rights were at center stage primarily at the rhetorical level and that they remained there so far as attempts at policy implementation were concerned only during the first eighteen months of his incumbency. After 1978 the rhetoric and practice were greatly modified; the former was curtailed because it was increasingly difficult to translate it into policy. Second, human rights as a policy during the Carter administration moved from receiving great emphasis to being "factored into" the foreign policy decision-making process. The Reagan administration's comparatively limited rhetorical commitment to human rights in U.S. foreign policy and much greater stress upon national security and the threat posed by the Soviet Union suggest less concern with the former. In his first two years, President Reagan indicated certain changes in the U.S. stand on human rights, principally a preference for unlinking foreign assistance from human rights and for quiet diplomacy. These changes illustrate an important question of foreign policy, which came forth during the 1980 campaign: How should human rights be balanced with other considerations in U.S. foreign policy? What, for example, is the proper balance or equilibrium between human rights and national security in U.S. foreign policy? Is it possible to reconcile the two?

This is a difficult question to answer in practice, for the balance can never be fixed or permanent, but is a constantly shifting mixture of the many facets of a state's foreign policy, which respond to the changing needs of the state and the challenges confronting it. Obviously, there are priorities, and national security must transcend all others if the very existence and survival of a state is in jeopardy. If survival is not at stake, human rights have an important place, particularly in the foreign policy of a state that is a superpower, a world leader, and one that has a democratic and representative system of government. Because of the nature of foreign policy, the shifting priorities, and the constant balancing and tuning required, there can be no consistent policy for dealing with human rights according to a fixed priority. The particular balance is a function of the circumstances in each case. For this reason double standards are inevitable. Certainly the national interest can be harmed by a preoccupation with human rights or with national security (unless survival is at stake), and the problem for the United States as a democracy and a superpower is the proper foreign policy equilibrium. Finally, the proper balance between human rights and national security to be achieved and translated into foreign policy will continue to pose a constant dilemma for the United States. It is likely that human rights "will continue to be an element of future American foreign policy," one of varying and limited priority, but one that "will continue to receive [some] attention in the policy-making process."[77] But there will be a much more restrained public articulation of a commitment to human rights in U.S. foreign policy.

Notes

1. Kenneth W. Thompson, ed., *The Moral Imperatives of Human Rights: A World Survey* (Washington, D.C.: University Press of America, 1980), p. 17.

2. Richard B. Lillich, "A United States Policy of Humanitarian Intervention and Intercession," in *Human Rights and American Foreign Policy*, ed. Donald T. Kommers and Gilburt D. Loescher (Notre Dame, Ind.: University of Notre Dame Press, 1979), p. 279.

3. There have been a number of recent books on human rights and U.S. foreign policy, some of them with identical titles. C. Beitz, *Human Rights and Foreign Policy: The Problem of Priorities* (College Park: University

of Maryland, 1978); Tom J. Farer, ed., *Toward a Humanitarian Diplomacy: A Primer for Policy* (New York: New York University Press, 1980); Kommers and Loescher, *Human Rights and American Foreign Policy*; Peter G. Brown and Douglas MacLean, eds., *Human Rights and U.S. Foreign Policy: Principles and Applications* (Lexington, Mass.: D.C. Heath & Company, 1979); Barry M. Rubin and Elizabeth P. Spiro, eds., *Human Rights and U.S. Foreign Policy* (Boulder, Colo.: Westview Press, 1979); and Sandy Vogelgesang, *American Dream, Global Nightmare: The Dilemma of U.S. Human Rights Policy* (New York: W. W. Norton & Company, 1980).

4. Statement by Professor Tom Farer quoted by Richard Lillich in "A U.S. Policy of Humanitarian Intervention," p. 278.

5. "Human Rights in the World Community: A Call for U.S. Leadership," 93d Cong., 2d sess. (1974), p. 13.

6. Quoted in Roberta Cohen, "Human Rights Decision-Making in the Executive Branch: Some Proposals for a Coordinated Strategy," in Kommers and Loescher, *Human Rights and American Foreign Policy*, p. 217.

7. Library of Congress, Congressional Research Service, *Human Rights and U.S. Foreign Assistance: Experiences and Issues in Policy Implementation (1977–1978)*, Report prepared for the Committee on Foreign Relations, United States Senate, 96th Cong., 1st sess. (1979), p. 17 (emphasis added). For an excellent discussion of the legislation, see, in addition to the Library of Congress report, pp. 16–29, Tom Harkin, "Human Rights and Foreign Aid: Forging an Unbreakable Link," in Brown and MacLean, *Human Rights and U.S. Foreign Policy*, pp. 15–26. For a list of all the pertinent legislation, see William Buckley, "Human Rights and Foreign Policy," *Foreign Affairs*, vol. 58 (Spring 1980), pp. 784–85.

8. Library of Congress, *Human Rights and U.S. Foreign Assistance*, p. 18.

9. In early 1974, there was only one full-time human rights officer in the executive branch—in the State Department's Bureau of International Organization Affairs. His duties involved the preparation of the government's position on human rights at the United Nations. The next officer added was in the legal adviser's office. For the background to the creation of the Human Rights Office, see John D. Martz and Lars Schoultz, eds., *Latin America, the United States, and the Inter-American System* (Boulder, Colo.: Westview Press, 1980), p. 187. For the expansion of the human rights machinery, see Cohen, "Human Rights Decision-Making," pp. 219–21.

10. Library of Congress, *Human Rights and U.S. Foreign Assistance*, p. 20.

11. A joint resolution is subject to the veto, which can be overridden by a two-thirds vote; a concurrent resolution requires a simple majority vote and is not subject to the veto.

12. Quoted in Martz and Schoultz, *Latin America, the United States, and the Inter-American System*, p. 176. Once Secretary Kissinger was out

of office, however, he presented his original and preferred position. Ibid., p. 177.

13. Quoted in Cohen, "Human Rights Decision-Making," p. 222.

14. U.S. Department of State, "Humane Purposes in Foreign Policy," News Release, May 22, 1977, p. 2.

15. Cohen, "Human Rights Decision-Making," pp. 222–23.

16. U.S. Department of State, "Arms, Economic Prosperity, and Human Rights," News Release, March 17, 1977, pp. 3–4. The new Section 502B in the Foreign Assistance Act of 1974 included language regarding U.S. "international obligations as set forth in the Charter of the United Nations."

17. Two leading scholars in international law, the late Professor Hans Kelsen and Judge Philip Jessup, had opposing views about the legal status of articles 55 and 56 of the United Nations Charter. While the former held that they were not legally binding, the latter held that they were. Hans Kelsen, *Principles of International Law,* 2d ed. (New York: Holt, Rinehart and Winston, 1966), pp. 226, 237; Philip C. Jessup, *A Modern Law of Nations* (New York: Columbia University Press, 1948), p. 91. And the United States, applying its distinction between self-executing and non-self-executing treaties, maintains that the Charter is *not* a self-executing treaty, which means that the human rights provisions require implementing legislation by the Congress. Traditional international law provides that a "declaration" does not impose a legally binding duty; instead, it is a moral obligation.

18. Thomas Buergenthal, "Domestic Jurisdiction, Intervention, and Human Rights: The International Law Perspective," in Brown and MacLean, *Human Rights and U.S. Foreign Policy,* pp. 111–20; and Lillich, "A U.S. Policy of Humanitarian Intervention," pp. 278–98.

19. The treaties drafted by the United Nations in the 1950s and 1960s are the following: Convention on the Political Rights of Woman; Convention on the Abolition of Slavery; Convention on the Status of Refugees; Convention on the Elimination of All Forms of Racial Discrimination; Covenant on Civil and Political Rights; and Covenant on Economic, Social, and Cultural Rights. All these treaties are in effect; the United States has ratified the first three.

20. In addition to the Genocide Convention, which has been before the Senate since the early 1950s, President Carter asked the Senate to consider four additional treaties: the UN Covenant on Civil and Political Rights; the UN Covenant on Economic, Social, and Cultural Rights; the UN Convention on the Elimination of All Forms of Racial Discrimination; and the American Convention on Human Rights (this convention went into effect in 1978).

21. In his 1978 letter of transmittal of four treaties to the Senate—the convention on racial discrimination, the two covenants on human rights, and the American Convention on Human Rights—President Carter, who had signed the last three in 1977, stated the following: "It is increasingly

anomalous that the list of parties [to the two covenants on human rights and the covenant on racial discrimination] does not include the United States, whose human rights record domestically and internationally has long served as an example to the world community." He proposed to the Senate that certain articles in the two covenants on human rights be classified as non-self-executing. U.S. Congress, Senate, *Four Treaties Pertaining to Human Rights: Message from the President of the United States Transmitting* . . . , 95th Cong., 2d sess. (1978), pp. v–vi, viii, x, xii, xv.

22. U.S. Department of State, Press Release, May 22, 1977, pp. 1, 3.

23. Concerning the development of the human rights bureaucracy, see Cohen, "Human Rights Decision-Making," pp. 226–36; and Library of Congress, *Human Rights and U.S. Foreign Assistance*, pp. 31–42.

24. Library of Congress, *Human Rights and U.S. Foreign Assistance*, p. 21.

25. Ibid., pp. 21–22. In carrying out the legislation applicable to the U.S. representatives to the multilateral institutions, the administration interpreted the words "to oppose" to include abstentions. See Elizabeth P. Spiro, "Front Door or Back Stairs: U.S. Human Rights Policy in the International Financial Institutions," in Rubin and Spiro, *Human Rights and U.S. Foreign Policy*, p. 137.

26. Quoted in Rubin and Spiro, *Human Rights and U.S. Foreign Policy*, p. 136.

27. Ibid., p. 146.

28. Mr. McNamara's reference above to the "Charter" meant the bank's Articles of Agreement, which prohibit political considerations from being taken into account in extending loans (article 4, section 10); the bank relies upon economic and technical criteria.

29. Sandra Vogelgesang, "What Price Principle? U.S. Policy on Human Rights," *Foreign Affairs*, vol. 56, no. 4 (July 1978), p. 833.

30. See Ernst B. Haas, "Human Rights: To Act or Not to Act?" in *Eagle Entangled: U.S. Foreign Policy in a Complex World*, ed. Kenneth A. Oye, Donald Rothchild, and Robert J. Lieber (New York: Longman, 1979), pp. 182–92; Library of Congress, *Human Rights and U.S. Foreign Assistance*, pp. 47–67; Abraham M. Sirkin, "Can a Human Rights Policy Be Consistent?" in Brown and MacLean, *Human Rights and U.S. Foreign Policy*, pp. 199–213; and Cohen, "Human Rights Decision-Making," pp. 224–25.

31. Stanley Hoffman, *Foreign Policy* (Winter 1977), pp. 3–26. For another very critical article, see Buckley, "Human Rights and Foreign Policy," pp. 775–96.

32. Vogelgesang, *American Dream.*

33. Charles Frankel, "Human Rights and Foreign Policy," *Headline Series*, vol. 241 (October 1978), p. 54.

34. U.S. Department of State, News Release, May 22, 1977, pp. 2–3.

35. Haas, "Human Rights," pp. 169, 185, 193. See also Hoffmann, "Hell of Good Intentions."

36. U.S. Department of State, "The Secretary of State, Speech: Human Rights Policy," Press Release, April 30, 1977, p. 1. Secretary Vance stated later in his speech: "In pursuing a human rights policy, we must always keep in mind the limits of our power and of our wisdom. A sure formula for defeat of our goals would be a rigid, hubristic attempt to impose our values on others. A doctrinaire plan of action would be as damaging as indifference."

37. Lars Schoultz, "U.S. Diplomacy and Human Rights in Latin America," in Martz and Schoultz, *Latin America, the U.S., and the Inter-American System*, p. 174.

38. Most of these cases are drawn from ibid., pp. 181–83, 195–97.

39. Ibid., p. 182.

40. "OAS Votes for Ouster of Somoza," *Washington Post*, June 24, 1979.

41. Schoultz, "U.S. Diplomacy and Human Rights in Latin America," p. 183.

42. Ibid., p. 196.

43. Library of Congress, *Human Rights and U.S. Foreign Assistance*, p. 82. Concerning bureaucratic politics, see Spiro, "Front Door or Back Stairs," pp. 134–35.

44. Some of the groups in the coalition are the following: Americans for Democratic Action; American Friends Service Committee; Center for International Policy; Clergy and Laity Concerned; National Council of Churches; Washington Office on Africa; Washington Office on Latin America.

45. See above and footnotes 17, 18, and 19.

46. Richard B. Bilder, "The Status of International Human Rights Law: An Overview," in *International Human Rights Law and Practice: The Roles of the United Nations, the Private Sector, the Government, and Their Lawyers*, ed. James C. Tuttle (Philadelphia: American Bar Association, 1978), p. 3.

47. Ibid., p. 7.

48. Sei Fujii v. State of California, 1952; for text, see *American Journal of International Law*, vol. 46 (July 1952), pp. 559–73.

49. See, for example, Bilder, "Status of International Human Rights Law," pp. 3–8.

50. *Congressional Quarterly Weekly Report*, vol. 38 (October–December 1980), p. 3284.

51. Ibid., p. 3353.

52. *Commentary* (November 1979), p. 42.

53. Ibid., p. 44.

54. "Envoy-Designate Would Be Selective with Aid to U.N.," *Washington Post*, January 8, 1981.

55. "Haig Says Teheran Will Not Get Arms. . . . Secretary of State at First News Conference Accuses Soviets of Promoting Terrorism," *New York Times,* January 29, 1981.

56. "Excerpts from Haig's Remarks at First News Conference as Secretary of State," *New York Times,* January 29, 1981 (emphasis added).

57. *Policy Review,* no. 3 (Winter 1978), p. 16.

58. Ibid., pp. 23–24.

59. U.S. Congress, House of Representatives, *Human Rights and U.S. Foreign Policy: Hearings before the Subcommittee on International Organizations of the Committee on Foreign Affairs,* 96th Cong., 1st sess., May 10, June 11, July 12, and August 2, 1979, p. 218.

60. "Panel Rejects Lefever by 13–4," *Washington Star,* June 5, 1981. The human rights constituency opposed him and influenced his rejection. See "Human Rights Community Expresses Concern over Lefever Nomination to State Department Post," Press Release of Ad-Hoc Committee of the Human Rights Community, February 24, 1981. In early July, it was announced that Dr. Lefever would serve as a consultant to Secretary Haig on terrorism, counterterrorism, and nuclear and nonproliferation issues. "Lefever Sworn In as Consultant to Haig," *Washington Post,* July 4, 1981.

61. "Demise of Human Rights Post May Result from Senate Panel's Rejection of Lefever," *Wall Street Journal,* June 8, 1981; "Reagan Weighs Plan to Abolish State Department Human Rights Office," *Washington Star,* July 7, 1981. Senator Howard Baker, the majority leader, and Senator Jesse Helms spoke in favor of abolishing the position.

62. *New York Times,* November 5, 1981; October 19, 1982.

63. Washington Office on Latin America, *Latin America Update* (May/June 1981), p. 1.

64. Ibid., pp. 3–4.

65. The war over the Falkland/Malvinas Islands was precipitated by Argentina's invasion and occupation in early April 1982 and by England's efforts to retake the islands. The United States announced its neutral position in the dispute, and Secretary of State Haig engaged in shuttle diplomacy in an effort to mediate. At the end of April, however, the United States sided with England. Argentina bitterly attacked the United States for this action and held it responsible for England's victory in June. Since that time the Reagan administration has been working to normalize and to improve relations with Argentina.

66. The summary was published by the Department of State, Bureau of Public Affairs, as Special Report No. 80, February 23, 1981. Critical evaluations of the validity of the White Paper were published June 8, 1981, in the *Wall Street Journal* and the *Washington Post.*

67. For the five criteria for certification, see U.S. Congress, House of Representatives, *Presidential Certification on El Salvador (volume 1): Hearings before the Subcommittee on Inter-American Affairs of the Com-*

mittee on Foreign Affairs, 97th Cong., 2d sess., February 2, 23, 25, and March 2, 1982 (1982), pp. 2–3.

68. The first two certifications prompted hearings before the Subcommittee on Inter-American Affairs in which both critics and defenders presented their views. Two volumes of hearings resulted; the testimony contained in ibid., volume 2, was presented in June, July, and August 1982.

69. "Administration Reiterates Aim of Scuttling Carter Rights Policies," *Washington Post*, July 10, 1981.

70. "U.S. Ends Opposition to Loans to Repressive Latin Regimes," *Washington Post*, July 9, 1981.

71. Ibid. In an eight-page "Press Guidance" paper prepared by the State Department, it was stated that "it is important to give a positive signal to Chile in terms of further improvement."

72. U.S. Congress, *Country Reports on Human Rights Practices For 1981: Report Submitted to the Committee on Foreign Affairs, U.S. House of Representatives, and the Committee on Foreign Relations, U.S. Senate, by the Department of State, February 1982*, 97th Cong., 2d sess. (1982). This report resulted in congressional hearings in which leading critics and defenders appeared, including Elliot Abrams. U.S. Congress, House of Representatives, *Review of State Department Country Reports on Human Rights Practices for 1971: Hearing before the Subcommittee on Human Rights and International Organizations of the Committee on Foreign Affairs*, 97th Cong., 2d sess., April 28, 1982.

73. U.S. Congress, *Country Reports*, pp. 1–11.

74. Ibid., p. 9.

75. For comparative figures and foreign aid charts for fiscal years 1978–1983, see Washington Office on Latin America, *U.S. Assistance to Latin America*, Occasional Paper no. 2 (May 1982).

76. *New York Times*, October 19, 1982.

77. Howard Warshowsky, "The Department of State and Human Rights Policy: A Case Study of the Human Rights Bureau," *World Affairs*, vol. 142, no. 3 (Winter 1980), p. 213.

9

Arms Control:
The Regional Alternative

JAMES H. WOLFE

The global theme of the Special Session of the United Nations General Assembly on Disarmament (1978), underscoring the long-term efforts of the United States to halt the proliferation of nuclear weapons, has led to the assumption that the expression "arms control" applies principally to worldwide endeavors to limit the production and deployment of the means of mass destruction first used at the end of World War II. The purpose of this essay is primarily to explore an alternative approach to arms control and secondarily to suggest in conclusion some structural reasons why the regional option fails to attract the attention it might otherwise merit.

During periods of Cold War and détente, U.S. policy has emphasized the conclusion of universal agreements designed to cope with the nuclear problem. The Nuclear Non-Proliferation Treaty (1968) is a successful example of this kind of diplomatic initiative. Conversely, steps designed to achieve arms control through incremental, regional arrangements have received comparatively low priority. If it is true, as Henry Kissinger has suggested, that the struggle for bureaucratic consensus may well produce a rigidity of policy, the structures and outlook developed in accordance with the global concern with arms control have obscured the advantages of spatially limited but often more realistic undertakings at the regional level.[1]

The author wishes to express his appreciation to the Institute for Sino-Soviet Studies of the George Washington University for its support of this project.

Terminology

The profusion of terms relating to disarmament and arms control necessitates a cursory review of concepts by way of introducing the pros and cons of regional accords.

Disarmament: the general and universal elimination of armed forces. Historically, plans to bring into being a world without armaments have possessed a utopian character detached from the reality of power politics. The air of idealism in which the Disarmament Conference (1932) of the League of Nations took place is illustrative of the point, and the comprehensive program sought by the United Nations Committee on Disarmament similarly remains an elusive goal.

Arms control: the effort either to restrict the expansion of armed forces or to prevent the deployment of new types of weaponry. In this instance the purpose is one both of reducing the probability of war and of limiting its impact. Thucydides described the classic instance in his discussion of the bipolar setting of the Peloponnesian War (431–404 B.C.) when he wrote that the Athenian decision to expand the city's fortifications contributed to an outbreak of hostilities with Sparta, for the latter regarded the mutual vulnerability of the two powers to attack as a form of security.[2] The assumption undergirding the treaty that limits antiballistic missile systems operated by the United States and the Soviet Union (1972) is analogous.

Arms reduction: an approach to arms control through the imposition of ceilings on the human and material resources devoted to military programs. The force ratio of 5:5:3 established by the Washington Naval Conference (1921–1922) for the capital ships of the American, British, and Japanese navies offers a prime example of the application of this technique of arms control. Similarly, the Treaty of Alliance signed by Cyprus, Greece, and Turkey in 1960 set a ratio of 3:2 governing the stationing of Greek and Turkish contingents, respectively, in the territory of the Republic of Cyprus. In 1974, the agreement reached in Vladivostok by President Gerald R. Ford and General Secretary Leonid I. Brezhnev also posited an arithmetic relationship regarding the total number of missiles to be available to each government. Multilateral efforts to impose cuts on the size of forces confronting each other in Central Europe similarly typify a regional application of the concept of arms reduction.

Arms limitation: a variation of disarmament related to reduction of arms but emphasizing, instead of levels of forces, the prohibition of specified types of weaponry or, alternatively, the narrowing of the definition of "military necessity" so that given categories of persons or property would not be subject to attack. The Geneva Protocol (1925), which prohibited the first use on the battlefield of poisonous gases and bacteriological agents, is representative of arms limitation in the outlawing of specific weapons. The Hague Convention (1904), which exempted hospital ships from attack, and the subsequent convention stipulating the rights and duties of neutrals in time of war (1907) illustrate the practice of endeavoring to remove certain groups from the zone of combat. The Geneva conventions (1929 and 1949) placed the sick, the wounded, and prisoners of war *hors de combat* and continued the tradition of arms limitation begun by the medieval Peace of God, which had protected the clergy and its property. The Treaty of Tlatelolco (1967) provided for the creation of a nuclear-weapon-free zone in Latin America and is a continuing example of arms limitation at the regional level.

Disengagement: a term popularized by George F. Kennan during the late 1950s, which refers to a reciprocal withdrawal or scaling down of armed forces throughout a region. The Gaitskell Plan (1957) was an early effort directed toward disengagement throughout Central Europe.[3] The assumption that a progressive imposition of ceilings on forces would induce a reduction in East-West tension failed to attract international support until 1973, when talks on mutual and balanced force reduction (MBFR) opened in Vienna. Closely related to disengagement is the practice of exchanging teams of observers to report on maneuvers of potentially hostile forces. The Helsinki Agreement (1975) provides for prior notification of maneuvers by forces of the North Atlantic Treaty Organization (NATO) or the Warsaw Pact as well as for the exchange of military observers by the two alliances. The further clarification of foreign policy objectives through the exchange of information by means of a hot line offers an additional variation on the theme of arms control.

Drawing upon the foregoing definitions, a model of a regional arrangement for arms control would possess the following structural characteristics: Arms reduction in such a setting could take the form of an across-the-board cut paring down the military capability of opposing coalitions. In addition to quantitative restrictions, a qualitative approach in the form of arms limitation affecting a particular mode of warfare is a logical complement. Specific types of weaponry classified as "offensive" rather than "defensive," for example, might be banned from the region covered by the treaty. The term "disengagement" offers policy makers a variety of options suited to local conditions. From the standpoint of pragmatic diplomatic bargaining the varying nature of regional arms-control agreements is undoubtedly an asset. Globally, however, this lack of uniformity may entail some complications.

Regional arrangements in international law derive support from both the Charter of the United Nations and localized collective-security agreements, such as the Charter of the Organization of American States (OAS; 1948). Explicit in the definition of the OAS and similar security communities is the proscription of the use of violence by one member against another; a limitation of this order on state power is in itself an institutionalized form of arms control. Basically, international law requires that a regional system not imperil the integrity of any given state, nor may it conflict with existing obligations of the signatory governments. Stated as principles, these stipulations appear straightforward enough, but in practice they are not always easy to realize. Most governments are unwilling to qualify their right to individual or collective self-defense, as guaranteed to all members of the United Nations under article 51 of the charter.

Case Studies

Efforts on the part of the United States to further the goal of arms control through regional agreements are numerous. The Rush-Bagot agreement (1817) between the United States and Great Britain led to the eventual demilitarization of the Great Lakes. The Antarctic Treaty (1959) offers a contemporary example of a local imposition of arms limitation as specified in article 1(1):

> Antarctica shall be used for peaceful purposes only. There shall be prohibited, inter alia, any measures of a military nature, such as the establishment of military bases and fortifications, the carrying out of military maneuvers, as well as the testing of any type of weapons.

Although the treaty does not cover all phases of activities in support of scientific research, such as possible intelligence gathering, the restrictions imposed on what a government may do are extensive. Because territorial claims on the continent are not recognized internationally, the legal status of Antarctica is analogous to that of celestial bodies, and the Antarctic Treaty is indeed a concomitant of the Outer Space Treaty (1967). Yet the Antarctic model may also be potentially important as an analogue of arms-control endeavors on other continents. Arms-control efforts in Central Europe, Latin America, the Middle East, and the Indian Ocean are possible examples.

Central Europe

Speaking in East Berlin on October 6, 1979, General Secretary Leonid Brezhnev raised the specter of nuclear war, then dramatically proposed a unilateral reduction of arms through the withdrawal from East Germany of 20,000 Soviet troops along with 1,000 tanks and other unspecified weapons.[4] Taking military realities into account, notably the buildup of Soviet theater nuclear weapons, the foreign and defense ministers of NATO, meeting in Brussels on December 12, elected to pursue two parallel policies: the modernization of the Atlantic alliance's own nuclear forces and, simultaneously, the initiation of negotiations directed toward an arms-control agreement for Central Europe.[5] Contingent upon Soviet capabilities and intentions in Europe and elsewhere, the West would retain its freedom of response. The subsequent Soviet intervention in Afghanistan validated this dualistic approach.

This sequence of challenge and response constitutes a recognizable pattern, which has been repeated several times since the de facto partitioning of Germany in the late 1940s. Faced with the possibility of West German rearmament as part of the Western reaction to the Korean conflict, Marshal Josef Stalin announced in 1952 that his government would assent to the political unification of the four Allied zones of occupation provided that the resultant state would be both neutralized and demilitarized. The Western Allies, reflecting the tensions of the classic Cold War period, rejected this note and pursued instead the ill-fated plan for a European Defense Community, which was tabled by the French National Assembly in 1954. After this temporary setback, the rearmament of the Federal Republic of Germany took place initially under the aegis of the Western European Union (1954) and culminated in the accession of the republic to the North Atlantic Treaty the following year.

The proposal to incorporate West Germany into the Western alliance prompted the Soviet Union to respond initially with a draft for a regional European system of collective security. As it became apparent that the political conditions attached to this initiative were unacceptable to the West, the Soviets sponsored a counterpart to NATO—the Warsaw Pact, which was proclaimed in 1955. The preceding year, at a conference of foreign ministers in Berlin, the Soviet delegation had put forward a plan for disengagement in the four zones of Germany coupled with the commencement of negotiations leading to a European security treaty.[6] Western governments were quick to stress the military inequity implicit in a disengagement scheme limited to Germany. Then, as now, Western thinking posited

213

a balanced geographical framework of arms reduction which would extend beyond Germany and into Eastern Europe. The Soviet initiative was too narrow in scope.

Speaking at a Warsaw conference of Eastern European governments in May 1955, Premier Nikolai A. Bulganin again linked the solution of the German question to a general conference on European security questions.[7] Two months later the heads of government of the four powers occupying sectors of Berlin met in Geneva and once again declared their willingness to effect the political reunification of Germany. Prime Minister Anthony Eden pointedly identified the chief problem confronting the conferees as the "unity of Germany." He proposed that a series of interrelated steps be taken on the German question so as to relieve the confrontation in Berlin and

> to make a practical experiment in the operative control of armaments. This, if locally successful in Europe, might, as it were, extend outwards from the centre to the periphery. If we can once establish a sense of security over the Continent of Europe—if we can create an effective system to reduce tensions here—can we not hope that this first success will be the preliminary for wider and more far-reaching understanding?[8]

The Eden Plan for the gradual and reciprocal reduction of armaments in Central Europe and the establishment of a system of control through inspection went considerably beyond Soviet initiatives both in geographic terms and in degree of verification. Above all, the concept of translating a local effort into a universal design for the relaxation of international tensions found its realization in the Austrian State Treaty (1955) and helped to stimulate the arms-control proposals of the Polish government.

Austrian State Treaty

In 1943, at a meeting of foreign ministers in Moscow, Eden had persuaded his American and Soviet counterparts, Cordell Hull and V. M. Molotov, to accept a declaration that the annexation of Austria by Germany in 1938 was null and void and that an independent Austrian Republic should be reestablished after the war. At the termination of hostilities the Red Army had occupied Vienna, and under Soviet auspices a provisional Austrian government took office. Like Germany, Austria was divided into four zones of occupation administered respectively by France, Great Britain, the Soviet Union, and the United States. Unlike Germany, Austria had a unified government that was able to function throughout the zones, with the result that the constitutional unity of the republic was never disrupted. After ten years of occupation the wartime Allies withdrew, thereby allowing Austria to rejoin the international community as a sovereign state.

The legal instrument that restored sovereignty to the republic was the Austrian State Treaty of May 1955. The occupying powers guaranteed independence and territorial integrity to Austria in return for self-imposed measures of arms control. Specifically, Austria committed itself to producing neither nuclear nor biological weapons and to denying these to her armed forces, along with all weapons of mass destruction, torpedoes and torpedo boats, naval mines, and artillery with an effective range greater than eighteen miles. The Austrian parliament promulgated a resolution obligating the republic to a foreign policy of neutrality, thereby complementing the military stipulations of the treaty with a necessary political statement. The combined result of the treaty and the resolution was to place Austria in a position of armed neutrality and to establish a model, albeit a limited one, of disengagement.

On May 18, 1955, three days after the signing of the Austrian State Treaty, President Dwight D. Eisenhower observed at a press conference,

> there seems to be developing the thought that there might be built up a series of neutralized states from north to south through Europe.
>
> Now, remember this: in the agreement of the neutralization of Austria, it does not mean a disarmed Austria. It is not a blank, it is not a military blank. It is on the order of Switzerland.[9]

A week later Secretary of State John Foster Dulles interpreted the president's remarks as applying solely to the countries of east-central Europe exclusive of Germany.[10] Given this limitation, neither the Eden Plan nor the proposals advanced by Bulganin would reach the stage of serious negotiation.

Eisenhower's comment may well have been prompted by the realization that Austria, along with Finland, might constitute a basis for a series of neutralized states running through Central Europe. The 1947 peace treaty between Finland and the Allies placed limitations on the size of Finnish armed forces and was accompanied by a political understanding whereby neutrality was the guarantee of independence. Finland accordingly did not become a member of the Warsaw Pact, and the Finnish adjustment to the reality of competition

215

among the superpowers added a new expression to the vocabulary of disengagement—"Finlandization." The 1981 suggestion by Brezhnev to Willy Brandt, president of the Socialist International and architect of West Germany's policy of reconciliation with Eastern Europe, for the creation of a five-country nuclear-weapon-free zone in Scandinavia is an extension of Finlandization. Notably, the area in question included neither Soviet territory nor waters adjacent to it.

To speculate on the reasons for the failure of the Austrian model to attract support outside of Scandinavia leads one to reflect on the implications of the asymmetry of forces at the disposal of the rival alliances. The members of NATO rightly recognized the projected military vacuum in Central Europe as a source of destabilization, and they rejected plans leading to the further weakening of their military position. But beyond the immediate considerations of strategy was the belief that the true goal of arms control was to prevent nuclear proliferation. This, in turn, required a global focus. Accordingly, a commitment to a worldwide concept of arms reduction, uniformly applied, was to overshadow in American thinking the more limited continental designs of the chancelleries of Europe. The exploitation of the difference between European and American spatial images associated with arms control is periodically a tactic of Soviet foreign policy. Nevertheless, the United States must recognize the needs of its allies and make an effort to develop the regional alternative to a global solution. Such flexibility was not characteristic of the United States in its reaction to the next major initiative toward disengagement.

The Rapacki Plan

In October 1957, the Polish foreign minister, Adam Rapacki, called upon the General Assembly of the United Nations to work toward the creation of a nuclear-weapon-free zone in Central Europe. The following February he conferred with the ambassadors of the United States, Great Britain, Canada, and Denmark along with those of the Soviet Union, Czechoslovakia, and East Germany. (West Germany did not then have formal diplomatic ties with Poland.) At this stage Rapacki elaborated his proposal to the General Assembly and stressed the need for regionalism as the correct approach to arms limitation. The nuclear powers were to agree through a multilateral treaty that they would deploy neither nuclear weapons nor support troops in the territories of the two German states, Poland, and Czechoslovakia. With respect to arms limitation the signatories would further commit themselves not to direct nuclear weapons toward objectives in the aforementioned states. Implementation and verification of the agreement would rest with an international control organ, whose staff would include not only representatives of the NATO and Warsaw Pact alliances, but also observers from nonaligned governments.[11]

The State Department and the Foreign Office responded by suggesting that the Security Council take up the question of disarmament. The exchange of views over the appropriate venue for discussions of arms control and the Western emphasis on general disarmament precluded extensive consideration of the Polish proposals. Undaunted, Rapacki formulated successive amendments through which he sought to cope with Western objections. He conceded the linkage between nuclear and conventional forces for purposes of arms control and suggested accordingly that his plan be implemented in two phases. Initially, the major powers would agree to freeze the nuclear arms available to them in the proposed zone, and the nonnuclear members of the opposing alliance systems would renounce all intention of acquiring these weapons. In the second phase the process of denuclearization would be fulfilled without qualification and in conjunction with a bilateral reduction of conventional forces.

The Anglo-American response again reflected considerable skepticism and stressed that Rapacki had failed to take into account legitimate Western security interests. To be acceptable, the plan would have had to encompass Eastern Europe as well as Central Europe. The pointed omission of the European republics of the Soviet Union plus Hungary from the nuclear-free zone undoubtedly constituted the principal objection of the West to the revised proposal. Furthermore, the State Department expressed doubts about the feasibility of a reliable system of verification.[12] In the face of these criticisms the Rapacki Plan ceased to attract diplomatic interest.

Fifteen years were to elapse before the United States and its European allies again treated the concept of arms control in a European framework as an important policy initiative. Confronted with domestic pressures for a unilateral reduction of armed forces in the aftermath of the intervention of the United States in Vietnam, an influential faction in the Senate, led by Mike Mansfield, endeavored to persuade the Congress to adopt a budgetary restriction on the level of forces stationed in the Federal Republic of Germany. The administrations of both Lyndon Johnson and Richard Nixon successfully opposed the movement for a unilateral cutback, thereby illustrating the difficulty inherent in formulating foreign policy by statute. Although the congressional initiative lost its momentum, funding continues to be provided for the support of diplomatic efforts to negotiate balanced arms reductions in Europe.

Mutual and Balanced Force Reduction

The national security policy of the United States contains an apparent contradiction regarding Central Europe, for it both stresses an expansion of NATO's capability to counter a hypothetical attack by the armies of the Warsaw Pact and also elevates to a major policy goal the need for a graduated reduction of international tension through a scaling down of opposing forces. Negotiations for mutual and balanced force reduction (MBFR) constitute the principal effort to achieve the second goal. Begun in Vienna in 1973, these talks are still in progress, but they have scarcely gone beyond the stage of diplomatic exploration.

The members of NATO that are directly participating in the MBFR talks include Belgium, Canada, the Federal Republic of Germany, Great Britain, Luxembourg, the Netherlands, and the United States. In conjunction with Czechoslovakia, the German Democratic Republic, and Poland, the Soviet Union represents the Warsaw Pact. Involved in the negotiating process are both the states of the reductions area—the Benelux countries, the Germanys, Czechoslovakia, and Poland—and those whose location on the periphery of this zone gives them a strategic interest in the discussions. Acting on behalf of the North Atlantic Council, an ad hoc group serves as the negotiating unit for NATO. In addition, the governments of the Atlantic alliance confer bilaterally with each other and, as the need arises, with the Soviet Union. The profusion of structures and the resultant complexity in lines of communication make negotiations on MBFR cumbersome at best.

In December 1979, Western negotiators outlined a two-phase plan calling initially for a reduction in ground forces by 13,000 U.S. troops and 30,000 Soviet troops in conjunction with the establishment of such confidence-building measures as verification and warning procedures. In the projected second phase the type and extent of reductions were left open. The following July spokesmen for the Warsaw Pact responded with a counterproposal encompassing a reduction ratio of 13,000 to 20,000, with the understanding that the Soviet quota would be over and above whatever forces were withdrawn from East Germany as a result of Brezhnev's 1979 announcement. The Eastern proposal also contained a provision to the effect that no single national contingent in NATO should exceed 50 percent of the alliance's total manpower, but references to confirmed data on levels of forces and to inspection for purposes of verification were lacking.[13]

Earlier discussions had already highlighted the difficulty of achieving a parity of forces in an asymmetrical setting. The original concept of the Warsaw Pact was that of a three-phase program under which both sides would reduce their air and ground strength by 17 percent. Since the result of these "balanced" cutbacks would be to fix the disequilibrium between the two alliances, the NATO powers rejected the Soviet formula. In June 1978, the Soviet Union and its allies modified their position and accepted the notion of a trade-off of Soviet tanks for U.S. nuclear warheads provided that all governments involved acknowledge as definitive the information on order of battle supplied by the Warsaw Pact—a stipulation that precluded further consideration of the idea.

Negotiations on MBFR are focused primarily on the questions of (1) securing reliable information on the strength of opposing commands, (2) setting ceilings on levels of forces, and (3) arriving at a formula for the progressive reduction of rival armies and air forces. It is notable that neither side has introduced the concept of arms limitation, which was the centerpiece of the Rapacki Plan. The exclusive emphasis on reduction of arms has contributed to an imbroglio in which the negotiators are unable either to agree on the extent of the forces available to the two alliances or to set a ratio of nuclear weapons to armored vehicles, which is a prerequisite for the implementation of the first phase of MBFR. The insistence of the Warsaw Pact governments on the need to impose special restrictions on certain national actors, such as the Federal Republic of Germany, further complicates the issue, because the NATO powers will accept only a system of uniform ceilings to be applied without national variation. Understandably, the immediate prospects for an agreement are not encouraging.[14]

Helsinki Agreement

The Conference on Security and Cooperation in Europe (CSCE) brought together the representatives of thirty-four European and North American countries, plus the Holy See, in Helsinki to conclude an agreement during the summer of 1975. While the conferees addressed an impressive array of topics, such as the inviolability of frontiers, international cooperation in science and technology, and human rights, detailed negotiations centered on questions of security and arms control.[15] Notification twenty-one days in advance of large-scale military exercises, for example, coupled with a planned exchange of observers suggested an innovative variation on the theme of disengagement in that verified prior warnings of troop movements tend to diminish the perceived threat of surprise attack. Beyond this commitment, the participating governments took no steps other than declaratory ones toward arms control, and the document itself represents an agreement on principles rather than a contractual obligation under international law. With a history dating from 1954, the goal of reducing tension through a general conference on European security continues to elude fulfillment.

The Helsinki Agreement did, however, provide a background for speculation regarding an arms-control undertaking by both German states. As part of the Paris Protocols of 1954 to the Brussels Treaty creating the Western European Union, Chancellor Konrad Adenauer declared that his government would not manufacture atomic, biological, or chemical weapons within its territory.[16] Although verification of analogous statements by East German spokesmen is lacking, the possibility of an arms-control agreement between the two Germanys continues to attract supporters, especially in the Federal Republic. The reluctance of the policy-making councils of the two major alliances to consider such an independent initiative makes the probability of an intra-German understanding conjectural.

In the 1980s the outlook for progress in the fields of reduction and limitation of arms in Central Europe is dim. On November 18, 1981, President Reagan delivered an address in which he proposed Soviet and American negotiations directed toward the reduction of nuclear and conventional arms in Europe.[17] He called for balanced and verifiable agreements under which the United States would cancel plans to introduce new missiles into Europe if the Soviets would dismantle intermediate-range nuclear missiles already in place. The declaration of martial law a month later in Poland undercut the political premise on which the success of such a far-reaching proposal depends.

Latin America

The Special Session of the United Nations General Assembly on Disarmament (1978) succeeded in creating a consensus among 149 participating delegations in support of an extensive series of declaratory recommendations.[18] Although most of these referred to global issues, regional arms-control arrangements did receive attention. On a presumed basis of "equality and parity" the session called for a reduction of the military potential of the two European alliance systems as well as for the progressive formation of nuclear-weapon-free zones. The Treaty for the Prohibition of Nuclear Weapons in Latin America, the Treaty of Tlatelolco (1967), serves as the primary example of the latter, and the General Assembly has proposed that the nations of Africa, the Middle East, South and Southeast Asia, and the littoral of the Indian Ocean also create "zones of peace." Ambassador Alfonso Garcia Robles of Mexico, the leading sponsor of the establishment of a Latin American zone closed to nuclear weapons, regards the treaty as a breakthrough, a model that merits emulation in other regions.[19] The experiment merits analysis of its purpose, geographical zone of application, obligations of the treaty partners, provisions for verification, and the international legal status of the agreement—that is, of the degree of adherence to it by nations within the hemisphere or with strategic interests in it.

Purpose. The twenty-one Latin American countries that have ratified the treaty seek to place this region outside the realm of superpower nuclear strategy. Their goal is both to stem the proliferation of nuclear armaments and to set an example worthy of emulation in other areas. Because of the reservations attached by some Latin American governments regarding their terms of accession to the treaty, its provisions currently fall short of full implementation. Nevertheless, this accord and its implementing organ, the Agency for the Prohibition of Nuclear Weapons in Latin America (OPANAL), constitute the most significant effort that the United States has supported toward regional arms control.

Zone of Application. The geographical scope is ambitious, for it covers 7.5 million square miles.[20] In addition to vast expanses of the Atlantic and the Pacific, the area encompassed by the agreement extends northward to a latitude of thirty-five degrees, which means that the coast of southern California and that of the Carolinas, Georgia, and Florida are covered beyond the narrow limit of the territorial sea. Efforts to deny these waters to, for example, the submarines of the nuclear powers are likely to be ineffective. The architects of the treaty would have served their purpose well had they exercised more restraint in delineating the zone of impact.

Treaty Obligations. The signatories hope to forbid both the manufacture and the deployment of nuclear weapons in any space over which they exercise de facto or de jure control. The problem arises with the interpretation placed on the concepts of "manufacture" and "weapons." Brazil has made clear its intention to purchase nuclear reprocessing and enrichment equipment from West Germany, and such apparatus might provide the fissionable material needed to build a functional nuclear bomb. Brazil's refusal to sign the Treaty on

Non-Proliferation of Nuclear Weapons (1968) may reveal long-range strategic designs. Argentina and Chile also pursue ambitious programs of nuclear research. Whatever the ultimate objectives of the three major Latin American powers may be, the complex and often speculative nature of the evidence invoked to designate a particular nuclear project as peaceful rather than military becomes apparent in this instance.

Similar conceptual difficulties arise in connection with the attempt to define a "nuclear weapon." Article 5 stipulates that such a weapon is a device "capable of releasing nuclear energy in an uncontrolled manner . . . and designed for military purposes." Delivery systems are excluded from the treaty limitations. The development, for example, of intermediate-range missiles mounting nuclear warheads is a subject left untouched by the Treaty of Tlatelolco. In comparison, it is noteworthy that in the SALT II Agreement (1979) the concentration was on missiles, and scant reference was made to warheads.[21] The difference in approach is illustrative of the recurrent emphasis placed by American and Soviet negotiators on the economic implications of arms control as opposed to the focus on research and technological development characterized by the Latin American nuclear-weapon-free zone. Presumably, peaceful nuclear explosions (PNEs) fall outside the limitations that the Latin American signatories have imposed on themselves. The exclusion of missiles and nonmilitary testing enables a ratifying government to develop the infrastructure required for strategic nuclear weapons—a lapse in drafting that several regimes may well exploit.

Verification. Established in 1969, the supreme organ of OPANAL is the General Conference, which represents all member states as equals. Because of a biennial schedule of meetings, the General Conference recognizes the necessity of electing a steering committee—the Council—to function as its executive arm on a continuing basis. Each serving for a term of four years, the five members of the Council meet regularly to direct the work of OPANAL, and on them falls the primary responsibility for the verification of the provisions of the treaty. The signatory states submit semiannual reports to the International Atomic Energy Agency in Vienna with copies to OPANAL certifying that activities proscribed by the treaty have not, in fact, been undertaken in the territories under their control. The Council may authorize an inspection of nuclear facilities to confirm or infirm the substance of a report rendered by any signatory nation, including one that is suspected of violations of the treaty. Presumably, the nation under scrutiny would grant unimpeded access to all its nuclear facilities. The reality of this provision, as expressed in the pertinent clauses of article 16, remains uncertain.

Argentina, Brazil, and Chile are locked in a competition to develop nuclear energy. Each may, under the treaty, build nuclear power stations. Breeder reactors and reprocessing facilities in such installations may provide the industrial infrastructure essential for the manufacture of the prohibited weaponry. How an international team could determine during an on-site inspection the uses to which reprocessed plutonium might be put poses a problem of verification that is unanswered by OPANAL.

Status of the Treaty. For the provisions of the treaty to take full effect, three preconditions must be satisfied: (1) all Latin American governments must ratify the agreement, (2) those countries outside the treaty area must accede to Protocol 1, whereby they accept the same obligations for their Latin American territories as do countries within the region, and (3) finally, the five principal nuclear powers must grant formal recognition to the denuclearized status of the zone. The cumulative effect of these conditions creates a vicious circle in which the signatories to the treaty limit their accession to the accord on the grounds that the superpowers have not committed themselves to respect the integrity of the zone, and the superpowers assert that they are unable to acknowledge unconditionally the nuclear-weapon-free status of Latin America because of the reservations of the signatory nations. Circular reasoning of this type enables regional powers to profess their loyalty to the ideal of zonal arms control as they pursue nuclear programs with military overtones.

The implications of this contradiction emerge clearly in the policy of the United States. Although accession to the treaty is open only to Latin American governments, countries not included in the zone may participate through adherence to one or both of the protocols. Protocol 1 applies to those countries which, although outside the prescribed nuclear-weapon-free zone, exercise authority over territorial entities within it. Great Britain, in 1969, and the Netherlands, in 1971, have ratified this protocol; France has not. On July 16, 1981, President Reagan promised to seek approval for ratification, and the Senate gave its unanimous consent on November 13.[22] Territories under the jurisdiction of the United States that are covered by this protocol include the naval base at Guantanamo, the Panama Canal Zone (until December 31, 1999), Puerto Rico, and the Virgin Islands. The denuclearization of these areas is now acceptable to American strategic planners, but restrictions on the transit of nuclear forces through the zonal seas are not.

Protocol 2 of the treaty provides a guarantee on behalf of external nuclear powers for the security of the zone. In the years 1971 to 1979, the United States, France, Great Britain, the People's Republic of China, and the Soviet Union have all become parties to this protocol, making it the only international undertaking that commits all these states not to use or threaten to use nuclear weapons in a given region. Like the treaty itself, the provisions of this protocol impose an arms limitation which remains in force indefinitely.

As a condition of ratification the United States reserved to itself exclusive legal competence regarding the determination of what constitutes deployment of nuclear weapons, thereby preserving its strategic option to transport them through the zone. Also, in the event of an armed attack by a Latin American country supported by a nuclear power, U.S. forces might employ a nuclear deterrent. Especially significant is an understanding on the part of the Senate that the United States does not recognize the presumed distinction between the development of nuclear technology for peaceful purposes and its military applications.[23] The framers of the treaty made precisely this differentiation by permitting PNEs but banning the testing of weapons. The reluctance of the United States to accept PNEs reflects its concern with uncontrolled nuclear proliferation and the spread of weapons capabilities to a number of countries (the nth-country problem). The readiness of the Federal Republic of Germany to provide Brazil with nuclear reprocessing equipment and assistance suggests that American reservations on this point may be well founded but are ineffectual.

Although the Treaty of Tlatelolco provides the sole working example of a regional arms-limitation agreement and one that merits consideration for emulation in other areas, the principal nuclear powers do not assign a high priority to this approach. The United States Arms Control and Disarmament Agency (ACDA) adheres to a pattern of organization that is adjusted to global policies. With the important exception of the standing delegation to the MBFR talks, the plan of organization of ACDA does not lend itself to a focus on regional problems. As a partial outcome of the Special Session on Disarmament of the General Assembly, Mexico and Venezuela proposed the establishment of a set of restraints on international transfers of conventional weapons. Although the United States and the Soviet Union held talks in 1977 and 1978 on criteria for the transfer of arms, these discussions were exploratory, and they lacked a particular focus on Latin America. The establishment within ACDA of an office devoted specifically to hemispheric affairs would lend structural support to its efforts to set regional limits on the burgeoning sales of arms.

Soviet policy on arms control reflects the same preoccupations with global concerns even though an unenthusiastic decision to ratify Protocol 2 was forthcoming in 1979. The principal Soviet objections to the treaty include an alleged failure to deal effectively with the question of transshipment of nuclear weapons through the zone and a pronounced skepticism regarding the vast expanses of the Pacific and Atlantic presumably closed to naval and air units armed with nuclear missiles.[24] An alliance with Cuba, coupled with growing naval strength, has caused Soviet strategic planners to regard the Latin American experiment with reserve. Nevertheless, the instrument of ratification was deposited at a point at which the SALT II negotiations appeared to have come to fruition. Support of a nuclear-weapon-free zone in Latin America is, of course, consistent with Soviet endorsements of the same status for Central Europe and other areas.

The treaty commitments of the superpowers to respect the banning of nuclear weapons in Latin America contrast starkly with the pressure for nuclear development among the industrial countries of the region. Among the hemispheric powers, Brazil may well have the most advanced nuclear program. Noting particularly the refusal of Cuba to sign the treaty, Brazil has declined to waive the stipulation that the limitation on the development of nuclear arms will take full effect only when all Latin American republics have become signatories.[25] Similarly, Argentina has signed but has so far refused to ratify the treaty, and Chile has attached preconditions to its ratification. Under international treaty law the result of these reservations is the same: Argentina, Brazil, and Chile are keeping their options open. Among these is the hypothetical possibility that any or all of the A-B-C powers could claim that the treaty became inoperative whenever a newly created state joined the Latin American community and was unable, for reasons of timing, to accede to the agreement immediately. The independence of Belize, achieved in 1981, is perhaps a case in point. Decolonization in the Caribbean could provide a pretext for challenging the validity of the treaty, because new states would not be parties to it. Finally, the fact that France has yet to ratify Protocol 1, which would denuclearize its Caribbean possessions, also provides a justification for arguing that the treaty is not yet in force. Legal considerations notwithstanding, the international politics of Latin America rests on the presumption of its status as a nuclear-weapon-free zone. A violation of the expectations of this community of states would probably bring with it sanctions that no power could disregard.

Summary

Efforts to negotiate regional agreements for the reduction and limitation of arms invariably center on the need to define carefully the following points: (1) the states eligible to become signatories, (2) the conditions under which the controls become operative, (3) the types of weaponry proscribed and formulas for mutual reductions in military capability, (4) the legal rights and obligations of member states, (5) the structures and processes established to implement the accord, including the questions of inspection and exchange of information, (6) the relation to powers outside the treaty area, and (7) the duration of the treaty itself. If the creation of a nuclear-weapon-free zone is the object of the agreement, the negotiators should clarify the distinctions between peaceful and military nuclear research, and they should differentiate between the deployment and the transit of banned weapons systems through the area in question.[26]

In view of the complexity of the foregoing, some commentators argue that it is easier to deal with the global limitation of strategic arms on the thesis that this problem can presumably be isolated, while a geographically circumscribed approach will fall short of realization because it is intertwined with the politics of a specific international subsystem.[27] Reflecting this interpretation, Ambassador William C. Foster, the U.S. delegate to the Eighteen-Nation Conference on Disarmament (1966), emphasized his government's interest in drafting a general convention on nonproliferation. Nevertheless, he did offer a qualified endorsement of an African denuclearization plan, subject to the establishment of a reliable means of verification.[28]

While strategic assumptions underlying détente may in part explain the reluctance of the United States to pursue the regional option, the literature on decision making offers another insight. Graham Allison's analysis of foreign policy behavior with the use of three models—the rational actor, organizational process, and governmental politics—illustrates clearly the resistance of bureaucratic structures to new directions.[29] Similarly, the case studies developed by Morton H. Halperin to depict the importance of roles and missions in the competition of bureaucracies for survival provide a basis for extrapolating what might occur if the priorities outlined by Foster were reversed.[30] A renewed emphasis on the implementation of regional commitments inhibiting the transfer of conventional arms would encounter stiff opposition from influential bureaucratic interests. The dynamics of organizational politics coupled with an understandable preoccupation with the "balance of terror" have led to a concentration on the SALT process to the neglect of more modest, but possibly more effective, regional arrangements.

A growing realization that the assumptions of mutual assured destruction (MAD) do not offer a plausible deterrent to all forms of aggression has led the Western powers to strive for a strategy based on a flexible response to a military threat in Europe. The growth of the Warsaw Pact forces in the 1970s, coupled with the Soviet deployment of SS-20 missiles directed against Western Europe, induced NATO to counter in 1979 with a decision to introduce, beginning in 1983, Pershing II and cruise missiles into its central sector. These missiles constitute NATO's projected Theater Nuclear Force and would have an effective range encompassing much of European Russia.

Geopolitics notwithstanding, developments in military technology also have symbolic overtones, and the rise of confrontational politics between the two alliance systems gives cause for concern.[31] Both sides now make uncertain gestures toward negotiations which would stay the escalation of weaponry. The dangers of a heightened arms race are such that renewed arms-control efforts in Central Europe deserve support. Success in Europe could provide an impetus for SALT III and for the formation of analogous regional undertakings in southeastern Europe, the Middle East, or the Indian Ocean.[32] In the language of nineteenth-century diplomacy, a détente occurs whenever two powers on a collision course reach a limited understanding that is based on a recognition of overlapping interests and on a subordination of emotion to statecraft. Regional arms control offers an opportunity to apply this lesson in the diplomatic method.

The focus on a global accord symbolized by the acronym START —strategic arms reduction talks—implies the assignment of a lesser role to geographically limited arrangements. On December 21, 1982, Yuri V. Andropov, having succeeded Brezhnev as general secretary a month earlier, called for the reduction of SS-20s in Central Europe to a level comparable to that of the combined missile forces of Great Britain and France in exchange for a U.S. pledge not to deploy Pershing II and cruise missiles in 1983 as planned. Adhering to a formula known as the "zero option," President Reagan reiterated his position that such an American commitment depended upon a Soviet willingness to dismantle all SS-20s. Governments of the major NATO partners supported the president, although opposition parties in London and Bonn alleged that his position was intransigent and disruptive of the negotiating process.

The standoff between the two alliances has stimulated private initiatives. Among those, the study group conducted by Swedish social democrat Olof Palme has attracted attention. The Palme Commission included former Secretary of State Cyrus Vance, Georgy

Arbatov, a foreign policy expert on the Soviet central committee, and Egon Bahr, the principal negotiator of West Germany's normalization treaties with Eastern Europe. Although the members did not arrive at a consensus on the need to remove all nuclear weapons from Europe, they did join in urging the creation of a denuclearized belt extending ninety-three miles on either side of the border between East and West Germany.[33] Whatever the merits of this proposal, it met with a cool reception in official quarters. The Eisenhower concept of a neutralized zone separating the two blocs is out of place in the confrontational politics of the 1980s.

Notes

1. Henry Kissinger, "Domestic Structure and Foreign Policy," *Daedalus: Conditions of World Order*, vol. 95 (Spring 1966), p. 508.

2. Thucydides, *The Peloponnesian War*, trans. Benjamin Jowett (New York: Bantam Books, 1960), p. 68.

3. Hugh Gaitskell, *The Challenge of Coexistence* (Cambridge: Harvard University Press, 1957), p. 65.

4. TASS (Moscow), October 6, 1979, as monitored by the Foreign Broadcast Information Service (FBIS), *Daily Report: Soviet Union*, vol. 3, no. 196 (October 9, 1979), p. F4. Brezhnev made a supplementary statement for *Pravda*, January 13, 1980, as monitored by FBIS, ibid., vol. 3, no. 009 (January 14, 1980), pp. A5–A6.

5. *Department of State Bulletin*, vol. 80 (February 1980), p. 16. An affirmation of this position appeared in the *Bulletin*, vol. 81 (April 1981), p. 28.

6. U.S. Congress, Senate Committee on Foreign Relations, *Documents on Germany, 1944–1959*, 86th Cong., 1st sess. (1959), p. 120.

7. U.S. Department of State, *Documents on Disarmament*, vol. 1, *1945–1956*, Doc. 113, Pubn. 7008 (1960), pp. 470–72.

8. Great Britain, Foreign and Commonwealth Office, *Selected Documents on Germany and the Question of Berlin*, no. 77, Cmd. 1552 (1961), p. 216.

9. *Public Papers of the Presidents of the United States: Dwight D. Eisenhower, 1955* (Washington, D.C.: National Archives and Records Service, 1959), p. 518.

10. Ghita Ionescu, "The Austrian State Treaty and Neutrality in Eastern Europe," Canadian Institute of International Affairs, *International Journal*, vol. 23 (Summer 1968), p. 415.

11. The text of the Rapacki Plan and related correspondence is in Andrzej Albrecht, *The Rapacki Plan: New Aspects* (Warsaw: Western Press Agency, 1963).

12. *Department of State Bulletin*, vol. 38 (May 19, 1958), pp. 821–23.

13. U.S. Congress, House Committee on Foreign Affairs and Senate Committee on Foreign Relations, *U.S. Arms Control and Disarmament*

Agency: 1980 Annual Review, Joint Committee Print, 97th Cong., 1st sess. (1981), pp. 108–12. For a critical analysis of the impact of MBFR on the strategic balance in Central Europe, see William B. Prendergast, *Mutual and Balanced Force Reduction: Issues and Prospects* (Washington, D.C.: American Enterprise Institute, 1978), pp. 35–47; and Jeffrey Record, *Force Reductions in Europe: Starting Over* (Cambridge, Mass.: Institute for Foreign Policy Analysis, 1980), pp. 67–70. The problem of equivalency of forces receives extensive treatment in Olga Šuković, *Force Reductions in Europe*, Stockholm International Peace Research Institute (Stockholm: Almqvist and Wiksell, 1974), pp. 74–100.

14. Joseph I. Coffey, *Arms Control and European Security: A Guide to East-West Negotiations* (London: Chatto and Windus, 1977), pp. 141–49; and John G. Keliher, *The Negotiations on Mutual and Balanced Force Reductions: The Search for Arms Control in Central Europe* (New York: Pergamon Press, 1980), p. 162.

15. U.S. Department of State, *Conference on Security and Co-operation in Europe: Final Act*, Pubn. 8826 (1975), pp. 84–87.

16. U.S. Department of State, *London and Paris Agreements, September–October 1954*, Pubn. 5659 (1954), p. 45. For a counterpart East German commitment, as yet unverified in practice, see Karlheinz Lohs, "Natur-wissenschaft und Abrüstung" [Natural science and disarmament], in *Zu Problemen der Abrüstung*, Academy of Sciences of the German Democratic Republic (Berlin: Akademie Verlag, 1978), p. 8.

17. *Weekly Compilation of Presidential Documents*, vol. 17, no. 47 (November 23, 1981), pp. 1273–77. For a discussion of the place of arms control in U.S.-Soviet relations, see Alexander M. Haig, Jr., "A Strategic American Foreign Policy," *NATO Review*, vol. 29 (December 1981), pp. 6–7.

18. United Nations, "Final Document of the Tenth Special Session of the General Assembly," *Disarmament: A Periodic Review*, vol. 1 (October 1978), pp. 55–59.

19. Alfonso Garcia Robles, *The Latin American Nuclear-Weapon-Free Zone*, Occasional Paper 19 (Muscatine, Iowa: The Stanley Foundation, 1979), pp. 13–21.

20. U.S. Arms Control and Disarmament Agency, "Treaty for the Prohibition of Nuclear Weapons in Latin America, 1967," in *Arms Control and Disarmament Agreements: Tests and History of Negotiations*, Pubn. 105 (1980), pp. 63–76.

21. U.S. Department of State, *SALT II Agreement: Vienna, June 18, 1979*, Pubn. 8986 (1979).

22. *Weekly Compilation of Presidential Documents*, vol. 17, no. 29 (July 20, 1981), p. 769; and *Washington Post*, November 14, 1981. For a summary of previous U.S. policy on Protocol 1, see John R. Redick, "Regional Nuclear Arms Control in Latin America," *International Organization*, vol. 29 (Spring 1975), pp. 429–31.

23. The text of the Senate resolution of April 19, 1971, is included in U.S. Arms Control and Disarmament Agency, *Arms Control and Disarmament Agreements*, pp. 77–78.

24. Y. Tomlin, "Nuclear-Free Zones: How to Make Them Effective," *International Affairs* (Moscow), vol. 8 (August 1975), pp. 69–71.

25. George H. Quester, *Brazil and Latin American Nuclear Proliferation: An Optimistic View*, ACLS Working Paper no. 17, Center for International and Strategic Affairs (Los Angeles: University of California at Los Angeles, 1979), pp. 20–24.

26. United Nations, General Assembly, 30th sess., 1976, *Special Report of the Conference of the Committee on Disarmament* (Supplement no. 27A, A/10027/Add.1), annex 1, pp. 31–33.

27. John H. Barton and Lawrence D. Weiler expressed a preference for the global approach in *International Arms Control: Issues and Agreements* (Stanford, Calif.: Stanford University Press, 1976), pp. 269–70. Alva Myrdal assigned more importance to regional agreements in *The Game of Disarmament: How the United States and Russia Run the Arms Race* (New York: Pantheon Books, 1976), pp. 194–204.

28. *Department of State Bulletin*, vol. 54 (January 17, 1966), pp. 103–5.

29. Graham T. Allison, *Essence of Decision: Explaining the Cuban Missile Crisis* (Boston: Little, Brown & Company, 1971), pp. 144–81 passim.

30. Morton H. Halperin, *Bureaucratic Politics and Foreign Policy* (Washington, D.C.: Brookings Institution, 1974), pp. 40–51.

31. Vladimir Petrov, "Dynamics of Confrontation" (Paper presented at the Eighth National Security Affairs Conference, National Defense University, Washington, D.C., July 13–15, 1981).

32. United Nations Centre for Disarmament, *General Assembly Resolutions on Disarmament—1979 Session* (Fact Sheet no. 11), p. 6; and Jozef Goldblat, *Arms Control: A Survey and Appraisal of Multilateral Agreements*, Stockholm International Peace Research Institute (New York: Crane, Russak & Company, 1978), pp. 206–10.

33. Cyrus R. Vance and Robert E. Hunter, "Arms-Control Steps," *New York Times*, December 27, 1982, sec. 1, p. A19; and "Ein Experiment mit kalkuliertem Risiko" [An experiment with a calculated risk], *Der Spiegel*, vol. 36 (May 31, 1982), pp. 38–40.

Contributors

FRANK B. FEIGERT is professor of political science, North Texas State University. His principal research interests are political parties and voting behavior. He has written and served as coauthor of texts on political analysis and political parties. His present research is focused on problems of rational evaluation of candidates and parties.

NORMAN A. GRAEBNER is Edward R. Stettinius Professor of Modern American History at the University of Virginia. He has written extensively in the field of American diplomacy and foreign policy. He is the author of a number of books, including *The New Isolationism* (1956), coauthor of *A History of the American People* (1970), and editor of several volumes, including *An Uncertain Tradition: American Secretaries of State in the Twentieth Century* (1961). He has also contributed to a number of historical journals and has served as a Fulbright lecturer and visiting professor at a number of universities.

GERARD J. MANGONE is H. Rodney Sharp Professor of International Law and Organization in the graduate professional College of Marine Studies and director of the Center for the Study of Marine Policy at the University of Delaware. He has been coordinator of ocean studies at the Woodrow Wilson International Center for Scholars; executive director of the President's Commission on the United Nations; consultant to the State Department, White House, and United Nations; faculty member or visiting professor at ten universities; dean and provost; and author, coauthor, or editor of twenty books on world affairs.

DEMETRIOS G. PAPADEMETRIOU is editor of the *International Migration Review* and is research scientist at the Center for Migration Studies in New York. He has taught at Duke University and the University of Maryland, and he is the author of several articles on the topic of international migration; at present he is conducting research, under a grant from the Ford Foundation, on the effects of emigration on the development of the sending societies.

233

DON C. PIPER is professor of government and politics at the University of Maryland. He pursues research in the fields of international law and international relations and has recently specialized in the problems of nationalization of alien property and foreign investment. He is the author of *The International Law of the Great Lakes*, is coeditor and coauthor of several other volumes, and has had articles published in a number of scholarly journals.

HARRY HOWE RANSOM is professor of political science at Vanderbilt University. He is the author of *Can American Democracy Survive Cold War?* (1963), *An American Foreign Policy Reader* (1965), *The Intelligence Establishment* (1970), and numerous articles and essays. He has taught at several universities and has been a consultant to the U.S. Senate Select Committee on Intelligence, congressional fellow of the American Political Science Association, and a fellow of the Woodrow Wilson International Center for Scholars.

RONALD J. TERCHEK, associate professor of government and politics at the University of Maryland, is primarily interested in political theory, political participation, and decision making. He has published in several scholarly journals and in several volumes; he is the author of *The Making of the Test Ban Treaty;* and at present he is writing a book tentatively entitled "Liberalism: Axioms and Assumptions."

LARMAN C. WILSON is professor of international relations in the School of International Service at the American University. His teaching and research are in two fields, international law and organization and inter-American relations. He is the coauthor of two books, the more recent being *Latin American Foreign Policies: An Analysis;* he is author of a recent OAS document, *The Inter-American System and Its Future;* and he has written a number of articles that have appeared in professional journals in Europe and Latin America as well as in the United States.

JAMES H. WOLFE is professor of political science at the University of Southern Mississippi. As a fellow of the Alexander von Humboldt Foundation, he studied and did research in Munich in 1964–1965 and 1972–1973. His publications include *Indivisible Germany: Illusion or Reality?* (1963), an essay on German corporatism in *Politics in Europe* (1974), and articles in several professional journals. He has served as a consultant to the Department of State and is now conducting research on constitution making in multinational states.

The following contributors were students of Elmer Plischke:

Frank Feigert
Demetrios Papademetriou
Don Piper
Ronald Terchek
Larman Wilson
James Wolfe

A Note on the Book

This book was edited by David Howell Jones
and by Gertrude Kaplan of the
Publications Staff of the American Enterprise Institute.
The staff also designed the cover and format, with Pat Taylor.
The text was set in Palatino, a typeface designed by Hermann Zapf.
Hendricks-Miller Typographic Company, of Washington, D.C.,
set the type, and R. R. Donnelley & Sons Company,
of Harrisonburg, Virginia, printed and bound the book,
using paper made by the S. D. Warren Company.

The Reagan Phenomenon—
and Other Speeches on Foreign Policy

JEANE J. KIRKPATRICK

In these speech/essays, Ambassador Kirkpatrick describes, assesses, and articulates the foundations of what she calls "the Reagan phenomenon" as it relates to the liberal tradition, Western values, America's goals, and U.S. foreign policy.

"She is at once informed, incisive, and challenging.... in a fresh and vigorous fashion.... This is a stimulating and valuable book, the work of an activist and participant that nevertheless has about it the qualities of scholarship and objectivity." *Contemporary Review* (London).

"Lucid, potent speeches.... Valuable reading on a number of levels."

"Ambassador Kirkpatrick...understands that truth is the main weapon of democracy."

Jean-François Revel, former editor, *L'Express*.

"The best thinking of the clearest mind in foreign policy today." William Safire, columnist, *New York Times*.

230 pp./1983/cloth 1361-9 $14.95

The Soviet Intervention in Afghanistan

ALFRED L. MONKS

This study examines the Soviet Union's military presence in Afghanistan in relation to Soviet global policies and military doctrine. It addresses these issues: whether Russia has historically sought control of Afghanistan, the timing of the invasion, the political and diplomatic consequences of the move for the Soviet Union, and the role played by Soviet military doctrine. The study begins with a historical perspective and concludes with some policy recommendations for the West. "A very useful book...admirably clear analysis." *International Affairs* (London).

60 pp./1981/paper 3431-4 $4.25

Judea, Samaria, and Gaza:
Views on the Present and Future

DANIEL J. ELAZAR, editor

Nine Israeli scholars present their views on this controversial Middle Eastern region. Part 1 examines the land and its resources; part 2, the economy, government, and social services; and part 3, planning for the future in Judea, Samaria, and Gaza.

Daniel J. Elazar is president of the Jerusalem Institute for Federal Studies.

"Useful to those interested in the thinking that is, and is not, being done in Israeli government circles. . . ."

Middle East Journal.

"Deserves to be read and considered thoroughly."

The Jerusalem Post Magazine.

"An interesting, refreshing, and original place to begin thinking new thoughts about the future of an old problem."

Annals of the American Academy of Political and Social Science.

222 pp./1982/paper 3459-4 $9.75/cloth 3458-6 $16.75

Human Rights and U.S. Human Rights Policy: Theoretical Approaches and Some Perspectives on Latin America

HOWARD J. WIARDA, editor

The debate over human rights and the place of human rights in U.S. foreign policy has been renewed in the struggle over human rights policy in the Carter and Reagan administrations and in the controversy over the appropriate stance of the United States, especially with regard to Latin America. This collection of seven diverse essays gives special attention to the consideration of such rights in Latin American policy, particularly with regard to the different approaches of the Carter and Reagan administrations. The book includes two essays by Jeane J. Kirkpatrick, the U.S. permanent representative to the United Nations, and essays by Mark Falcoff, Michael Novak, Edward A. Olsen, Richard Schifter.

Howard J. Wiarda is a resident scholar at AEI, director of the AEI Center for Hemispheric Studies, and professor of political science at the University of Massachusetts.

"Well worth reading."   *Orbis.*

96 pp./1982/paper 3481-0 $4.25

Dictatorships and Double Standards: Rationalism and Reason in Politics

JEANE J. KIRKPATRICK

In a series of essays, UN Ambassador Jeane J. Kirkpatrick argues forcefully and persuasively that in modern politics the rationalist spirit has, with dangerous effect, played too strong a role. In its rigid adherence to utopian ideals of human behavior and social processes, excessive rationalism has wrought havoc upon U.S. policy both at home and abroad. Whether her subject is U.S. policy toward our allies, or the nature of totalitarian thought, or the problems of party reform, Ambassador Kirkpatrick writes with clarity and insight in these essays—together they represent a comprehensive statement of principles by the most powerful woman in American government today.

"Temperate, well-reasoned and extremely challenging. There are no easy ways to dismiss what she is saying."

New York Times.

"[The views are] presented with striking clarity, forcefulness, and realism. Highly recommended." *Library Journal.*

"Learned and assertive." *The New Yorker.*

Co-published with Simon & Schuster.

270 pp./1982/cloth 0-671-43836-0 $14.95

U.S. Arms Sales Policy: Background and Issues

ROGER P. LABRIE, JOHN G. HUTCHINS, EDWIN W. A. PEURA, with DIANA H. RICHMAN

Among the topics examined in this volume are: U.S. arms sales policy in the postwar period; differences on arms sales between the Carter and the Reagan administrations; existing legislation and government review processes for arms sales; and political, economic, and security arguments for and against arms sales restraints.

"A clearly written overview...brings together and summarizes concisely a wide range of political and economic arguments on this complex topic....The book also contains an extensive, up-to-date bibliography."

Naval War College Review.

87 pp./1982/paper 3491-8 $4.95

• *Mail orders for publications to:* AMERICAN ENTERPRISE INSTITUTE, 1150 Seventeenth Street, N.W., Washington, D.C. 20036 • *For postage and handling, add 10 percent of total; minimum charge, $2* • *For information on orders, or to expedite service, call toll free* 800-424-2873 • *Prices subject to change without notice* • *Payable in U.S. currency only.*